RELIGION
and
COMMUNISM

RELIGION
and
COMMUNISM

*A Study of Religion
and Atheism
in
Soviet Russia*

by
Julius F. Hecker, Ph.D.

HYPERION PRESS, INC.
WESTPORT, CONNECTICUT

Library of Congress Cataloging in Publication Data

Hecker, Julius Friedrich, 1881-
  Religion and communism.

  Reprint of the 1934 ed. published by Wiley, New York.
  1. Russia--Religion--1917- 2. Church and State in Russia--1917- 3. Communism and religion. I. Title.
  BR936.H28 1973   274.7   73-842
  ISBN 0-88355-037-7

Published in 1933
by Chapman & Hall, Ltd., London, England.

First Hyperion reprint edition 1973

Library of Congress Catalogue Number 73-842

ISBN 0-88355-037-7

Printed in the United States of America

To

JOHN HAYNES HOLMES,
Poet and Preacher,

to whom Truth is God
and the witness thereof—Religion.

PREFACE

In the Soviet Union, in every sense—geographical, racial, cultural—East and West meet. But whilst face to face with one another, as yet, of these two, there is no synthesis. On the contrary a bitter conflict rages between the mystic, ascetic, life-denying, other-worldly ideal of the East and of Old Russia, and the rational, Marxian, will-to-power, life-asserting passion of the West and of New Russia. Will the latter triumph, crushing the other? Or will there emerge from this conflict a higher, synthetic culture, rich in strength, thought, beauty? It is hoped that the study pursued in this problem will serve in throwing some light upon this question.

The fate of Religion under Communism is of great concern to many earnest and thinking people. I, personally, have always considered it a problem of major interest and throughout the last fifteen years have continually studied it from one aspect or another. In this present work I have been compelled, by the limitations of the volume, to confine myself to Religion and Communism in the Soviet Union. Much also could be learned from the views of Western thinkers upon this problem; nevertheless, the Soviet Union is the only nation that on an enormous scale is actually carrying out the destruction of organized religion in order to clear the ground for the newly developing Communist social order.

This book attempts to tell the story of the conflict between religious thought and organization and radical atheist thought and Communist organization.

In a previous book, *Religion Under the Soviets* (published in U.S.A. in 1927), I showed the status of religion as it then existed in the Soviet Union. When that book was being written organized militant atheism, sponsored by the Communist Party, was only beginning to take shape. Since then it has become a far-reaching movement and now has probably attained its maximum development; hence, major attention

PREFACE

is given here to the study of the anti-religious forces which, however, can only be understood upon the background of the religious history of the Russian people.

The facts presented may appear alarming as regards the outlook for religion in the Soviet Union. That there may be no doubt as to the actual situation I am giving in the appendices a translation of the most important Party pronouncements upon the subject; also the decrees of the Soviet Government which clearly show the legal position of organized religion in the Soviet Union and the conditions under which it is permitted to function. Finally I give the legislation by which a government department has been set up to regulate the functioning of religion within the existing laws. All these documents deserve attentive study.

Students wishing to continue the study of this subject and who possess a reading knowledge of Russian will find a selected bibliography in my *Religion Under the Soviets*, and a more extensive bibliography in the recent work of Professor N. M. Nikolsky, *History of the Russian Church* (1931). The anti-religious developments of recent years are best reflected in the Russian monthly review, *Antireligiosnik*, which has been issued in Moscow since 1926. The aspect of Communist philosophic theory, which must be grasped in order to get the philosophic bearing underlying the study of Communism and Religion, is treated in my *Moscow Dialogues*, a series of Discussions on Red Philosophy.

In this volume it has been my earnest desire to treat the subject as objectively as possible without denying my own convictions in the matter, which are the result not merely of theoretic study but of a long, painful readjustment of my own mind throughout many years or direct contact with both Religion and Communism in the Soviet Union.

J. F. HECKER.

Moscow, *February*, 1933.

CONTENTS

	PAGE
PREFACE	ix

CHAPTER

I. THE PROBLEM STATED 1

II. THE RELIGION OF THE PEOPLE 13
Pagan Survivals—Ecclesiastical Culture—Ikon and Relic Worship—Doctrinal Peculiarities—The Ethics of the People.

III. CHURCH AND STATE 37
Church and State under Feudalism—Centralization of State and Church Authority—The Church and the Institution of Serfdom—Bureaucratic State Control of the Church.

IV. NONCONFORMITY IN RUSSIA 56
Differentiation of Old Believers—Extremist Sects—The Evangelical Sects.

V. THE BEGINNINGS OF THE ANTI-RELIGIOUS TRADITION 76
Foreign Sources of Russian Atheism—The Beginnings of Russian Enlightenment—The Russian Voltairians—The Masonic Reaction—A. N. Radischev, First Martyr of Revolutionary Thought.

VI. RELIGION AND THE REVOLUTIONARY MOVEMENT . 102
The Decembrist Movement—The Narodnik Movement—The Conspiracy of Ideas.

VII. INTELLECTUALIST GOD-WRESTLERS AND SEEKERS AFTER GOD 128
The Church and the Intellectuals—The Neo-Christians.

VIII. TOLSTOY'S RELIGIOUS ANARCHISM 155
Tolstoy's Religious Development—Tolstoy's Contact with the People—Principles of Tolstoy's Religious Philosophy.

IX. COMMUNIST THEORY OF RELIGION . . . 174
Communist Philosophy of Life—Dialectics and Religion—Socialist God Builders.

CONTENTS

CHAPTER	PAGE
X. THE CONFLICT OF THE CHURCH WITH THE REVOLUTION	189

The 1917-18 Council of the Church and the Re-establishment of the Patriarchate—The Counter-offensive of the Revolutionists—The Church and the Famine of 1921—The Living Church Movement.

XI. THE ANTI-RELIGIOUS MOVEMENT . . . 215

Numerical Strength of the Union of Atheists—The Atheist Youth Movement—Atheism in the Red Army—Atheism among the Minor Nationalities—The Atheist International—Chief Causes of Atheism.

XII. COLLECTIVIZATION AND ATHEIST PROPAGANDA . 232

The Effect of Collectivization upon Religion—New Tactics of Anti-religious Propaganda.

XIII. ORGANIZATION AND METHODS OF ANTI-RELIGIOUS PROPAGANDA 246

Special Educational Activities—Anti-religious Literature—Anti-religious Museums—The Fine Arts as Weapon of Anti-religious Propaganda.

XIV. THE OUTLOOK 266

APPENDIX I. Important documents relating to Religion issued by the U.S.S.R. Communist Party:

(A) Programme and Rules of the U.S.S.R. Communist Party of Bolsheviks 275

(B) Problems and Methods of Anti-religious Propaganda (Theses adopted at the Party Conference on Anti-religious Propaganda and at the General Committee of the U.S.S.R. Communist Party, April 27-30, 1926) . . . 275

APPENDIX II. Decrees and Stipulations of the Soviet Government relating to Religion and the Church:

(A) Decree of January 23, 1918, "On Freedom of Conscience and Religious Societies" 289

(B) Decree of the All Russian Central Executive Committee and Council of Peoples Commissars of the R.S.F.S.R. about Religious Organizations, April 8, 1929 290

(C) Decree of the All-Russian Central Executive Committee and the Committee and Council of Peoples Commissars of R.S.F.S.R., relating to the formation of a Central Commission on Religious affairs 293

INDEX 297

CHAPTER I

THE PROBLEM STATED

Is civilized humanity in need of religion ? This question is more and more often asked by thinking people and variously answered. The mystics and representatives of organized religion generally reply by a categorical affirmative. Others accept it conditionally, as in the case of such confirmed rationalists as Bernard Shaw who, while rejecting every form of organized religion, proclaims a still vaguely defined religion of the " life force." Others, like the Comtian and modern humanists, raise humanity upon the pedestal of deity and proclaim a religion without God, or dedicate their altars, as did the classic Athenians, to the unknown and unknowable God.[1] In Western civilization there are but few really confirmed atheists among liberal intellectuals ; the Communist movement alone declares itself unreservedly and categorically against every religion, whether orthodox, humanitarian, or philosophical.

[1] Among the English Moderns, *Julian Huxley* may be cited as quite representative of this trend of thought. In *What Dare I Think*, pp. 187 ff., he emphasises that religion is not a divine revelation but " a function of human nature . . . first, a reaction of the human spirit to the facts of human destiny and the forces by which it is influenced ; and secondly, a reaction into which there enters a feeling of sacredness."

Canon *Charles E. Raven*, the brilliant representative of the hypothesis of emergent evolution in Anglican theology, is, in my opinion, inconsistent in making his doctrine the basis of theism. It is more akin to pantheism and lends itself much more to the Humanist interpretation of religion than to Orthodoxy. Canon Raven seems to recognize this, when he says in his *The Creator Spirit*, " From embryo to saint is man's Pilgrim's Progress ; if we could see it whole and complete, we should resolve the antithesis of organism and environment, of nature and nurture, of freedom and determinism, of process and deity " (page 87).

" We must learn to appreciate earth if we are to be fit for heaven ; and for me the revelation of it is so overwhelming that there is often little room and little desire for more. *Is this Pantheism ?* No doubt good folks will say so " (page 107, italics are mine).

Our problem is, therefore, first to demonstrate the reasons which have led the Communist movement to this uncompromising stand; and secondly, to examine, in the light of modern social science and philosophy, whether there is no error in the Communist reasoning, or perhaps some misunderstanding in the concept of religion as understood by Communists who reject it, and as affirmed by others who offer a different interpretation. This necessitates an agreement in terminology.

What do we really mean by religion? Scores of definitions have been formulated and new ones added by almost every thinker upon the question. Some of these definitions, true enough, are little more than rhetorical phrases, whilst others emphasize some one special aspect which happens to seem most important to its author.

If we turn to the German classical idealist philosophers, we find that Kant held religion to be a right attitude of the will growing out of the belief in the morality and sovereignty of the moral order. Schleiermacher, rejecting Kant's moral theory of religion, sought its origin in the sense of piety, which he described as a feeling of dependence and a direct relation to the absolute, ultimate reality. Hegel, differing from both Kant and Schleiermacher, exalted the intellectual aspect of religion as the grasp of eternal truth. Thus *will*, *feeling* and *reason* have been respectively emphasised as the sphere of religion by the classical writers of the German idealist school.

When we turn from the philosophers to the sociologists and anthropologists, we find them advancing the view that religion is primarily a social product. Durkheim, for example, makes the authority of the social group itself the source of religion; the sacred is the socially sanctioned. Other sociologists, like Benjamin Kidd, see in religion an ultra-rational sanction for social conduct in the individual; Franklin H. Giddings defined religion as "belief in the possibility of life"; similarly Reinhold Niebuhr says that "at its best religion is both a sublimation and a qualification of the will to live."[1] Charles A. Ellwood, another sociologist, associates religion with the whole of

[1] Reinhold Niebuhr, *Does Civilization Need Religion*, p. 26.

human nature and the social life of man. To him religion is a many-sided phenomenon. Tersely expressed, Ellwood accepts Barton's formulation, " Religion is man's attitude toward the universe regarded as a social and ethical force." [1] Similar definitions are advanced by many other modern students. Thus says Caird : " A man's religion is the expression of his ultimate attitude toward the universe, the summed-up meaning and purport of his whole consciousness of things." [2] These definitions are either too broad or too narrow when compared with what, historically, religion has been in the experience of the race. Professor John Oman is quite right when, sharing Runzes' point of view, he believes that religion includes so many manifestations that it is quite impossible to give it an all-embracing definition. He therefore prefers to speak of a religious attitude of mind as a guide in the sphere of religion : " If we have a religious interest and a religious attitude of mind, we shall know what belongs and what does not belong to religion." [3] This point of view makes religion depend upon subjective criteria with an ever-shifting scale of values. What to one appears to be superstition, or the phantom of a diseased mind, or a surpassed or sublimated sex impulse, seems to another a religious reality of eternal value.

Oswald Spengler approaches the problem of religion as a stage in the cultural development of the human race, and he defines religion as the awakening of man at a time when he masters his being, negates and destroys it.[4] That is, when he overcomes his animal consciousness. Fear and love are accordingly the basic emotions of religion. It is the desire to free oneself from the anxieties and torments of consciousness, the desire for relaxation from the tension of thought and

[1] Charles A. Ellwood, *The Reconstruction of Religion*, p. 26.
[2] Caird, *The Evolution of Religion*, Vol. I, p. 30.
[3] J. Oman, *The Sphere of Religion, Science, Religion and Reality*, edited by Joseph Needham, p. 262. Cf. also *The Natural and the Supernatural*, p. 7.
[4] " Religion nennen wir das Wachsein eines Lebewesens in den Augenblicken, wo es das Dasein uberwaeltigt, beherrscht, verneint, selbst vernichtet." Oswald Spengler, *Der Untergang des Abendlandes*, Vol. I, p. 323.

meditation born out of fear, the desire to solve and annihilate the consciousness of the loneliness of the ego in the cosmos. It is the desire to escape the conditional state of nature with its existence, old age and death. Religion overcomes this fear by understanding its causes. The theoretic critic becomes the seer; the technician, the Priest; the discoverer, the Prophet.[1] Thus at the root of all religions we find an unconscious impulse, an inner urge to come to terms and adjust oneself to that which is not like oneself but something altogether different, one may call it the Universe. The mode " of coming to terms " and of associating with " the other " inevitably developed into a cult and worship. This Spengler calls the function of the " technician." This element of worship must not, by any means, be ignored as many of the modern definitions ignore it. In our opinion it is the chief attribute of every religion and there is none without it.

Finally there is an effort towards a rational interpretation of the subjective and social experience just mentioned. This prepares the ground for a theology and inevitably appears at a certain stage in the development of organized religion. Thus we find that religion is equally the product of emotion, of will and of rational interpretation. It has its subjective experience and its objective roots, its intellectual formulation and its social application. The many sidedness and the subtleties of religious experience undoubtedly account for the great variety of definitions. If judged by its effects, we find that to one religion means unquestioned passive submission to tradition and custom; to another it is an instrument of escape from the hard and unpleasant realities of life; to a third it may be an inspiration to action; to a fourth a soporific, an opiate to dull the reason or excite the imagination; to a fifth, religion is a force of control over others, a class implement of exploitation; to others it is the means to mystic contemplation, æsthetic enjoyment, satisfaction of cosmic curiosity, and so on.

In recent years students of the psychological origins of religion have endeavoured to discover traces of God by an

[1] Cf. *ibid.*, p. 324–27.

intuitive irrational approach, considering the nature of religion as outside the scope of rational concepts.

Among the serious scholars who have devoted themselves to the study of the irrational origins of religion should be mentioned Professor Rudolph Otto of Marburg, author of *Das Heilige* and *Das Gefühl das Uberweltlichen*.[1] Otto's hypothesis is that man is endowed with a *sensus numinis*—that is, a sense of awe—an innate characteristic revealing itself in a longing for the " otherworldly," the " sacred," or the " divine," for something which is " altogether different " from the nature of man ("*das ganz andere*,"[2] to use one of Otto's favourite expressions). Thus Otto's hypothesis is that " religion begins of itself."[3] This does not mean that man from the outset was equipped with a ready-made religion, but it means that he is endowed with its basic element, which is present in the most advanced religion as well as in its most primitive forms. This basic element is the *sensus numinis* from which, when it creates " Wunderwesen," develops the concept of God, an awe-inspiring being to which man is irresistibly drawn, his reactions ranging between terrifying fear and self-effacing love. In his extensive research into the great Oriental religions and into the various forms of Christian mysticism, Otto discovers undeniable traces of this *sensus numinis*, and since his hypothesis is a serious challenge to the atheist position of Communist scholarship, we shall try to indicate how this challenge may be answered from that quarter.

It can easily be shown that human qualities such as reason, ethical evaluation, and religious and æsthetic appreciation, all have a prehuman basis. No serious scholar, whatever his speciality, will deny that man has originated from some common ancestor of the anthropoid ape family. If we are to accept some *sensus numinis*, or let us call it a religious instinct, in man, naturally we must ask what is its animal base? To say that it is an *a priori* quality of human nature is not a satis-

[1] In England a similar theory has been developed by Professor John Oman. See the latter's *The Natural and the Supernatural*.
[2] *Das Gefuhl das Uberweltlichen*, p. 2.
[3] *Ibid.*, p. 1.

factory answer. Man is a continuation of the animal species, but he is possessed of a new quality which cannot be reduced to the animal without a remnant. Now this remnant of the irreducible new qualities of man consists in his reason and his ethical, æsthetic and religious sense. While human reason can never be reduced to animal reason, it cannot be understood without first understanding the animal brain. Human reason therefore presupposes animal reason, but in man it appears raised to a higher power. What has raised it? What has broken the continuity and brought about the mutation of its human quality? The Communist answers that such is the Dialectic Law of the transition of quantity into quality; the larger human brain has a new quality which the animal brain cannot possess. Higher organization of organic matter simply reacts that way. Such is the law of nature. Now if human intelligence is a mutation and an offspring of animal intelligence upon a higher plane, the *sensus numinis*, in our opinion, is equally an offspring of a former animal characteristic. Otto describes the *sensus numinis* in its primitive form as an emotional stupifaçtion of awe and fear.[1] This is a commonly observed animal characteristic. The bird is stupified in the presence of a snake and is unable to fly away. The terror of natural phenomena acts upon animals in much the same way as upon human beings. I do not deny that human " awe " has a new quality which differentiates it from animal fear, just as any other animal instinct in man takes on a new quality. What in the animal appears as a stupefying fear in the presence of the unexpected and the terrifying, in man becomes the seed of religion, of *numinus* awe. It provides a perfect analogy to Kant's moral sense or categorical imperative, which in its animal state is known to us as " social instinct," but which in the human state is a conscious social responsibility, i.e. a categorical imperative. In the animal state, the *sensus numinis* is " stupifying fear "; in the human stage, it is a conscious appreciation of this fear and a reflection upon its *wunder-*

[1] *Ibid.*, p. 3. Otto says: " Emotionen des numinosen Staunens und der Scheu."

wesen. Such an interpretation makes any *a priori* category of the *sensus numinis* unnecessary, neither does it minimize the religious sense any more than it minimizes the moral sense, or human intelligence, because of its animal antecedents. All human psychic characteristics are new qualities, but these qualities only arise upon some biological or social animal base. They are a continuity and yet something new. To those reasoning from the dialectical hypothesis of evolution there is nothing mysterious in these mutations. It is a well-observed law of nature.

While Communist theory recognizes the many-sidedness and the subjective elements in religion, it tends to simplify the matter by exposing its objective roots, which it traces to the social economic conditions, and is confident that with the change of these objective conditions the subjective experience will undergo a cardinal change, discarding religion altogether.

To the query—does modern civilization need religion?—the Communist answer is *yes*, so far as decaying capitalist civilization is concerned. There, under pressure of crisis, in an atmosphere of uncertainty and fear, religion serves as an escape mechanism for the classes which history has already condemned. It also is still a necessity to certain elements of the petty bourgeoisie and those of the backward toiling classes who have not as yet grown class-conscious and are held down by traditions. In a socialist society the uncertainties, fears and isolations of the individual vanish, and religion, at least as it has been known so far, is certain also to disappear. The class-conscious workers are guided by an atheist ideology which nevertheless gives them direction to a purposive life.

On the contrary Reinhold Niebuhr, in his able study on the fate of religion under modern civilization, believes that religion, while in a state of decay in capitalist society, may still have chances of rejuvenation. He points to the crushing influence which machine civilization, backed by modern science, revealing an impersonal universe, has had upon the integrity of human personality. In such a universe the human spirit seems to be reduced " to a mere effervescence to outlast the collocation of forces which produced it."[1] Depersonalization of the universe and depersonalization of civilization through the machine are the forces which impede personality and threaten to crush it. Niebuhr takes personality for " that type of reality which is self-conscious and self-determining,"[2] and he cannot think it could be valid except in a universe where creative freedom is developed and maintained not only in individual life but in the universe as well. These complaints indicate revolt against mechanized civilization and a mechanistically determined universe.

According to this reasoning, if religion is to survive, it must create a new metaphysics which must meet these demands of personality. This is one aspect of the problem. The other is the fact " that more men in our modern era are irreligious because religion has failed to make civilization ethical, than because it has failed to maintain its intellectual respectability,"[3] and here is the real tragedy of religion in the modern world. Organized religion, by logic of class society, has come under control and has been put to the service of the decaying ruling classes to which the ethical demands of a socialized democracy has no promise nor appeal. To begin with, the masses of industrial workers drift away from the Church and grow indifferent to religion. Can anything reclaim them ? Niebuhr answers in the affirmative. He says : " the quest for what is not real but always becoming real, for what is not true but is always becoming true, that makes man incurably religious."[4] It is the quest for the ideal implicit in human nature. Every organism is urged to move on towards its own completeness which calls for moral purpose and ethical freedom. This makes man rise above the present conflict, maintained by a religious hope, preventing despair. Religion is generated by the desire for perfection and freedom, which cannot be realized in this world as it is constituted ; therefore men have always become " otherworldly," finding compensation in the unreal and mystical.

[1] Reinhold Niebuhr, *Does Civilization Need Religion*, p. 5.
[2] *Ibid.*, p. 6. [3] *Ibid.*, p. 12. [4] *Ibid.*, p. 239.

What can the Communist answer to this enlightened opinion of a thoughtful observer? We believe he would say that Communist philosophy has for its goal the conquest of those two major evils of capitalist civilization which Niebuhr has detected; the first of which is a depersonalized civilization growing out of the subjection of the individual to the machine. The Communist system makes the machine servant and not master, and through its aid man is freed from dependence upon nature, making it possible to overcome class society, since classless society is the one condition of true freedom. Secondly the dialectic philosophy of Communism has overcome mechanistic metaphysics and has endowed the universe with a law which gives meaning to cosmic necessity and makes a self-directed, purposeful life possible. In Communist classless society, escape to another mystic world becomes unnecessary, since man shall have here the freedom to live a full life. This in itself will deprive religion of the soil in which it grows and it is bound to wither away. The Communist answer to our query is that *a classless Communist civilization will have no religion, but it will have a spiritual culture and an integral philosophy of life.*

The student of Communist atheism is struck not only by this clearly thought out theory but also by the militant tactics of Communist atheism and by that elaborate machine which is systematically at work to wreck the still existing institutions of religion and to uproot their every vestige. There was nothing ever like it in the history of the human race. In the Soviet Union, religion is at present put to the supreme test of its vitality. It may have resources which to us have so far remained hidden and which may now reveal themselves, but the known forces which have produced the historic religion of the Russian people have exhausted themselves and Communism is digging in that country the grave of Orthodox religion. During the last fifteen years already half the Russian churches have been closed, destroyed or put to other uses. This process still continues, though at a somewhat slower rate. Nevertheless it seems that in another generation religion, as organized at present, is doomed to disappear.

To appreciate fully the significance of this process, the tragedy of religion in Russia must be studied against its historic background. In the first chapters of this book we shall, therefore, sketch the one thousand years development of Russian Christianity from its inception to the present, showing how it was embraced by the people and what was its social significance.

The relation of State and Church in Russian history calls for special attention, for the present plight of the Church is in a large measure the result of this unholy alliance. It also brought into existence the Nonconformist movement, the evangelical forms of which are to some extent holding their own against the competition of Communist propaganda. For the present at least Evangelical Christianity, for reasons which we shall show later, has a better chance of survival than the historic Orthodox Church.

Apart from the Evangelical mass movement and the popular religion of the people, are the remnants of the old intelligentsia, showing desperate efforts to adjust their religious demands to modern science and the encroachments of mechanical civilization. Impotent to cope with these, many of the intellectuals sought refuge in apocalyptic mysticism or, as in the case of Tolstoy, in resolutely rejecting modern civilization altogether and reverting to primitive, pre-capitalistic, rural forms of life. While the influence of the intellectualist " God-wrestlers and God-seekers," as they were called, is practically nil in the Soviet Union, it flourishes among the Russian immigrants in Western Europe and America.

Parallel to the development of the religious thought and tradition we must sketch the anti-religious tradition in Russia, which had its beginnings in the 18th century and has culminated in the Communist anti-religious movement. The clash of the Church with the Revolution also had its long history. The uncompromising enmity of the proletarian Revolution to the Church has its sources in this struggle which lasted for nearly a century.

In the chapters dealing with the anti-religious movement we describe the methods and organization of this extensive movement and show the conflict which is now raging between militant atheism and religion in the Soviet Union. It is our aim not to obscure this issue but to present the existing situation with all its tragic consequences to the Church, not only in the Soviet Union but throughout the world, wherever Communist propaganda and organization exist, as for example, in Central China where a population greater than that of the United Kingdom and France together is held under Communist control and is being rapidly Sovietized, where also the anti-religious policy of the Party is carried out equally well, although with greater caution than in Russia itself.

In our study we also pay attention to the description of the Atheist International which pursues the task of organizing proletarian freethinkers and atheists all over the world. Militant atheism is directed not only against organized Christianity but against every other religion. In the atheist centres in Moscow, Leningrad and other large cities, specialists are at work studying methods to combat Judaism, Islam, Buddhism, Shamanism, and the other great religions of the East.

There is a tendency among some writers on Communism [1] to ignore the religious issue, or to regard it as a misunderstanding, interpreting Communist opposition to organized religion as an opposition to the abuses of religion but not to religion in its pure state. This is a great error. Communists, particularly Lenin, have always emphasized that reformed, modernized, socialized and every other improved religion, is worse than the old orthodox, reactionary religion. As a matter of fact, Communists are much more tolerant to reactionary religion than to any of its modernized and philosophically improved forms. Lenin fought hard to eradicate within his own Party every vestige of the old religion and prevent the appearance of any new socialized and modernized form.

The Communist intolerance towards religion has led critics to the conclusion that Communism must be itself a new world religion. For, they argue, the Communist claims alone to hold the *truth* and that intolerance is the first and sure attribute

[1] For example, Middleton Murry in *The Necessity of Communism*.

of any new religion. To prove this it is shown that the aims of Communism do not differ from those of Christianity at its best. Communist theory presupposes a belief in the possibility of a good, free, ethical life and its faith in the common man as the hope of the future is altogether unwarranted from the scientific point of view ; it spurs the faith of its adherents to the point of missionary zeal and martyrdom, the like of which the history of religion alone presents its parallels ; finally Communist theory is apocalyptic in outlook, for it expects to reach its goal only after a desperate bloody conflict with its class enemies, a parallel to the apocalyptic battle of Armageddon.

These comparisons and parallels are thought provoking. The Communist optimistic faith in the common man is not denied ; on the contrary it is Communism's fundamental working hypothesis, which it continually checks by experience and from experimental work carried out in special psychological laboratories. But the Communist himself objects to calling his creed and movement a religion. He does not object to calling it an ideology, which he construes upon scientifically tested facts, and he employs in his service experimental science to a degree which no other social movement has ever done. One thing he does openly confess, and in this respect Communist teaching is not unlike religious dogma, it is frankly *partisan*, it accepts its proletarian class bias and scornfully rejects any so-called objective, impersonal, or super-class science and philosophy.

Communists greatly dislike religious terminology. In this respect they suffer from acute logophobia, a prejudice against unpleasant terminology. This is of course quite human and a common ailment of most people. In our study we shall avoid treating Communism as a religion, either in terminology or through psychological analogy. To do so would not help in solving our problems but rather obscure the issue. Of course Communists are human beings and whatever difference in theory and opinion the opposing philosophies may possess, there still remains the basis of common humanity, on which we shall always be able to meet and understand one another.

CHAPTER II
THE RELIGION OF THE PEOPLE

THE religion of the great mass of Russian people, including the Ukrainians, the Georgians, and some of the other minority races of the former Russian Empire, is nominally orthodox Christianity as taught by the so-called " Holy Orthodox Church," or the " Greek Orthodox Church." It was introduced into Russia from Byzantium at the time when the rivalry between the Eastern and the Western sections of the Christian Church was nearing its breaking point; the final severance took place in 1054. The Byzantine emperors were hard pressed by the advancing Moslems and the continuous raids of barbarians, and sought the support of the latter by their Christianization. Thus, at about the middle of the 10th century, the people of the Balkans were Christianized, and there were also groups of Christians in Southern Russia, particularly amongst the roving warriors.

The official date of the baptism of the Russian people is given as 988. This was a mass performance ordered by the ruling prince, Vladimir of Kiev, who undertook this religious reform of his people partly from personal leanings towards the Christian cult, but chiefly because of political considerations, wishing to establish closer contact with the Byzantine Emperor whose sister he married. He wanted also to be sure of the loyalty of his army, which by this time had many Christians in its ranks. Princess Olga of Kiev, who became a convert to Christianity in 955, had also a share in persuading Vladimir to become a Christian. Later she was canonized and is venerated as the first Russian Christian saint.

One of the peculiarities of the Russian Orthodox Church, by which it was marked from its very inception, was its close organic relation to the State and to the patronage of the Crown. In this it differed from its rival in Rome, where the Church maintained a relative independence from the State and sought always to rule princes and emperors, rather than be ruled by them. Another peculiarity of the Russian Church is the fact that the Christianity it adopted at the close of the 10th century was the religion of a declining State, rapidly losing the once glorious traditions of the Byzantine Empire. For these reasons the religion which Vladimir took over from Byzantium was already a completely stereotyped orthodoxy, lacking the fervour and the youth of its apostolic days. Finally, being imposed upon the people by order of a despotic ruler, it was simply grafted upon the existing paganism, much of which has survived to this day in the religious cult and the customs of the common people.

PAGAN SURVIVALS

The Pagan Slavs had not a very highly developed religion. They worshipped Perun, the thunder god, together with many spirits of nature. There was also a cult of the dead and an ancestor veneration, together with a preanimistic worship of the uncanny and of the awe-inspiring generally. Russian folk lore shows many survivals of totemic ideas. Animals were generally considered friendly and helpful. They are tenderly called " godmother wolf," " godmother fox," " czar bear," and so on. The horse was always considered a symbol of power, because its early owners were usually knights and princes. The he-goat enjoyed particular popularity; to him were ascribed powers to scare away bad spirits and to aid in the growth of crops. The last ears of grain gathered from the fields were braided into his beard and he was presented with a freshly baked loaf of bread. To this day, in some parts of Russia, village youths dress in goatskins and, with the he-goat as mascot, they wander through the fields singing : " Where the goat passes, the grain will grow."

There was strength in this Christian paganism. It was due to its antiquity, its quaint beauty and, in spite of its boasted orthodoxy, its independence from speculative thought, from puritan morals and individualism. The syncretism of the old Slavic paganism with Byzantine Christianity, which became the Russian orthodox religion, has many elements of a crude anthropomorphism and religious materialism which, however, was quite suited to the primitive economy and social life of the peasants and the town folks of feudal times. They still worshipped and appeased the spirits of the hearth, the field, the forest, the waters, etc.; they used magic and incantations against illness, "bad luck," the "evil eye," drought and flood and other forces of nature against which primitive man felt himself impotent. Even such a subtle concept as the "Grace of God" was understood quite materialistically; to this day Samara peasants close windows and chimneys and plug up cracks in the walls when the priest is invited to say prayers in the house. These precautions are taken to make sure that as little as possible of the " grace " of the prayer may escape through any possible opening in the house.

To satisfy the demands of these primitive needs the priest functioned similarly to the former magician and medicine man. He had the power of " grace " which was bestowed upon him by the mystery of ordination, and he was attired, besides, in sacerdotal vestment, equipped with a holy cross, an ikon, sacred ointment, and holy water. All these invested him with powers of " grace " which, when administered with the proper " words " and " signs," were able to give the coveted protection and relief. The personality, wisdom and moral quality of the priest as a man had nothing to do with the efficacy of " grace "; as long as the ritual was carried out according to the old traditions and the price of the performance was not too exorbitant, the parishioners were entirely satisfied.

Up to the 18th century illiterate village priests were quite the common rule. Before ordination they had to learn the words of the service by heart and they repeated them ever after with but the least idea of their meaning. This semi-paganism of the masses was not denied even by such an authority on Russian Orthodox Christianity as the famous

High Procurator of the Holy Synod, Pobyedonostzev, who practically ruled the Church and the State for two generations. Pobyedonostzev, who died in 1907, said: " Our clergy teaches little and seldom. The Bible does not exist for the illiterate people. . . . In far off parts of the country the people understand absolutely nothing as to the meaning of the words of the service, not even the Lord's Prayer, which is often repeated with alterations which altogether destroy its meaning. And yet, in all those primitive minds there is erected, as in ancient Athens, an altar to the unknown god, and they resign their lives to providence as a matter of course."

The original Slavic cult of the dead has fully survived and has merged with the Christian cult. The primitive idea of the soul was crudely materialistic. It was thought to be like a bee or a tiny mouse, or a butterfly, or a small bird, which lived in the little nest formed between the neck and the chest. When man slept or died, this little soul-animal went from him. Death differed from sleep only in so far as in sleep the departure of the soul was temporary and in death permanent. Under Christian influence the soul changed its shape from an animal to a *pneuma*, an intangible something, but none-the-less real and hence to be cared for.

In some of the more backward sections of the country, like White Russia, the care of the soul of the departed is still taken quite seriously. It begins even before death has set in. It is considered highly important not to lose sight of the soul; therefore into the hands of the dying person is pressed a burning candle. As soon as death has set in, the flame of the candle is extinguished and the direction of the departing smoke indicates the direction in which the soul has fled. If the eyes of the deceased happen to remain open this is considered a sure sign that the departed is looking for some mate to take with him, so the eyes of the dead are quickly shut and sometimes such heavy objects as large copper coins are placed upon the eyelids to keep them down. The deceased is washed and dressed by strangers, not by relatives, for it is feared that any discomfort to the dead during this performance may arouse his wrath and it is therefore thought safer to employ strangers, whom the dead does not know, to render him this last service. On the contrary the night watches are held in the presence of relatives to assure the dead of their affection for him. Psalm readers are employed to read to the dead for his solace and this is continued day and night as long as the deceased is in the house. After the burial, memorial services and feasts are held and some of the food is deposited on the grave. These ceremonies are repeated on the ninth, the twentieth and the fortieth days, when it is believed the soul finally departs from the earth. But the return of the dead is considered always possible, and therefore semi-annual memorial services are conducted.

In White Russia, according to Professor N. M. Nikolsky,[1] the cult of the dead is still practiced on " ancestral days." In spring and autumn, particularly during the latter season, a family feast is arranged, for which occasion a thorough cleaning of the premises is undertaken. Plenty of food and drink is served, and when the family is gathered about the table the family head opens " the soul trap," a small opening in the ceiling, and the ancestors are invited to join the feast. The head of the family speaks thus : " Holy grandfathers we call you, holy grandfathers come down to us. There is everything our house possesses, holy grandfathers we beg you, if you wish, to come down to us ! " During the meal all present throw morsels of food and drink under the table and after the meal the ancestors are requested to depart with the words : " Holy grandfathers, you have come down here, you have drunk and eaten, fly back home. Tell us what else you want, rise then, rise to heaven ! " This survival of pagan rites illustrates how the Christian ideas of the immortal soul fitted in well with the primitive Slavic cult of the dead.

Under the patronage of the ruling princes the Church grew in wealth and power. The dreary landscape of the Russian plains was soon dotted with quaint onion-shaped domes which in towns and settlements produce a beautiful skyline. Not all

[1] N. M. Nikolsky, *History of the Russian Church*, 1931.

of the Slavic tribes, however, accepted the new religion as resignedly as the people of Kiev. Novgorod, report the Chroniclers, was baptized with the aid of the sword and with fire. And from the Northern Rostov three bishops fled for their lives when they tried to burn up the old idols of the town. But in time the Christian Byzantine cult attracted the people by its gorgeous beauty and ceremony, though the teachings of the Church remained quite unintelligible to the barbarian Slavs. Hence, their " conversion " remained but an outward affair and gradually merged with the old folk lore. The affection which the people had to the new ikon cult was not unlike that which they cherished for their former family idols and fetishes. Their old magic rites and feast days were simply re-christened with new names. This, of course, is not only peculiar to the Slavic Church. It was the case wherever there was compulsory or mass conversion of savage or barbarian people.

The early Russian Church deserves credit for much colonizing in the remote parts of the great Russian country. Monastic settlements sprang up in the wilderness, becoming the nuclei for trade and frequently developing into large towns and cities. The Church quickly realized its advantages as a colonizer. Everywhere it went it established titles to enormous tracts of land. By the 17th century, it actually owned one-third of all the land in Russia, besides thousands of peasant serfs ; but subsequently it lost a part of the land by expropriation measures carried out by the Tzars since the 18th century, and particularly during the reign of Catherine II, who turned much of the land over to the crown and its favoured nobility.

ECCLESIASTICAL CULTURE

Cities like Kiev, Novgorod, Moscow and most of the older cities of Russia, were culturally speaking ecclesiastical towns. Their most valued property was held by the church. For example, in Moscow a generation ago, at a time when the population was about half a million, there were in this city 10 cathedrals, 15 monasteries, 9 convents, 2 deaconess centres,

351 churches and 33 chapels, with 1,233 clerics, besides several thousand monks, nuns and professional choristers, supplying the music to the churches.[1] The ringing of the bells of these many churches, their gorgeous processions on feast days, the splendour of their music and the mysticism of the ritual, filled the atmosphere of the city and gave it a quality of its own. The old Moscow was limited to the walls of the Kremlin; within it there is still a mass of church buildings and palaces with little space for residential purposes. But as the city grew to wider circles around the Kremlin, churches were planted at every city gate and along the main thoroughfares.

The Mother Church of Moscow is the old cathedral of the Assumption of the Holy Virgin in the Kremlin. Its foundation dates back to early 14th century. Many times it was destroyed and again rebuilt. It was often looted by invaders, but the piety and patronage of the ruling princes always re-endowed this ancient church. The last to loot it was Napoleon who, from this church alone, took as much as 1,300 pounds of silver, 720 pounds of gold and many precious stones. This enormous amount of metal was used for decorating the altar gates and the sarcophagi of the Muscovite princes and patriarchs, who were interred in the walls of this church, which is decorated by as many as 375 ikons, besides fine fresco ornamentation on the walls, the dome, and the pillars.

In this church took place the gorgeous ceremonies of the Tsars' coronations and the anointing of the Patriarchs and Metropolitans. Frequently great processions made their start hence to various parts of the town and to the river Moscow to bless its waters. These processions were held in commemoration of great historic events in the national history, such as the liberation of the city from the invading Tartars, the Poles and, last of all, Napoleon; also during such great church festivals as Easter and New Year.

In these " Processions of the Cross," as they were called,

[1] This data does not include churches and clergy of other creeds such as the Old Believers, and other dissenters, Roman Catholics, Protestants, Jews, etc.

usually participated all the clergy of Moscow, all the fine choirs and thousands of people. One orthodox writer called these processions " the church in motion." He writes : " What temple walls can include so many sacred objects, so numerous a congregation of clergymen, singers and such a mass of people as a procession of the cross." Festive ringing of the numerous bells of the Kremlin and nearby churches announced the starting of the procession. It was led by gorgeously vested choirs of boys and men. The clergy, headed by a bishop, followed in full vestment; zealots of the faith carried the sacred ikons, crosses and richly decorated gonfalons. The whole was a most impressive spectacle. In the centre of the procession, raised upon a high dais, were carried the sacred " miracle working " ikons of the Vladimir Virgin and the Iberian Virgin; the first was housed in the Cathedral of the Assumption in the Kremlin, and the other, called " The Gatekeeper," was for centuries in a little shrine outside the gate leading to what is now the Red Square. The dais was carried in such a way as to leave a passage below it, and particularly fervent believers in the miraculous power of those images prostrated themselves upon the pavement and lay there in expectation that the sacred ikons, in passing over them, would take with them all their infirmities. Women " possessed " shrieked hysterically at the sight of these venerated images and frequently raised the accompanying mob to a pitch of fanaticism. Male bystanders, watching the procession, had to remove their headgear or run the risk of having it knocked off by zealots in the mob. Thus the piety and religious zeal of Russian orthodoxy showed itself.

IKON AND RELIC WORSHIP

Another favoured expression of the religious fervour of the Russian Christians was their passion for making pilgrimages to sacred shrines and places throughout the country. They were always in search of the miraculous. This encouraged particularly monastic centres and convents to possess some miracle working ikon or relic, the latter usually consisting of an " in-

THE RELIGION OF THE PEOPLE

corruptible " saint—a mummified body, which was considered a sure sign of sanctity. This belief originated in the naive interpretation of the scriptural passage which says, " nor wilt thou suffer thine holy one to see corruption." Naturally monasteries which could not dig up real mummies were tempted to fraud, and frequently exposed to the miracle-hungry mob some dummy specially prepared for them. In addition cures of cripples were instigated, and all kinds of other sensational miracles performed. Of course, there were occasionally real cures ; for faith, even in a dummy saint, may remove mountains and the power of auto-suggestion can do many wondrous things.

One of the queer results of this rivalry for sacred ikons and relics is that during feudal times ruling princes frequently undertook raids and besieged towns and monasteries to capture some particularly popular relic or ikon, or, if it proved impossible to get them by force, to obtain these sacred objects by fraud or bribe. The belief in the magic power of these pictures and bones was so strong that no warrior felt secure in going to battle unless some such relic was carried in the ranks ; most of the famous ikons of Russia have a great war history behind them. Many of the sacred virgins are credited with victories over invaders or as conquerors of new territories and peoples.

It may be of interest to hear the histories of some of these ikons.

We have already mentioned the Vladimir ikon of the Holy Virgin, housed in the Kremlin Cathedral of the Assumption. It is credited with existing as long as Christianity itself. It is supposed to have been painted by St. Luke and presented to Mary the mother of Jesus. Mary seeing this painting of herself greeted it with the words : " Behold from henceforth all generations shall call me blessed," and then added, " the grace of him whom I have born and mine will abide with this ikon." In the 5th century, under Emperor Theodosius the Younger, this ikon was taken from Jerusalem to Constantinople, and in the middle of the 12th century it was brought to Kiev, to Prince Ury Dolgoruky, where it was for a short time exhibited in a virgin's convent. Soon afterwards Prince Andrew, the son of Ury, went on a campaign to the North and took this ikon with him for protection. On reaching the principality of Susdal, within ten miles of the town of Vladimir, the horses which carried the ikon refused to go further and Andrew took it for a hint that the Virgin wanted to rest there. This was corroborated to him in a vision in which the Virgin stated that she wished her ikon to remain in Vladimir. Prince Andrew was obedient and at once ordered for her the erection of a habitation in the form of a church. He enshrined his ikon most lavishly in silver, gold and precious stones. Thirty pounds of gold alone, says the historian, were used for this purpose. Thenceforth the ikon became known as the Vladimir ikon of the Virgin. Her fame spread far and wide and she was the object of the envy of many princes. She participated in many battles and not a few victories were accredited her; but she also suffered some reverses. In 1237 the Tartars besieged and captured the city of Vladimir; of course they looted and destroyed the church, taking with them the precious ornaments of the Virgin. Somehow the ikon miraculously survived and soon was rehoused in a new church and splendidly redecorated by the ruling Prince George of Vladimir.

In 1395 the fierce Tamerlane swept with his horsemen over the Russian plains, setting Moscow as his goal. Basil, the ruling prince of Moscow was greatly frightened; his only hope, he believed, of escaping destruction was to appeal to the principality of Vladimir for the aid of the Virgin. A delegation of high clerics from the Kremlin cathedral was hurriedly despatched to Vladimir and by threats and bribes succeeded in extracting the Virgin from the town in spite of the weeping and lamentation of the population. So great was the crowd accompanying the ikon that it took ten days to carry her in procession to Moscow. When she approached the city gate, innumerable people lined both sides of the road kneeling and crying, " Mother of God! Save the Russian land! " The high nobility and all the clergy of Moscow met the ikon and accompanied her in a gorgeous " procession of the cross " to the Cathedral of the Assumption where she was duly enthroned. While this was taking place in Moscow, Tamerlane was dozing in his tent, but was startled by a vision of a high mountain moving towards him, from which descended a company of saints carrying golden crosiers; over them hovered, in beaming light of indescribable magnificence and splendour, a woman surrounded by hosts of warriors. Frightened he called his sages into council and asked them what this vision might mean. They answered, " This woman of heavenly splendour which you have seen is the God Mother, the protector of Christians, and therefore we shall not vanquish them." To the surprise of everybody Tamerlane ordered his retreat and, concludes the chronicler: " For the sake of the virtuous life of Prince Vasily Dmitrievitch God honoured him and spared the Russian land from the invasion of godless Temir-Aksaka (Tamerlane) by the coming of the miraculous image of His (Christ's) Pure Mother, painted by his own divine spokesman, Luke."[1] The street by which the Virgin entered Moscow in 1395 is to this day called Sretenka, that is " the street of meeting "; and the gates of the city through which she had passed are called the Sretenka Gates. To commemorate the event, a fortlike monastery was built near this gate and was called the Sretensky Monastery. Thenceforth the ikon remained in Moscow and is credited with many miraculous deeds in saving the city from invaders. Before this ikon, princes, tsars and warriors swore allegiance to their country. It is still housed in the Kremlin Cathedral of the Assumption of the Holy Virgin. The ikon in itself is a small painting on a wood panel, twelve by seven inches; it represents the Virgin with the infant Christ clinging close to her neck. The ikon is mounted in a silver case and the panel is decorated by precious trimming of gold and precious stones valued at $100,000.

This Vladimir Virgin, while very popular with the Muscovite rulers, is by no means the only attraction of its kind in

[1] See F. I. Rychin, *Guide Through Moscow Sanctuaries*, pp. 23–24.

Moscow. There are hundreds of other ikons of the Virgin, the Saviour and of popular saints, which enjoy as great and perhaps greater popularity among the people than the one just described, and reproductions of which are found in practically every Russian household.

The curious thing about these sacred panels is that copies of them, if properly prepared and blessed, are just as effective in their miraculous power as the originals. A good case in hand is the ikon of the Iberian Virgin. It is a copy from the original, miracle-working ikon of the Greek monastery on Holy Mount Aethos. This ikon was called by the Greeks the Portaitissa of Iberia, that is, the Gate-keeper of Iberia. The monks of Mt. Aethos, being in constant need of money, made an offer to the pious Tsar-Alexis to prepare for him a copy of the sacred ikon in return for the privilege of coming to Russia to collect alms for their monastery. They assured the Tsar and his chief adviser, the later Patriarch Nikon, that the copy would have all the merits of the original. In a letter addressed to the Tsar and to Nikon, Pakhomius, the Father Superior of the Monastery, gives a detailed description of the Mt. Aethos recipe for transferring the wonder-working quality from the original to its copy. We shall quote somewhat extensively from this most curious historic document, first published in 1879.

"In response to Your Majesty's will and the word from the saintly Lord Archimandrite Nikon of the new Spassov monastery, I, on my arrival into our monastery gathered our whole fraternity of three hundred and sixty-five brethren for much prayer and song, lasting from evening until sunrise. We blessed water with holy relics (that is, bodily remains of dead saints) and poured this holy water over the sacred miracle-working ikon of the blessed God-bearer, the old Portaitess; we collected this water into a great basin and again and again poured it over the new ikon, made of cedar wood. Then we gathered this water into a basin and zealously celebrated divine and holy mass. After the holy mass we gave this holy water and the holy relics to the ikon painter, the Reverend Friar and

Holy Father, Lord Yamblikhon Romanov, in order that he, after mixing the holy water with the relics and the colours, might paint the holy and blessed ikon, in order that the panel and the colours be joined with the holy water and the relics. And in painting this holy ikon, he partook of food only on Saturdays and Sundays and completed it in great silence with joy and vigilance."

The letter adds that while Romanov was painting the ikon, Pakhomius and the three hundred and sixty-five brethren conducted prayers from dark until sunrise twice every week and daily celebrated holy mass till the ikon was completed, which was within two weeks.

It must not be thought that I am unearthing these medieval saint stories to make sport of the credulity of the people, reviving tales otherwise long forgotten. This is not the case. The Iberian Virgin survived the Revolution and its shrine remained at the gates leading into the Red Square until 1930, when the Soviet Government removed it to make room for a wider street. And even now it still continues to " work its miracles," although in a much quieter place than before, being housed in a small chapel situated in a blind alley, not far from the Nikitskaya Street almost opposite the building of the Conservatory of Music. Although there are no street signs which would indicate the whereabouts of the ikon, thousands of devotees manage to discover her, and the chapel is open from morning until night every day, and many services are conducted there which are specially ordered and paid for by the faithful.

To the orthodox Christian prayer seems possible only in the presence of an ikon. In medieval times, 13th to 16th centuries, it was customary that each parishioner, besides his household ikon, had also his ikon hanging in the church, to which he prayed during the service without regard for the priest or anyone else. Trouble arose when someone else dared to pray to an ikon not his own. This meant to steal the " grace " from it and was greatly objected to by the owners. The sight of such a service with each worshipper turning in a different direction must have been ridiculous, but even to this day it is not unusual to find people praying before a favoured ikon in some corner of the church all by themselves while the service is chanted by the priests. The ikon is thus more than a reminder of the presence of God; it is possessed of God and full of " grace." The ikon lives, feels, sees, and hears. It watches over the home life and is pleased when tapers are lit before it or when it is clothed in silver, gold and precious stones. These beliefs are so ingrained in the mind of the people that they still linger on and even intelligent people cling to them, who otherwise appear quite rational beings.

The religious practices of the people with their ikon and relic worship, their feast days, and sacerdotal functions are of a purely utilitarian nature and are designed as protection against evil spirits, disease and famine. The dogma of the church is of secondary importance. Orthodoxy is rather understood as conformity to the old rites and practices and has little or nothing to do with the teachings of the Bible and the basic dogma of the church. The Bible is practically unknown and not read by the people. Bible-reading Christians were always under suspicion of evangelical sectarianism, and as a matter of fact the Russian evangelical sects originated with the introduction and the spreading of the Bible by foreign societies.

DOCTRINAL PECULIARITIES

If we turn to the teachings of the Russian Orthodox Church, we find it emphasises the static aspects of religion. It considers its chief function is to conserve the truth which was put into its trust by the Fathers of the Church. There are no new truths to discover and even the thought of such a thing is heretical. On the occasion of the ninth centenary of the " conversion of Russia," one of the solemn pronouncements made by representative clergymen was expressed in the following words: " The Orthodox Church alone has preserved the divine doctrines just as they were committed to her, and will preserve them unchanged to the end of the ages, without adding to or taking from them a single iota, inasmuch as she is the pillar and ground of truth, inasmuch as the spirit of God which dwelleth within her preserveth her from all error."

This is precisely the doctrinal position of the Greek Orthodox Church. It considers its task to *preserve*, not to develop or search for truth. Therefore the learning of Orthodox theologians limited itself to the apologetic function of guarding against any possible innovation. By the " Divine Doctrine," which is mentioned in the above statement, is meant the Nicene Creed and the canons of the Seven Ecumenical Councils.[1] The doctrines of the first four of these Councils were raised by the Emperor Justinian, as confirmed by the Fifth General Council, to the level of the Holy Scriptures, and this ruling has been accepted by the Russian Orthodox Church.

Let us briefly recall what doctrines were developed in these Councils, which as we have seen, are still valid in the Russian Church, and which it intends to preserve unchanged to the end of the ages. The first General Council of Nicaea in 325, because of its Catholic representation, was unquestionably the most important of the doctrine-making Councils. The principal problem it attempted to solve was to give definition of the Godhead, which to the philosophically-minded Greeks seemed to be of the highest importance and about which passionate controversies were carried on by the followers of Arius and Athanasius, especially at Alexandria, the most prominent centre, in the early centuries after Christ, of philosophical and theological speculation.

As is well known the controversy turned on the relations of the Divine Persons in the Trinity, dealing in the most subtle shades of meaning of words for which only the Greek language finds expression. And yet this excess of dogmatism in the most abstract region of human thought was elevated, subscribed, sealed, and guarded by anathemas as " Divine Doc-

---

[1] These Councils are known according to the names of the cities in which they were held : in Nicaea in 325 ; in Constantinople in 381 ; in Ephesos in 431; in Chalcedon in 451; in Constantinople in 553 and 680; in Nicaea in 787.

trine," of which the Greek Orthodox Church of to-day is the most ardent supporter.[1]

Although the makers of the Creed intended to have it stand unaltered for " ever and ever," there were, nevertheless, certain additions and subtractions made at the Fourth General Council in 451. From that time on it has stood unaltered.

Other problems which occupied these Councils pertained largely to the condemnation of heretics, i.e. those ecclesiastics who did not yield to the rulings of the majority in the controversies. Besides this, the Councils regulated the conduct of the clergy and gradually developed the Greek Orthodox system of ecclesiastical hierarchy. Thus the institution of the patriarchate was established at the Fourth General Council in 451. The Seventh and last General Council recognized by the Russian Church sanctioned the veneration of sacred pictures and condemned the iconoclasts who would destroy them.

This was in the year 787. Since then the Holy Spirit ceased to reveal " Divine Doctrine." Orthodoxy was stereotyped and theologians of the Church for almost twelve centuries have spent their energies in guarding against adding or taking from it a single iota.

This stereotyped doctrinal position of the Eastern Church, Greek and Russian, explains some of the peculiarities which distinguish it from those of the West, whether Roman Catholic or Protestant. It is particularly marked by the absence of

[1] The Creed, which was the final outcome of the heated debates of the ecclesiastics at Nicaea, reads as follows :

" We believe in one God, the Father Almighty, Maker of all things both visible and invisible ;

" And in one Lord Jesus Christ, the Son of God, begotten of the Father, *only begotten that is to say, of the Father, God of God,* Light of Light, very God of very God, begotten not made, being of one substance with the Father, by whom all things were made, *both things in heaven and things in earth*—who for us men and for our salvation came down and was made flesh and was made man, suffered, rose again on the third day, and went up into the heavens ;

" And in the Holy Ghost.

" But those that say ' there was when He was not,' and ' before He was begotten He was not,' and that ' He came into existence from what was not,' or who profess that the Son of God is a different ' person ' or ' substance,' or that He is created, or variable, are anathematized by the Catholic Church."

a learned clergy. There is no need for them, since no new truth is to be discovered. There exists some scholarship to perpetuate the traditional theology and guard against heretics who might undermine the Orthodox faith, but for original thinking there is neither need nor place in the Orthodox Church. This may account for the fact that the few original religious philosophers Russia has produced were all laymen; the best known of these are the Slavophil Khomayakov and, more recently, Vladimir Soloviev. The Russian Church, unlike the Churches of the West, has developed no institutions of secular learning There were never Church Colleges and Universities in Russia, and even the former theological seminaries and academies, which generally maintained a fair standard of scholarship, have ceased to exist and seem not to be missed whatever by the Church, which manages very well without a learned clergy.

The monasteries, which in the West were generally centres of learning, were not so in Russia, at least not with respect to letters. The learned monk was looked upon with suspicion. " Book cunning " could easily lead to spiritual pride, and was considered a weapon used by the devil to drag the souls of men to hell.

A narrative of the monks of the famous Petchersky Monastery tells how one of their brothers, named Nikita, had a vision of an angel who told him to become learned in order that he might instruct the people who came to him for advice. He set out to learn the Scriptures by heart and actually could recite the whole of the Old Testament. The Brethren suspected that it was the devil who seduced Brother Nikita to this folly and by persistent admonition and prayer succeeded in driving off the evil spirit from the learned Nikita, " and," ends the narrative, " Nikita lost all his knowledge."

Thus, because of the absence of learning, the Russian Church was not only unable to develop further the religious ideas she had received, but she was even unable to preserve them unchanged. Paul Miliukov, the historian of Russian civilization, makes the assertion that the Russian Church " necessarily adopted very easily and involuntarily the dogma of her former pagan creed. She attained this result by dint of simplifying Eastern Christianity and reducing it to a state of complete materialization. Simplified and materialized, the oriental creed has become a particular and national type of Russian orthodoxy."

The veneration of ikons and relics, which if properly understood has æsthetic and symbolic value for the faithful, has lost most of its spiritual quality in the practice of the Russian Church. The ikon, as we have shown, is such an important factor in the religious life of the Russian people that we must know the teachings of the Orthodox Church in regard to its purpose. As always the Church reverts to the interpretation and sanction given to the use of ikons by the General Councils. We already know that the Seventh General Council, which met at Nicaea in 787, occupied itself with the iconoclastic controversy and decided in favour of the veneration of sacred pictures. The arguments presented at the Council favouring the veneration of pictures are still advanced by the Russian Church.

St. Methodius of Constantinople, one of the champions in the defence of sacred images at the iconoclastic controversy, writes to his opponents : " You say that this veneration of the images has made gods of them ? But it is you, yourselves, who ought to teach the people in what way it is befitting to honour them. For, supposing that some villager or country boor were to meet a servant of the King, and should worship him as if he were the King himself, and should say to him, ' Have mercy on me, most gracious Majesty,' would you order that both the servant who received this homage and the man who offered it should be punished with death (on a charge of *laesa majestas*) ? Certainly not, inasmuch as he did it in ignorance. But it is the business of those who know to explain to the inexperienced that this is not the King ; inasmuch as the King lives in his palace and no one sees him except at such time as he chooses to show himself outside. And so you should teach those who in ignorance make a god of an image of Christ, that it is not Christ in the flesh but only an image of him. For Christ is in Heaven, and no man seeth Him, so far as I know, until He appear in His second coming to judge the world. And this they would certainly understand, and would regulate their worship accordingly. For this is what Bishops are meant for, namely to teach the people to believe and pray."

Thus in the early Church pictures were maintained principally on the ground of their practical utility. Images were the books for the unlearned and, in truth, the images in the older churches do represent the orthodox plan of salvation and the history of the Church. A classic illustration is furnished by the Moscow Cathedral of the Assumption and is considered to be a perfect model of the orthodox idea of a Christian church. Its iconostasis, that part of the church where the altar is situated, is divided horizontally into several tiers or stages, upon which in long rows are mounted the various ikons. The basic idea expressed in the pictures (ikons) is the beautiful and truly Christian doctrine of " the Communion of Saints " down through the ages.

The upper tier represents the saints of the era before Moses, with the Lord of Sabaoth in the centre. There are Adam, Seth, Enoch, and Abraham, Isaac and Jacob, who symbolize continuity of holiness proceeding from the Father of All Life. The next tier represents the saints of the Old Testament Church, from Moses to Christ, with the Holy Virgin in the centre. The prophets on either side of her hold scrolls containing the Messianic hope. In the tier below is pictured the story of the Gospels in twelve great events.[1] On the fourth row (immediately above the royal gates) the Christian Church itself is depicted by the reign of Christ who is seated on a heavenly throne as the everlasting High Priest making intercession for our sins; on either side of Him stand, in position of prayer, His Mother and St. John the Baptist, as two representatives of human perfection, the nearest intercessors before Him on behalf of sinful man. On both sides of them are

[1] These events are celebrated in the twelve principal feasts of the Orthodox Church. Easter is called the " Feast of Feasts."

ranged all the Apostles, beginning with St. Peter and St. Paul, as preachers of the Gospel of Christ and builders of His Church. Thus, beginning from above and descending upon the inner wall of the nave is depicted the gradual growth of the Church as the invisible Communion of Saints.

The four central pillars of the church are representative of the Martyrs, whose blood has been the strength of the Church; on the royal gates in the iconostasis are the ikons of the Annunciation and the four Evangelists; on the south wall are paintings of the General Councils, whose doctrines and canons contain the teachings of the Orthodox Church, and on the west wall is represented the Last Judgment. Besides these, there are many other ikons and paintings, representing madonnas and saints who were important factors in the making of the Russian Church and State.

The doctrinal interpretation of the ikons, however, goes beyond the ideas of symbolism. According to St. John Damascene, whose point of view triumphed at the Seventh Council, the *ikon became an object of incarnation of the Logos*. This idea must have much to do with the belief in " God-manifested " ikons, now prevalent in Russia. There are scores of ikons in Russia which the Church claims were not made by man but were sent down by God from Heaven. This is proved by their wonder-working power. I doubt whether the Fathers of the Councils would have accepted these myths, but in Russia they are but a natural development of the idea which was advocated by St. John Damascene, and are a clear case of what Milukov calls the materialization of the Christian ideas in Russia.

Next to this ikon worship the doctrine of prayer for the dead is of the greatest importance in the practice of the Orthodox Church. We have shown that it fitted in well with the traditional ancestor worship and the care of the departed. The enormous wealth of the Church has grown chiefly out of the exploitation of this superstition. Princes and rich men frequently endowed monasteries and churches on condition that daily prayers should be said for their departed souls.

The doctrine of retribution for sins committed on earth and the possibility of being relieved from punishment by the prayers of the Church was a mighty weapon in the possession of the clergy, who exploited it to its utmost capacity. Even to this day the income of the clergy is mostly obtained from this source. Most orthodox Russian families still maintain the custom of having the priest, at least once a year, pray for the departed members of the family. These indulgences sold by the Church had, of course, their immoral effect on the people and largely account for the glaring amorality of Russian Christians.

THE ETHICS OF THE PEOPLE

Religion had little to do with shaping the moral code and practices of the Russian people. Systematic teaching of the decalogue and the Sermon on the Mount and other Christian precepts was almost impossible in the early Russian Church owing to the gross ignorance of the clergy, the absence of schools, and of the institution of preaching, besides the general illiteracy of the people and of the majority of the village clergy. The traditions of the Slavic tribes, with their primitive economy and social organization, did not fit in with the ethic of the early Church. It remained thus in abeyance and the social relations of the people were commonly regulated by time-honoured customs and social expediency.

Russian folk lore with its tales, sayings, rhymes and proverbs, contains the wisdom of the people. Lovers of antiquity [1] have collected these and their analysis shows that these sayings generally met the social and moral demands of the groups which produced them. Some of this folk lore antedates the introduction of Christianity into Russia, but much of it is a syncretic product in which the primitive ideas are intermingled with Christian concepts and with words from the Bible. In their scope they deal with practically every human need and interest. There are sayings which pertain to God, to the

[1] There are some ten thousand such proverbs published in the collections of I. I. Illustrov, V. Dal, I. Snegirev, T. I. Buslaev, B. Perogovsky and others.

loyalty of the group to its rulers, to marriage, the rights of property, to crime, taxation, validity of contract, taboos of certain foods and drinks, poverty, sickness and health. Eminent Russian jurists [1] believe that Russian common law had its origin in Russian folk lore. Sayings about diseases and their cures contain not a few very correct observations and good advice to which any physician could subscribe to-day.[2]

The proverbs relating to God emphasize characteristics which were common to despotic rulers : " There is but one God and one Tsar " ; " God in the heavens, the Tsar on the earth " ; " All is in the power of God and the Tsar " ; " The Tsar is terrible but God is merciful " ; etc. Scores of other proverbs draw these analogies between God and the Tsar, but there are also many which suggest other more democratic characteristics, e.g. " Man for himself, but God for all " ; " Man walks, but God leads " ; " Man proposes, but God disposes." Divine care and mercy to the poor find frequent expression in the proverbs : " God who gave us teeth will also give us the bread " ; " God gave the body, he will also give health " ; " God is not poor, His mercy is not scanty." While God's power is emphasized, there are also proverbs which encourage man's own efforts : " Who lives purely is aided by God " ; " Who guards the truth is rewarded by God " ; " Who guards himself is guarded of God " ; " God is not in force but in truth," and so on.

The Christ of the proverbs is ever the suffering and forgiving Christ : " Without a cross, without a Christ " is a favoured saying. Sin and crime are almost synonymous ; but the sinner is not ostracized, he is thought of as " the unfortunate " and rather pitied than despised. Sin is taken as

[1] Thus Professor Gorushkin of Moscow called attention to it. He says : " In reading the old proverbs, one finds in them truth which cannot be refuted, and one must recognize in them the spoken law. In the past they must have had the power of law. This may be proven by the fact that many of their principles are incorporated by us in the code of laws." Similar opinions are expressed by Professors T. Moroshkin, P. Chubinsky and N. Taganev.

[2] Professor of Medicine, Dr. N. T. Vysocky, made some valuable collections of proverbs pertaining to health and hygiene, diseases and their remedies.

quite inevitable in life : " God alone is without sin " is a much-quoted proverb. " Where there is prohibition, there is sin " ; " If you do not sin, you do not repent—if you do not repent, you cannot be saved " ; this is the logic of orthodox sinners, and " As there is no fire without smoke, there is no man without sin." " Even the archbishop, when hungry, steals," runs one saying.

Talk about " sin " is commonplace in Russian orthodox circles but the emphasis is rather on forgiveness and mercy : " Quarrel with sin but be reconciled with the sinner " ; " Mercy over sin is like water over fire." While compassion with the sinner is characteristic the proverb does not encourage mingling with the evil-minded : " The evil man is like charcoal, if it does not burn you it blackens you " ; " Lying down with the dog, you will rise with fleas."

Sociability, neighbourliness, hospitality, friendship, pity, forgiveness, humility, patience, simplicity, etc., are the virtues praised in the proverb : " To a united fold the wolf is not awful " ; " Good to us and good to all, this is the lawful life " ; " Where there is love, there is God." The spirit of forgiveness was once dominant with orthodox Christians. It reflected itself in the common speech of the people. Thus the farewell word at parting is to this day *proschaitey*, that is, " forgive." The Russian forgives and forgets quickly. The Revolution with all its cruelties has not left the people hateful. The victorious as well as the defeated classes have quickly forgotten and forgiven their mutual grievances. The frightful humiliation to which the Church has been subjected since the Revolution she has borne with patience and accepts it as a chastizement for her past sins.

To say, however, that the Russian has a deep sense of moral responsibility would not conform to the facts. The supernaturally sanctioned categorical imperative of the Protestant peoples is not the ethics of the Russian Orthodox Christians. The servile status of the peasant and worker masses during the feudal and bourgeois epochs of Russian history constituted no proper social basis upon which to develop a strictly individualistic ethic with a profound respect to individual property and the sanctity of personality. Now the social revolution has swept away the old. A transitional stage, in which an adjustment in social relations is taking place, is also shaping a new morality. The future ideals of moral criterion are not yet clearly defined, but the fact remains that with the new social order a new ethic also is being created.

CHAPTER III

CHURCH AND STATE

THE unholy alliance of Church and State in Russia had much to do with the progressive paralysis of the Church and its present impotence. The Church from its very inception in Russia was tied to the throne. The Christianizing of the Russian people, as we have seen, went on under the direct initiative of the ruling princes and from the very beginning the Church leaned upon the strong arm of the State. At times in Russian history the throne has been empty or has been occupied by weaklings, and on these occasions the Church took over the rudder of State ; but the nobility, as a class, was too strong and too jealous to leave the State an exclusive prey of the Church, and so the arrangement was never more than temporary. Again there were occasions when the throne of the Tsar and the throne of the Patriarch were occupied by members of the same family, as was the case with the first Romanovs ; Michael I was the son of the Patriarch Philaret and in actuality the Patriarch ruled the country. Throughout these vicissitudes of the Russian Church and State there was never any separation between the two ; but, generally speaking, the State grew the stronger and, in the early 18th century, brought the Church completely under its domination, making it practically a department of State, something of a police force over the consciences of the people.

Following the parallel developments of Church and State in Russia we may divide their history into the epochs of feudalism, the period of centralization of power in State and Church, the period of serfdom, and finally the bureaucratic period of control of the Church by the State.

CHURCH AND STATE UNDER FEUDALISM

Feudalism flourished in Russia between the 13th and the 15th centuries. Throughout this period the Church, though still nominally under the reign of the Patriarch of Constantinople, was actually dependent upon the local feudal princes who resented the interference of the alien Patriarch The invasion of Russia by the Tartars and the pressure of the Moslems on Constantinople made contact with the Byzantine Mother Church very difficult. As a result the Russian Church began to be ruled by Russian bishops chosen by the ruling princes. These bishops were mostly former boyars or rich merchants, whose custom it was to enter the monastery at the decline of life. Frequently they founded their own monasteries, ruling them as Fathers Superior and holding themselves quite independent of the diocesan bishops. The diocesan bishops thus had practically no power over the monasteries founded by the princes ; the monks therein were mostly from the following of the prince, and peasants were admitted only to do the hard work for their former feudal masters.

The administration of bishops consisted chiefly in collecting income from the Churches in the given dioceses. The feudal princes and rich landlords often built their own churches and selected their own priests, but in doing so they had to come to terms with the bishop to have these priests ordained and the churches consecrated. This could be done only by a bishop, who charged the feudal lords fixed fees for this service as well as for every visitation of the parish. In addition, the bishop collected tithes from the local priests and received large incomes from the Episcopal estates, many of which were given them by princes and rich merchants. Some of these estates were very large. Records of the 17th century show, for example, that the Bishop of Vyatka owned 30 villages with the lands and the forests surrounding them. To the fifteen bishops of that period belonged 28,000 homesteads in towns and villages and the Patriarch himself owned 7,000 households. The bishops sublet these properties or exploited them after the fashion of the boyars and princes themselves, through a special agency of tax collectors.

The princes retained the rights of *dominium directum*, collecting a tax from the properties of bishops. They also claimed the right of driving undesirable bishops from their principalities. The relation of the Superiors of monasteries to the prince was similar to that of the bishops. Under these feudal conditions the Church lacked real unity, and the rivalry common between the feudal principalities also characterized the Church. Each of the princes wanted to possess some popular wonder-working relic or ikon. If there were no such local objects the Prince sought to obtain them by bargaining with neighbouring princes and bishops and occasionally organized raids to capture the coveted sacred objects by force.

During the feudal period many local cults with their own patron saints had developed. Very often these saints were former local princes who were venerated for their piety and their lavish support of the Church, which declared them as patron saints. Indigenous Russian Christianity was strikingly backward in intellectual achievements. Most priests were as illiterate as their parishioners, and the bishops and theologians of the Church discussed problems of symbolism as of chief interest : such as the sign of the cross, whether it is to be made by two fingers or by three ; the wearing of long untrimmed beards and the prohibition of trimming them since this would mean, they argued, mutilating the image of God, whom man was to represent, and who, in the ikons, was always painted with a full beard like their own. To the reading of prayers was attached particular magic power. It was supposed that there were certain prayers which, when read often enough, would " possess " man of God, and salvation would surely be attained by the number pronounced during a lifetime. These same prayers when read for the soul of the departed had a similar effect. Because of this the number of professional prayer-makers, i.e. monks, was rapidly increasing and resulted in the abuse of the monasteries and their huge accumulation of wealth.

CENTRALIZATION OF STATE AND CHURCH AUTHORITY

At the end of the 15th century the Princes and Metropolitans of Moscow undertook the work of centralizing the power of the State and the Church. This was done mostly by conquest of the weaker princes. In Moscow at the time reigned the shrewd John III surnamed " Kalita," which means " money-pouch," so-called for his frugality and parsimony. He was backed by Metropolitan Jonah, whose ambition it was to make the Russian Church independent of Byzantium and elevate Moscow to the position of a third and final Rome. He began to propagate the idea of the Apostasy of the Byzantine Church from the orthodox faith, and explained the fall of Constantinople as the consequence of its impiety and heresy. In a pastoral letter to his bishops, he made the accusation : " You know yourselves, my children, what the Royal City (Constantinople) had suffered from the siege of the Bulgarians and the Persians, who for seven years held it as in a net ; yet, it stood as long as the Greeks maintained their piety. But when they had lost their faith, you know what they had to suffer and how they were captured and killed ; what became of their souls, God alone knows." The conclusion was plain. Russia had nothing more to expect from the Greek Church, which had lost its birthright. The State must take the welfare of the Russian Church into its own hands. More than this, it must become the guardian of the orthodox faith for the world. Constantinople, the second Rome, had fallen, but there was Moscow with her " most pious " princes; she was chosen to be the third Rome, that should last till the coming of the Lord. And her Princes were to be the " true Christian Emperors " and the guardians of the cross.

John III liked the idea and resolutely undertook to make himself " the all-pious " Emperor of Orthodox Christendom. To facilitate his ambitions, he arranged for his marriage with Princess Sophia of Constantinople (1467) and commenced to build his great Cathedral in Moscow, which was to replace the desecrated Cathedral of Saint Sophia of Constantinople.

Whilst John, " the money-pouch," was successfully freeing the Russian Church from the Byzantine domination he conquered, with equal success, one after the other of the northern principalities. He did not destroy their sanctuaries or their sacred ikons, but collected them in Moscow and placed them in his new Cathedral of the Assumption which became the central pantheon of Russia. In this manner he brought the ikon of the Virgin from the Vladimir Cathedral, the ikon of the Saviour from the conquered Novgorod, the ikon of the Virgin from Pskov and a similar one from Smolensk. These local shrines, which were once the glory of feudal princes, were now to add to the splendour and power of the Moscow metropolis. At the same time John sought to attract to his court the wisest of the clergy and gladly listened to their philosophizing upon the coming of the third Rome—Holy Moscow. A very interesting example of this is left to us in a letter of the learned monk Philotheus to John III. He says: " The Church of ancient Rome was destroyed in consequence of the heresy of Apollinarius and the Constantinopolitan Church of the second Rome was cut to pieces by the axes of Hagar's posterity. But this Holy Apostolic Church of the third Rome (Moscow)—to wit, of the autocratic power—shines more brightly than the sun of the whole universe. . . . Two Romes have fallen; the third stands upright, and there is no fourth to come; thou art the only Tsar of the Christians in the entire world." Under these circumstances the domination of the Church by the State was successfully carried on by the Muscovite princes. What was commenced by John and his faithful ecclesiastics was completed by the Tsars who followed him.

John IV the Terrible continued the policy of gathering Russia about Moscow and driving away the Tartars. He also emphasized the independence of the Russian Church from Byzantium. It was under his reign that the myth of the preaching of St. Andrew, the Apostle, on the banks of the Dnieper was circulated and, of course, readily believed. " Why do you refer us to the Greeks ? " answered the Tsar to the

Papal envoy Possevin, who wanted the Russian Church to follow the Greeks in regard to the Council of Florence. " The Greeks are no Gospel to us ; we believe not in the Greeks, but in Christ. We received the Christian faith at the beginning of the Christian Church, when Andrew, the brother of the Apostle Peter, came to this country on his way to Rome. Therefore we received the Christian faith at the same time as you in Italy." [1]

In this manner the direct Apostolic origin of Russian Christianity was theoretically established and the claim of the Tsars as the true and only Emperors of Orthodox Christianity strengthened.[2] To complete the independence of the Russian Church and give proof of its orthodoxy, the ecclesiastics felt the need of real, canonized, Russian saints, since until that time the saints and martyrs venerated by the Church were all foreign, mostly Greeks, which appeared as if the Russian Church itself was barren of holy witnesses for the Christian faith. To overcome this difficulty, the Russian bishops began to inquire about Russian saints venerated by local communities, and what great deeds of piety they had wrought. In the year 1547 a general Council was called at Moscow and the bishops reported on their researches, which yielded twenty-two saints. These the Council canonized. The search for saints was continued in the following year, and in 1549 the Council met again and canonized seventeen more Those prelates who dared to oppose the Moscow hierarchy in its efforts to elevate Moscow to the rank of the third Rome were anathematized by the Council. This opposition, the first known to the Church, came from the south-east. On the lower Volga was a monastic settlement

---

[1] There is no shadow of historical evidence in this myth of Andrew visiting Russia. But it is true that in the South there were scattered Christian communities and isolated Christians long before Russia officially accepted the Christian faith from the Greeks.

[2] The Greek Church held that there could be only one Christian Emperor. In 1393 the Greek Patriarch wrote to Basil I, prince of Moscow : " It is impossible for Christians to have a Church without a Tsar, for the State and the Church are in close union and cannot be separated. . . . The Apostle Peter said ' Fear God, honour the Tsar.' He did not say ' Tsars,' but ' Tsar,' in order that none should consider the Tsars of different people, showing by this that there is but one Tsar in the world."

founded by Nil Soroky, a man of deep spiritual insight and learning. He attracted an able following and for half a century opposed the imperialistic tendencies of the Moscow nationalist-ecclesiastics, until he and his followers were finally suppressed by the Moscow Councils.

The Volga monks opposed too close a union between Church and State, and demanded that each be independent of the other. The pastors of the Church, they said, should not fear the temporal power, but should stand for what is right in the Kingdom of the Spirit; the ruler of the State should be no judge in spiritual affairs; religion is a matter of individual conscience, and the State should not persecute anyone for his religious opinions.

One thing still was lacking in the Russian Church. It had no Patriarch of its own and was compelled to recognize the Patriarch of Constantinople. To find one was no easy matter, for it needed the consent of the Byzantine Patriarch. Boris Godounov, the shrewd pretender to the Russian throne, finally succeeded in obtaining the consent of the Greek Patriarch Jeremiah, who in 1589 had come to Moscow to collect alms for the impoverished Byzantine Church. The Moscow hierarch, Job, was consecrated First Patriarch of Russia and thus the dream of Russian ecclesiastics for independence and dignity was attained. Simultaneously with this achievement was created a situation which inevitably led to the decline of the Russian Church.

There were now in Russia dual powers: the Patriarch and the Tsar. Thus, as the Patriarchs began to assert their spiritual sovereignity, rivalling the Tsars in the splendour of their court, it soon became evident that a conflict was inevitable.

During the troubled times which followed the extinction of the Rurik dynasty, when all kinds of pretenders reigned in Moscow, order was restored by the strong hand of the Patriarch Philaret, who placed his youthful son, Michael Romanov, on the throne, but in the practical sense reigned himself as long as he lived. Under Alexis, the second of the Romanovs, Nikon was made Patriarch and was unquestionably the ablest of Russia's ten Patriarchs. Historians frequently called him the Thomas à Becket of Russian Orthodoxy. He was the first to clash with the Tsar and the nobility, who feared this mighty man as a super-autocrat. That there was good reason for this fear is apparent. Nikon was conscious of the dignity of his office and his power. Once, when irritated by the insubordination of the Tsar's powerful boyars, he said: "Know ye not that it is not we who receive the sublime sacerdotal authority from Tsars or Emperors, but on the contrary those who govern are anointed to rule. By the same token it is clear that priesthood is a far greater thing than royalty." This was dangerous doctrine. The timid Tsar feared the Patriarch, whom he had loved in his youth. But he did not hinder his boyars, who plotted Nikon's downfall and finally succeeded. Nikon's defeat irrevocably established the supremacy of the State over the Church and prepared the way for abolishing the Patriarchate altogether. This was accomplished by Peter the Great a few decades later.

Nikon was the last of the influential Patriarchs. He is frequently thought of as the reformer of the Russian Church. It is true that he made many changes in the outward form of the orthodox cult. This, as we shall see later on, aroused the protests of the conservative zealots and paved the way to a schism which alienated a large portion of the most devout members of the Church and irreparably destroyed the unity on which it had justly prided itself.

THE CHURCH AND THE INSTITUTION OF SERFDOM

The 17th century is called, in Russian Church History, the Epoch of the Russian Patriarchy. It could equally be called the Epoch of the Triumph of Serfdom in Russia. During this century the centralized power of the Moscow Tsars, backed by the nobility and the upper hierarchy, steadily oppressed the free peasants and forced them into servitude, robbing them of their possessions and their lands. By this time the Patriarch, the bishops, and the monasteries owned about one million serfs, roughly eight per cent. of the population. These they exploited as did the boyars and princes and, of course, it was to their mutual interest to maintain the dignity of the Church and of the Throne, both of which blessed and protected the institution of serfdom.

Thus the Church, depending for protection of its property upon the Tsar, became his willing tool. At this time it was already an established prerogative of the crown to select the candidates for the Episcopacy, the Patriarchal throne, and for every other important ecclesiastical position. The Tsar began to be likened to God's plenipotentiary on earth and this doctrine, advanced by the Church, maintained itself till the final fall of the autocratic regime in 1917. Naturally the double yoke of Tsar and Patriarch, oppressing the serfs and the lower clergy, who themselves were kept in much the same condition of servitude as the peasants, could not but generate great discontent and protest.

The first manifestation of mass protest against these evils in the Church started at the end of the 14th and continued throughout the 15th and the 16th centuries. It first appeared in the so-called Strigolnik movement, named after the trade of its founder, Karp, who was a clothmaker, " stregat " meaning to shear the woollen cloth ; probably, also, it had its first adherents amongst the clothmakers. The Strigolnik movement spread from Pskov to Twer, Novgorod and Moscow, and was considered quite a dangerous heresy, chiefly directed against the feudal abuses within the Church. It was predominantly a lay movement and penetrated the trade guilds. Agitation was carried on against the upper hierarchy which was abusing its power in ordaining priests for money, these orders being frequently purchased by unworthy men. These first Russian protestants took recourse to the Bible and found its texts sufficient support against the whole system of the hierarchy in the Church. They pointed out that the Apostle Paul encouraged laymen to teach and to preach and condemned drunkenness and the love of money. Since their priests, they argued, are drunkards who eat and drink with unworthy men and take gold and silver by taxing the living and the dead, they are but wolves in sheep's clothing, and there is no need for them at all. These laymen took over the Church services and even administered the sacraments. They preached against the cult of the dead and prohibited prayers for the departed. Some of the extremists among the Strigolniks rejected the Church altogether as not necessary to salvation. Here in a very crude form we have all the chief arguments advanced ever since by Russian sectarians against the Church.

Still the traditional faith in the Church and its cult was very strong and there were relatively few laymen who were able to read the Bible and possess one. Whilst everything remained much the same and the priests were not too exorbitant in their demands, the people, although greatly dissatisfied with the clergy, tolerated the existing conditions.

A new occasion for a mass movement of dissent from the Church was presented by the so-called reforms of Patriarch Nikon, which called for considerable changes in the ritual and texts of the service book. As we know, during the period of feudal decentralization, many local cults had developed which deviated considerably from the Byzantine ritual. Nikon wished to revise the old books and create an improved uniform service in all the churches. The chief objection of the masses and of the village clergy to these reforms was as regards the changes in the traditional sign of the cross, which had hitherto been made by the first two fingers and which Nikon demanded to be made by folding the thumb and the first two fingers, thus symbolising the Holy Trinity. A further grievance was due to changing the Slavic spelling of the name of Jesus from " Isus " to " Iīsus." This additional " ī " seemed an outrage to the believers, robbing the name of " Isus " of its old magic spell. These and other innovations were resented not only by the laity but equally by the semi-illiterate village clergy to whom the demands of the Patriarch seemed beyond the possibility of fulfilment. They had learned the old texts of the ritual by heart and now the new reforms demanded from them a knowledge of reading which went beyond their capacities. They also resented the ever-increasing taxations of the

Church by the Episcopacy and their progressive degradation to servitude. This, together with the general protest of the impoverished peasants and the revolting townsfolk, started that mass dissenting movement from the patriarchal Church which in history is generally known as the Old Believers schism. Simultaneously it was a mass movement to escape the unbearable conditions of serfdom and expressed itself in an exodus of thousands of peasants from their old habitations to the unoccupied frontiers, to the wilds of Siberia, and to the Southern steppes.

The outstanding leader of this schism was the Moscow Arch-Priest Avvakum, an uncompromising zealot and martyr for the old faith. He enjoyed considerable popularity also among some of the Moscow boyars who were in opposition to Nikon and who sought to overthrow the power of the Patriarch and persuade the Tsar Alexis I to reinstate the old customs of their faith. They actually succeeded in accelerating Nikon's downfall, but they were not able to stop the reform measures which by this time had gained considerable support among the upper classes and the city clergy. The Council of 1666–1667, called to settle the schism, condemned the dissenters, together with Avvakum and with many others, who were driven into exile.

The Solovetsk Monastery on the White Sea Islands was one of the strongholds of the old faith. The monks revolted against Nikon's reforms and destroyed the new service books, resisting with armed force the Tsar's orders to accept them. The Solovetsk monks particularly disliked Nikon because he robbed their monastery of the remains of the martyred Metropolitan Philip of Moscow, who had been murdered by order of John the Terrible for daring to reprimand the despot for his evil deeds. Under the Romanovs, this Philip was canonized as a saint and martyr, and many pilgrims from all over Russia went to Solovetsk to worship at his sarcophagus. The Solovetsk revolt was crushed and the instigators executed. The year 1666, during which the Council of the Church condemning the dissenters had assembled, was considered a mystical number, a sure sign of the coming of Anti-Christ and the approach of the end of the world. The ideology of the Anti-Christ developed during the siege of the Solovetsk monastery, and the writings of Avvakum are full of most vehement denunciations of the Patriarch and Tsar as the ambassadors of Anti-Christ. For many years this preacher of righteousness was kept in an underground prison, and finally burned in 1681 for his continuous attack upon the new faith and the Tsar. Some of Avvakum's sermons were preserved and found wide circulation among the people; their apocalyptic revolutionary doctrine was very dangerous to the existing order and called forth severe persecution of the Old Believers.

Avvakum taught that there was an alliance of the State and the Church against the people. The servant of Satan is not only Nikon but the Tsar who gave Nikon the liberty and was one with him in corrupting the old faith. Nikon and the Tsar are the two horns of the apocalyptic beast; the Tsar and the Patriarch drink the blood of the Holy Witnesses of Jesus and are drunk with it. The Tsar and Nikon and all other authorities have bowed to Anti-Christ and follow him. This teaching was later developed by Avvakum's pupils. The Anti-Christ was defined as the Satanic Trinity of the serpent, the beast and the false prophet: the serpent is Satan, the beast is the cunning Tsar, and the false prophet is the Patriarch.

Avvakum and his pupils urged the faithful to flee from Anti-Christ and his servants, and burn themselves alive rather than surrender. As a result a mass exodus to the wilderness commenced. The discontented peasants and artisans left their homesteads and fled from the pursuing authorities. When captured they tried to prevent it by setting alight the houses into which they had fled. This was called the baptism by fire and was considered as the supreme stage of piety. During this epidemic of self-burning, not less than 9,000 fanatics perished in the latter part of the 17th century alone, and there were repeated new outbursts throughout the 18th century.

BUREAUCRATIC STATE CONTROL OF THE CHURCH

Peter I was determined to modernize Russia. He recognized in the Patriarchate not only a dangerous rival to the absolutism of the throne, but also the greatest obstacle to his modernizing reforms. With the aid of several ecclesiastics, who lent themselves as willing tools to his wild schemes, he abolished the Patriarchate, and in 1720 brought the Church under the complete control of the State. In place of the Patriarchate he organized a governing College of Ecclesiastics, under the guidance of a layman appointed by himself. This institution was later called the Holy Synod and was patterned upon the models of Protestant State Churches. The purpose of this reform was to subject the Church to the interest of the State and use it to strengthen centralized autocratic sovereignity. Peter had little interest in purely spiritual matters, and therefore neither he nor his successors ever meddled with the doctrines or ritual of the Church. In fact, the Holy Synod had no authority to decree doctrines, but was simply the governing body of the Church, and in this capacity controlled by the State. The future history of the Church proved that it was made a very efficient tool to prolong the despotism of the Russian Tsars long after autocracy had not only ceased to be a necessity but had become the greatest hindrance to progress. That the State control over the Church hampered to a great extent its spiritual development will subsequently be shown. Peter's ecclesiastical coup has been the principal cause of the spiritual decline of the Russian Church. To understand this, we must fully understand the organization and functions of the Holy Synod.

The Holy Synod was composed of all classes of the clergy, all appointed by the Emperor, but not for the same term. There were two kinds of members, active and assistant, the former permanent and the latter consulting and temporary. The number of members was also unlimited and could be enlarged or decreased at the will of the Emperor. The Metropolitans of Petrograd, Moscow and Kiev were considered permanent members. The same status was provided for the Exarch of Georgia.[1] The Metropolitan of Petersburg was honoured with the title of the " first member," and as a rule, with the presidency. The other active members were five or six Archbishops, Bishops and Archimandrites, and were appointed for a specific term. Finally, there were several members of the white (married) clergy, one of whom usually acted as confessor to the Emperor.

The assistant members of the Holy Synod, who were mostly bishops and influential priests, were consulted only when needed. The general executive of the Holy Synod was the High Procurator, representing the Emperor. Peter described the functions of the High Procurator as " the eye of the Tsar," and his duty was to see that the affairs of the Church were carried on in conformity with the Imperial decrees. He held the rank of a Minister of State, and was represented in the State Cabinet, with responsibility to none except the Emperor. Laymen were appointed to this high position, and Peter, as well as other Tsars, preferred military men of firm character who could control the clergy by military discipline. Thus it happened that under Nicholas I a spurred and sabred officer, Count Protassov, occupied the post of High Procurator and presided over the shepherds of the Church.

The power and range of functions of the High Procurator were extraordinary. Nothing could be done in the affairs of the Church without his consent; no act of the Synod was valid without his signature; he exercised his special power of veto if any act of the Synod, in his opinion, did not conform to the laws of the State.

The affairs which came within the jurisdiction of the Holy Synod were of several categories, such as those pertaining to censorship of religious books and periodicals, the administration of justice in cases of clerical misconduct and heresy, and the like. These duties were disposed of principally by the

---

[1] The Church of Georgia is much older than the Russian Church. Its head is called Exarch. When Georgia was incorporated into the Russian Empire, the Georgian Church was supervised by the Holy Synod, yet maintained relative independence.

ecclesiastical members of the Synod. Matters pertaining to education, finance, and so forth were attended to by the Procurator and his large staff of assistants and clerks. The affairs of the Church were centralized to such a degree that no Bishop could travel beyond the boundaries of his diocese without first getting permission from the chancellery of the Holy Synod. Some ten to fifteen thousand cases had to be disposed of annually, and each case had to pass numerous stages of the bureaucratic machinery.

In the provinces, branches of the Holy Synod were organized, called the " Diocesan Consistories," which were patterned upon the Holy Synod and were to assist the Bishop of the diocese. They were presided over by lay appointees of the High Procurator of the Holy Synod, and occupied themselves principally with matters of clerical discipline and cases pertaining to marriage and divorce, with the Holy Synod open as the higher court of appeal.

The fact that the Emperor appointed all bishops on nominations made by the Synod, and at his will bestowed the dignities of Archbishop and Metropolitan, who in turn were called into membership of the Holy Synod, make it apparent that the governing hierarchy and the Holy Synod lent themselves as willing tools to the interests of the autocracy. The State was not slow to use the clergy for its advantage, often at the expense of the welfare of the nation and the Church, and the unity which the system promised to produce was only external.

The more spiritually minded ecclesiastics resented this servitude to the State, and the schism which commenced as a protest against the innovations of Patriarch Nikon in the 17th century widened on the new issue of State control. Peter was branded Anti-Christ, and the number of adherents to the schismatics grew in leaps and bounds and continually drained the Church of its best spiritual resources. This state of affairs was bound to accelerate the decline of the national Orthodox Church.

The iron despotism of Nicholas I roused the Russian intellectual class to take up the fight against autocracy which, in spite of all repressive measures, continued until the old regime was vanquished in the successful proletarian revolution of 1917. The Russian autocracy, struggling for its existence, enlisted the hierarchy of the Church and the Holy Synod to fight its battles. This led to the darkest period in the history of the Church; its unholy alliance with the State undermined its influence upon the people, and prepared the ground for a mass atheist propaganda.

The man who led the Church during this worst reactionary period was the High Procurator of the Holy Synod, K. P. Pobyedonostzev, who died in 1907. He was an able administrator and considerably erudite; he was loyal to the crown and the autocracy, and loved the State Church; he enjoyed the complete confidence of the Imperial family and was entrusted with the education of the Tsars Alexander III and Nicholas II.

Pobyedonostzev, in his continuous efforts to uphold the existing order, was particularly severe upon the sectarians, the revolutionists, and the Jews, whom he considered enemies of the Church and the autocratic State. He inspired repressive legislation and organized his "missionary departments," which were principally used as secret service agencies of the Holy Synod. The ordinary clergy was enlisted in this widespread persecution. The priests were requested to co-operate with the secret service of the Tsar and inform the police of any revolutionary propaganda carried on in their parishes. As a result of their information, more than 10,000 school teachers were imprisoned or sent into exile.

Believing that ignorance was the best safeguard against revolutionary propaganda, Pobyedonostzev suppressed the zemstvo (public) schools and made great efforts to organize a parochial school system under the supervision of the parish priests. By rigid censorship he tried to control also the thinking of the more educated classes. The higher clergy, in general, followed his leadership, and became zealous advocates of his reactionary policies. Some went so far as to abuse the most sacred institution of the Church, the confessional, for spying purposes, and the blood of many innocent victims may be charged to this heinous espionage. It is true that such abuses were not frequent, and that there were not a few even among the higher clergy who protested against this prostitution of the Church to the interest of autocratic despotism, but they were quickly silenced by the almighty Holy Synod. Such men were Father Tikhovinsky and Gregory Petrov, and their names will go down through history as martyrs and prophets for righteousness.

The lower clergy, particularly the village priests, who had little to gain from official favours and who depended largely upon the goodwill of their parishioners, generally showed passive resistance to the efforts of the State to abuse their office for political purposes. By tradition and habit they had no interest in politics and generally ignored the political efforts of the Holy Synod and the high clergy. It is true that in the elections of 1912 their participation as electioneers for the government parties had increased. Yet, even then, many participated not out of conviction but because of pressure from above.

The crowning shame of the Church was the unspeakable Rasputin scandal at the Court of the late Tsar, which humiliated the Church and dragged it to the lowest depth. Nicholas and his consort, Alexandra, were by nature superstitious and their perpetual fear for their lives and their throne made them susceptible to occultism. Some mystical personalities were always kept at Court, who, by their prophecies and spiritualistic messages, guided the family affairs of the late Tsar. For a while the renowned charlatan-spiritualist Philippe controlled the situation. Then Hiliodor, of Tzaritzin, was for a while the favoured " saint," but was soon replaced by his rival, Gregory Rasputin, mockingly called " Grishka." Rasputin was a licentious, ignorant, and drunken peasant, who came to power because of his forceful and brutal personality and animal magnetism, which lured hysterical women into his net. He was brought to Moscow by a rich woman who had met the " holy man " on one of his pilgrimages in Siberia. Later he was introduced to Court on the occasion of the illness of the young heir, for whose health and life the Empress continually worried. Somehow Rasputin succeeded in arresting the frequent hemorrhage from which the Tsarevitch suffered and which the physicians were unable to prevent. This assured the Empress of his " supernatural " power. Rasputin made her believe that not only the life of the boy but also the security of the Empire depended on him. She clung to the impostor until his tragic end, when he was brutally murdered with the aid of some members of the Imperial family. Rasputin was shrewd enough to exploit his position as " spiritual " adviser of the Empress. No favour which he asked for himself or his friends was refused him. Office-seekers in the State and Church therefore sought his aid by flattering him and begging his blessing. Those who dared oppose him were instantly removed or discharged at his will. It is even believed that the transfer of the Grand Duke Nicholas, the Generalissimo of the Russian Army, to the Caucasus was at Rasputin's suggestion.

The reputation of the Church suffered greatly from its tolerance of Rasputin. Members of the Holy Synod did not dare to oppose him for fear of their positions; and when Samarin, the highly respected High Procurator of the Holy Synod, was not friendly enough to Rasputin's favourites, he was dismissed. Through Rasputin's influence unworthy men were made Bishops and even elevated to the rank of Metropolitan. Thus Bishop Makarius, who was accused of having set fire to the Tomsk Theatre in 1905, while a popular meeting was being held, causing the loss of many lives, was made Metropolitan through the influence of the all-powerful Rasputin. All Russia was indignant at the dictatorship of the " Holy Devil," as his rival Hiliodor called him, and when finally he was murdered there was general satisfaction excepting on the part of the Court camarilla, the Empress and Emperor, who greatly mourned their " saint." The position of the Church, already weakened by its long servitude under State control, was greatly shattered by Rasputin's unholy dictatorship. When the Revolution broke out the best elements of the Church welcomed the change, but the higher clergy which was accustomed to leaning upon the mighty arm of the State was of different opinion. It feared for its power and generally protected the counter-revolutionists, who promised to re-establish their former favoured position.

Thus, by virtue of historical circumstances, the Church became a mighty national institution and its development was parallel with the growth of centralized government in Russia. From its very beginning the hierarchy of the Church was closely associated with the secular power, and finally, under Peter I it was definitely degraded to a tool of the State. Since the Church was prostituted to autocratic despotism, the ill repute of the old regime was attributed to the Church as well as to the temporal power. The alliance of Church and State proved a failure in Russia as it has in other nations. Now, freed from its old bondage, the Orthodox Church has received a new lease on life. Has it any vitality left to prove its right to existence? Future history will prove this. For the present it has been rapidly losing its influence on the masses and has not shown any definite signs of rejuvenation.

CHAPTER IV
NONCONFORMITY IN RUSSIA

Where no channels exist for the legitimate expression of grievances in the affairs of State and Church, dissenting movements and schisms naturally arise. Russia, less than any other European nation, had such legitimate channels and for that reason nonconformity and the development of a great variety of sects was a common phenomenon in Tsarist Russia.

Nonconformity in Russia had two main branches, one developing from the Old Believers movement and the other forming under the influence of German Evangelical immigrants from the West. As we have shown in the preceding chapter, the Old Believers found some of their adherents amongst the Moscow nobility but chiefly amongst the town traders and artisans, and to a still larger extent amongst the oppressed peasants. The boyar Old Believers soon reconciled themselves to the established Church; their social position did not favour associating with dissenters from amongst the common people. Nonconformity in Russia flourished, therefore, amongst the middle and lower classes; in this respect it did not differ from the nonconformist position in the West and it had also the same social and economic effects. The higher moral standard of the nonconformists, their mutual help and solidarity, made them prosperous and they soon became the leading merchants, manufacturers, and bankers of Russia. Whilst the well-to-do Old Believers were much more willing to compromise, the dissenters from amongst the poor artisans and serfs were following more extreme tendencies by developing a great variety of sects. These avoided every contact with " Anti-Christ "; no true dissenter would allow himself to be counted in the census, nor accept a passport stamped with the "seal of Anti-Christ"; they refused to pay taxes, and when oppressed by the authorities, migrated to remote parts of the country to escape their reach. Thus a movement, with every surface indication of black reaction, developed oddly enough into religious, social and political radicalism, bordering on philosophical anarchy. It is no exaggeration to say that here were the dim beginnings of the revolutionary movement in Russia, which after centuries of struggle destroyed that hated reign of the Anti-Christ—the autocratic State.

DIFFERENTIATION OF OLD BELIEVERS

Only one of the bishops, Paul of Kolomna, was excommunicated with the Old Believers. He was imprisoned and died in captivity without chance of consecrating a successor to perpetuate the Apostolic succession of the orthodox hierarchy. By this tragic incident the Old Believers were left without an Episcopate, and consequently without a priesthood able to consecrate and administer the sacraments. What was to be done? Some of the Old Believers contended that Christianity is impossible without a priesthood, and suggested, in order to perpetuate the Old Faith, that they call priests from the State Church: "For having followed Nikon's heresy," they argued, "has not forfeited the apostolic power, the succession, the right of consecrating bishops and ordaining priests by the imposition of hands. Their ordinations being valid, all we have to do in order to have a clergy is to bring back to us, and to the ancient rites, the priests of the official Church." The more radical faction argued differently: "Not so," they said, "by giving up the ancient books, by anathematizing the ancient traditions, the Nikonians have forfeited all rights to the Apostolic succession. The official clergy is no longer a Church, it is Satan's synagogue. All communion with the ministers of hell is sin, consecration at the hands of these apostate bishops, pollution. By sanctioning the anathemas hurled by the Russian prelates against the ancient rites, the Eastern Patriarchs have become participators in their heresy. With the fall of the Episcopate, orthodoxy has perished. There is no longer an apostolic succession, a lawful priesthood."

Upon this issue the Old Believers split; the one party, holding to the hierarchy, was called *Popovtzy* (Priestly), the other *Bespopovtsy* (Priestless). The *Popovtzy* decided to have priests by any possible method, from the official Church; by means of bribes, or by harbouring fugitive priests, they actually succeeded, although with great difficulty, in obtaining enough priests to continue the Church services and the sacraments, until in the middle of the last century they were greatly relieved by securing an independent priesthood. In their ignorance the Old Believers believed that the Orthodox Church of the Near East had remained true to the Old Faith, and therefore searched for a bishop in the ranks of the Serbian and Greek prelates, after great effort securing the services of the former Bishop of Bosnia, a Greek, Ambrose by name, who for some reason had been deposed from his office by the Patriarch of Constantinople. They established and richly endowed a monastery in Bielo-Krinitza, in the former Austria near the Russian frontier, which became the seat of their bishop and from which centre their Church was administered. In this manner the " priestly " faction of the Old Believers was able to maintain itself without deviation from its traditions and beliefs.

The Old Believers, who were puritanic in morals, became very prosperous and established many richly endowed monasteries, convents, schools, and orphanages. They have been particularly active since the beginning of this century; and when after the 1905 revolution the old restrictions against their building churches, publishing literature, and openly agitating for their ideas were removed, they flourished greatly. The strength of the Old Believers rested largely in that, unlike the State Church, their work was almost entirely carried on by the laity. Their priesthood existed only to administer the sacraments and render such services as the canons forbade to the laity. Their great wealth, particularly of the Moscow following, permitted them to educate their children well, and at the beginning of this century there was a young generation of Old Believers who presented an unusual blend of ancient piety with modern liberal ideas and high cultural standards. Some of the noblest creations of Russian art, such as the Moscow Art Theatre, were founded and financed by the cultured following of this sect. In politics and social reform they united with the liberals and gave not a few able fighters to the Revolution.

Related to the priestly Old Believers, and as a connecting link between them and the State Orthodox Church, was the movement of the *Edinovertsy* or " United Faith."

It dates back to the year 1800, when under the tolerant reign of Alexander I, a group of Moscow Old Believers appealed to the State Church to permit them to have churches in Moscow with a bishop and priests provided by the State Church. They were willing to accept the priests without the usual anti-Nikonite anathemas so long as they consented to conduct the service according to the old cult.

The Government recognized in this compromising proposal an opportunity to drive a wedge into the ranks of the Old Believers, and therefore agreed upon the compromise, supplied priests, but did not keep the promise to provide a special bishop. This was only done by the Sobor of 1918, over a hundred years after the original agreement.

There were relatively few outside Moscow who voluntarily joined the *Edinovertsy*, so the Government tried to force membership in the new church. Under Nicholas I, who persecuted those Old Believers who refused to enter the *Edinovertsy* Church, they were exiled; their churches were turned over to priests of the State Church, who began to function as *Edinovertsy* priests, that is, according to the old rites. This was a hard blow to the Old Believers. Nevertheless, many would not submit and they continued their services in secret places and with fugitive priests.

The " Priestless " (*Bezpopovtsy*) faction deviated much further from the Mother Church and split into numerous sects, some following very radical tendencies. Their slogan was "Flee the world, no compromise with Anti-Christ." Having repudiated the priesthood, they inaugurated a lay leadership of elders who conducted Church services as far as the traditions of the Church permitted. This consisted in the reading and expounding of the Scriptures and in baptizing the converts, which functions had always been recognized as admissible to the male laity of the Greek Orthodox Church. The *Bezpopovtsy* went further and permitted women to conduct the services. Baptism was generally maintained as a sacrament, although there was divergence of opinion as to its mode. Some adhered to the Greek Orthodox form of three-fold immersion of infants, but refrained from the unction with holy chrism because unable to consecrate it; others required immersion of adults at night in a running stream; others, again, baptized themselves with their own hands. The remaining sacraments [1] were either abandoned altogether or interpreted spiritually. Thus certain sects confessed to an ikon in the presence of an elder who acted as adviser and spoke these words: "May thy sins be forgiven thee."

The rejection of the priesthood and the sacraments prepared the way for all kinds of radical ideas, particularly in regard to marriage. Some repudiated it altogether and demanded absolute celibacy. Others permitted concubinage as a means of protecting the weakness of the flesh; others again argued that marriage is not at all a sacrament, but a civil union for the propagation of the race, which is to be entered upon with the consent and blessing of the parents and kept sacred by solemn oath of the man and the woman. The lay marriage regulations of the Old Believers did not lead to the immorality expected by many of their critics. The lack of legal constraint to make marriage indissoluble was offset by custom and the patriarchal form of family life which largely survived among the Old Believers. Amongst those who demanded absolute celibacy, reversion into licentiousness occurred frequently and in turn

[1] The Greek Orthodox Church recognized seven sacraments: Baptism, Chrism (also applied to baptized infants in place of Confirmation), the Eucharist, Penance, Orders, Honourable Marriage, and Unction of the Sick and Dying.

reacted into fanatical asceticism, which finally culminated in the radical sect of the Castrators or Eunuchs.

The Priestless were much more antagonistic to the established order and the State. From its ranks movements arose to "flee from the world and the reign of Anti-Christ." The extreme faction was led by a certain Theodosius (1706), whose call was: "Save yourself by flight into the wilderness, and if you are sought for by the authorities, burn yourself, or perish by starvation, and you will gain the crown of martyrdom." The idea of redemption by suicide and "fiery baptism" took hold upon large masses of extremists. They interpreted literally the Bible text: "The Kingdom of heaven suffereth violence, and the violent take it by force." To save their children from the accursed reign of Anti-Christ, these fanatics killed them, and whole families and communities volunteered to sacrifice themselves unto God as burnt offering. They shut themselves into barns and houses and then set them afire, guarding one another from escaping the ordeal. Others fled to the wilderness and perished of starvation and cold. It is estimated that 20,000 men, women and children exterminated themselves in this manner. Many other thousands perished at the hands of their official enemies.

The Old Believers found their adherents mostly amongst the North Russians, to whose morbid nature a religion demanding so much sacrifice had a special appeal. Fleeing from their persecutors the Old Believers pushed farther and farther north, settling finally in the forest region of the Upper Volga, the Ural, and along the coasts of the White Sea. Others migrated to the south-west towards the Polish border, some crossing the frontier into East Prussia, where they are living in communities to this day. The more restless went further east into Siberia, and found also adherents among the Cossacks of the Don region and the Caucasus. Wherever they settled in the wilderness, they established villages of a more or less communistic type, and by hard work and co-operation quickly prospered. Their accomplishments as pioneers and colonizers were extraordinary, and to them principally was due the

Russianizing of the great area of the North and of Siberia, which until then had been populated only by widely scattered Finnish and Tartar tribes.

Catherine II, who prided herself on her religious liberality, was lenient with them and permitted them to have their settlements even in Moscow. Wealthy Old Believers endowed cemeteries near Moscow, for they are very particular about burying their dead in ground specially consecrated for this purpose, in conformity to their creed. Within the cemetery walls they built churches and around these sprung up settlements, to which the faithful flocked and which to this day are the principal centres of their movement. For the Priestly there is the *Rogozhsky* Cemetery and for the Priestless the *Preobrazhensky* Cemetery, both near Moscow.

EXTREMIST SECTS

About the year 1770, a certain Euphemius rose in protest against the compromises of the settlers in Moscow. He denounced city life as Babylon and called upon the faithful to abandon landed property, which he considered to be the chief tie that held people down to settled life. " The land was, is, and ought to be God's," he declared, " man should use it collectively, but never own it."

Under the slogan, " Leave thy father and mother, take up thy cross, and follow me," the disciples of Euphemius incited the faithful to flee from the towns and villages and take up a nomad life. They were called *Beguny* (Runners) or *Straniki* (Wanderers), and no doubt their preaching had much to do with the spread of Communistic and anarchistic ideas among the Russian peasants. The convert who entered the community of " true Christians " and became a " wanderer " was initiated by a ceremony of the " Wanderer's Baptism," which was performed at night in out-of-the-way places. He destroyed his passport and received in its place a piece of paper on which was drawn a cross and some such sentence as : " This is the true passport, endorsed at Jerusalem." The " wanderer " carried a wooden bowl and spoon and a small ikon. They were supposed to be celibates, but in case of " weakness of the flesh " they tolerated illicit relations which, they argued, were better than marriage, " for a married man gives himself up to evil forever."

As the sect spread it appeared impossible for all its adherents to take to the road; moreover, since they must have friends where they could obtain food and shelter, they developed a second category of " residents," or hospitalers, whose duty was to assist the " wanderers " with food and protection against the police who had strict orders from the Government to arrest the " holy tramps " and those who aided them. The " residents " were considered as novices of the sect and did not attain perfection until they abandoned their homes and took the wanderer's staff, which often they did only in old age or when feeling that their life was coming to an end. The Government tried its utmost to exterminate this sect, but the more the " wanderers " were persecuted the more adherents they gained, as was the case during the oppressive reign of Nicholas I. Here was an inevitable reaction to the existing social order with its serfdom, long military service, and bureaucratic oppression. The " wanderers " were rustic revolutionists, who slowly undermined the authority of the State and Church with their philosophy of Anti-Christ and the Communistic ownership of the land.

Besides the radical " wanderers," many other sects and groups formed within the Old Believers movement. Thus there were the *Gapers*, who believed that God cannot deny to the faithful the flesh and blood of His Son. At their Holy Thursday Service they stood with their mouths wide open, expecting that angels would come and feed them with the Holy Sacrament for which their souls were hungry.

The sect called *Molchalniki* (The Mutes) demanded vows of silence, but otherwise pursued a life similar to the " wanderers " and was probably only a variation of that sect. Many were arrested, but in spite of the severest tortures they could not be forced to speak.

The *Nyemoliaki* (Non-prayers) was a mystical sect carrying

the spirit of denial to its logical consequences. They rejected every outward form of worship and ritual and gave to scripture but an allegorical and rationalistic interpretation. They regarded everything as " spiritual " and believed they lived in the age of the Holy Ghost, where worship and understanding may be carried on only through the Spirit.

Like the " Non-prayers " were the *Denyers*, who believed that since the commencement of the reign of Anti-Christ all sacred things had been removed to heaven and therefore worship is possible only in direct communion with the Saviour.

Akin to the mystical sects which developed within the ranks of the Old Believers was the widely spread spiritualistic sect of independent origin known as the *Hlesty* or Christs. They were first heard of at the end of the 16th century. Unlike the Old Believers they were from the beginning radically opposed to the ritualism of the Church, and their whole teaching has little in common with the doctrines of historical Christianity. Some students of this sect believe that it has many ideas in common with early Gnosticism. *Hlesty* means flagellators; the name has been attached to them because of their habit of whipping themselves into frenzy at their " spiritual " orgies. They prefer to call themselves *Ludy Bozhye* (People of God), or *Khristovtchina* (Community of Christ). The *Hlesty* have no books so as not to hamper the freedom of inspiration and revelation. " The book of life," they say, " which we must learn to read is written within our hearts." According to their tradition, the true faith was brought down by God Himself from heaven during the reign of Peter the Great; God had descended to a Mount in Vladimir, and there took human form. In his incarnate state He became known as Daniel Philippovitch, who had said of himself: " I am the God announced by the prophets, come down on earth the second time for the salvation of the human race, and there is no God but me."

Daniel Philippovitch was a soldier in the army, and having deserted he declared himself the new incarnation of " Lord God Sabaoth." When a hundred years old, says the tradition,

Daniel begot a son, the Christ, and then re-ascended to heaven. This son was known by the name of *Ivan Suslov*, a serf of the Narishkin family, and he appears to be the principal prophet of the sect. He selected twelve Apostles and decreed twelve commandments, which were handed to him by " The Lord God Sabaoth," i.e. Daniel Philippovitch. Ivan Suslov, the first Christ, according to the tradition of the *Hlesty*, was flogged and persecuted and twice crucified, but rose each time and lived long on earth until he finally ascended to heaven to reunite with his father. The *Hlesty* believed that every man or woman may aspire to divinity and become either a " Christ " or a " Mother of God." Divination is the result of a holy life, and the sect has produced already many Christs. The commandments of the *Hlesty* form an ascetic code, prohibiting the use of alcoholic drinks, attendance at feasts and weddings, marriage, and sexual intercourse; also they forbid stealing and taking an oath.

Their principal ceremonies are secret rites accompanied by great excitement and ecstasy. They gather at night in secret places in white garments. Forming a circle, the participants begin to sing and revolve, at first in measured time, then slowly increasing in velocity until they work themselves into frenzy and exhaustion. The convulsions, screams, and sobbings of the hysterical men and women are taken for manifestations of the presence of the Holy Spirit. That these nightly orgies of emotional excitement end at times in immoral practices is probable, and mainly upon this suspicion they were suppressed by the authorities. The lure of the *Hlesty* practices was so enticing that they found their way into convents and monasteries, and even into the drawing-rooms of higher society and the court. Lifeless orthodoxy among the masses, and the equally lifeless scepticism in higher circles, made high and low alike receptive to any such cult. The *Hlesty* have survived the Revolution and continue to exist in some communities, chiefly rural, of the U.S.S.R.

Similar to the *Hlesty* are the *Skakuny* (The Jumpers). They appeared at first in Petersburg, and their origin is traced to foreign influence. They spread first among the Protestant Finns, but later also amongst the Russian population. The *Skakuny* worked themselves into ecstasy by singing and leaping; they also were accused of sexual licentiousness. Their custom was to come to their secret meetings in couples, and when they had reached the point of ecstasy they gave themselves to the celebration of the " Love of Christ " in darkened rooms. The Government investigation of these sects found that there were tendencies towards both asceticism and sensualism. The ascetic groups were a variety of Quakers whose services consisted, according to their testimony, " in sacred singing and reading of the Bible, accompanied with salutes of brotherly love and endearments of Christian charity; also in pious discourses from preachers whom the Spirit moves to stand up before the meeting; lastly, in prayers with quaking of the body, bending of the knees, and prostrations with weeping, groaning, or invocations, according to the feelings called forth by the preachers' words." Other groups, consisting mostly of younger people, had little of the mystic flavour and gave themselves over to sexual licentiousness under cover of a religious meeting. These sects organized themselves secretly into lodges which the *Hlesty* called *Korables* (Ships). Each " Ship " was presided over by a prophet or a prophetess, and the whole movement was governed by a " Christ."

A more recent offshoot of the *Hlesty* is the sect of the *Sholopats*, first heard of about 1850. They were pronouncedly Communistic and held all things in common.

The *Pliassuny* (Dancers) are also related to the *Hlesty*, although outwardly they remained within the Church. There are many other varieties of the same tendency.

As a reaction to the sensualism of the *Hlesty* and *Skakuny*, must be considered the ascetic sect of self-mutilating eunuchs, called *Skoptsy* (Castrators) or " White Doves," as the adherents of the sect preferred to call themselves. They made their appearance about the year 1770. The founder of the sect was a member of the Petrograd community of *Hlesty*, an illiterate peasant, Selivanov by name. He proclaimed himself ' God of Gods and King of Kings," who had come to gather the faithful and with their aid and under their tutelage establish the Kingdom of the Messiah in Russia. Selivanov added to his divine honours also the honours of the " Tsar of Russia," for he was considered the reincarnation of Peter III, who came to claim his throne usurped by Catherine II. The fundamental doctrine of the *Skoptsy* was based upon the literal interpretation of a few Bible texts ; Matth. xix, 12, being the basis of their faith and practices : " For there are some eunuchs, who were so born from their mother's womb ; and there are some eunuchs, who were made eunuchs of men ; and there be eunuchs who have made themselves eunuchs for the Kingdom of Heaven's sake. He who is able to receive it, let him receive it."

They hold that the carnal union of the first parents of mankind was the " original sin." They preach and practice self-mutilation, believing that by means of a surgical operation they can attain perfect holiness and purity and become like angels. Their zeal for converts knows no obstacles. Like most Russian sectarians, the *Skoptsy* are millenarians ; they believe that " Christ " will come and the reign of the " White Doves " will commence when their converts will have reached the prophetic number of 144,000. They zealously work to complete this number and spare no effort to reach their goal.

Being continually watched by the police, they organized secretly, and like the *Hlesty* call their lodges *Korables*. The Petrograd Lodge, which was headed by a " Christ," was entitled the " Royal Ship." Like the *Hlesty* they clad themselves in white gowns and employ the rotary dance to attain their ecstasy. Women are admitted to the sect on an equal basis with men and are very prominent, some of them being titled " Mothers of God." Their mutilation consists in cutting off the breasts so as to unfit them for nursing children. The bloody initiations take place in hidden places at night, the victims being operated on when the ecstacy reaches its highest pitch. The *Skoptsy* are generally prosperous and they help one another in business.

Outwardly they appear to conform to the social order. They marry and sometimes have children before they submit themselves to the expiating sacrifice. After emasculation they are, of course, readily recognized by their flabby faces and effeminate voices. They knew how to keep out of gaol by bribing the police. They bloodily revenge themselves against those who dare to betray them. Shortly before the Revolution there was a movement among them which repudiated physical mutilations and interpreted the Scriptures spiritually ; this promises to convert the *Skoptsy* into a community of voluntary celibates and to make an end of their savage practices. They are not extinct as yet, but the social conditions which favoured their appearance have now radically changed.

The 17th century, so prolific in religious movements, called into life also a number of sects which in their doctrinal ideas are not unlike those of the Quakers. The Russian *Dukhobory* (Wrestlers of the Spirit) is a sect which probably deviated from the *Hlesty* movement. Tolstoy became interested in them when he learned of their doctrines of the Kingdom of God within man and of their Communistic principles, at which he had arrived himself in his search for the true religion. The *Dukhobory* believe that God is inseparable from man and that independent of man He does not exist. The Holy Trinity is memory, reason and will. They deny the supernatural life and seek to make their paradise on earth. They worship God in man and their services consist in reverential bowing and mutual salutations. In the earlier history they also had their " Mothers of God," and even their present leaders enjoy much the same respect as the " Christs " of the *Hlesty*. They repudiate the authority of Scriptures and believe in the " living book " within the hearts of men. They are vegetarians, pacifists, and preferably Communists. Because of their resistance to the State, they have been severely persecuted. With the aid of Tolstoy, a considerable number of them emigrated to Canada, where they live prosperously and generally maintain the Communistic order.

Just as the Revolution has thrust a rough and sudden hand

into the ordered affairs of the Orthodox Church, so too has it crashed bewilderingly into the obscure activities of these many sects. Within them, also, there is the struggle between the younger and the older generations. The Old Believers have their progressive youngsters who would make common cause with the reformers within the Orthodox Church, while the elders threaten to join hands with the reactionary elements of the Tikhon faction. But generally the Old Believers have lost the impetus which formerly inspired their struggles. Their old enemy, the former State Church is now as weak as they are themselves. Moreover, the Old Believers, who in the cities were supported by rich merchants and manufacturers, have now lost this support and their former prosperous settlements are now quite desolate. There are few prospects of their revival, nevertheless no student of modern Russia who would go behind the scenes can afford to neglect the tremendous influence wrought by the sects on the life of the people.

THE EVANGELICAL SECTS

The vernacular Russian Bible was first published by the Holy Synod in the early 19th century, sponsored by Alexander I, who sympathized with Evangelical pietism and was tolerant towards the various dissenting sects. The Bible, which was widely distributed by such organizations as the British and Foreign Bible Society, made the Evangelical mass movement in Russia possible, and at present the various Evangelical sects have no less than five or six million adherents in Russia. These Evangelicals must be distinguished both in origin and in spirit from the schismatic mystical or rationalist bodies previously described.

The oldest of these are the *Molokans*, " the milk drinkers," so called because of their habit of drinking milk on fast days, a custom prohibited by the Orthodox Church.

Quakers who have visited the Molokans say that in many respects the beliefs of the Russian Evangelists are similar to those of their own Society of Friends. The *Molokans* claim as their spiritual fathers Semenov, first martyr for the Evangelical faith in Russia, who was executed in Tambov in the 16th century, and Dr. Tverentinov of Moscow, who in the reign of Elizabeth felt the influence of Protestantism from the West. Dr. Tverentinov's extracts from the Bible served as a religious text-book. The organizing work for the *Molokans*, at the beginning of the last century, was done by Simon Ukleyn, a peasant who agitated against the orthodox cult and called upon his followers to " live the life of the spirit " and become " Spiritual Christians." Ukleyn denounced all sacraments and any formal cult ; he recognized the Bible as the source of apocalyptic hope and accepted it in its allegorical rather than its literal sense. In respect to the social order of his time he was almost as intolerant as the *Dukhobors*. He declared that all people were equals, that there should be neither rich nor poor, neither commoners nor aristocrats, neither slaves nor masters ; war, the taking of the oath and military service were contrary to the will of God and to desert the army was to do the right thing. In emergency *Molokans* may submit to the monarchical rule, but only to such of its decrees as are not contrary to the Divine law. Ukleyn won his thousands. Alexander I regarded his teachings with tolerance and, in response to a petition from the *Molokans*, permitted them to settle in remote districts along the Volga and in the Taurien Province. Later they suffered renewed persecution and many were exiled to Siberia where their descendants still live in close communities ; some migrated to the United States. A *Molokan* community, by reason of its pacifist religious views, furnished some of the most notable American conscientious objectors during the World War.

The growth of the Baptist movement in Russia was largely at the expense of these *Molokans*. It began with German pietist colonists, Stundists and German Baptists in the 18th century. Energetic, well-organized, aflame with prophetic zeal, the Baptist missionaries were able to take over the administration of religious affairs from the hands of the easy-going *Molokans*. As a result, you rarely come upon a *Molokan* meeting-house without finding a Baptist chapel in the same community.

With the restrictive measures against Evangelism removed, as a result of the revolutions of 1905 and 1917, the Evangelists have turned their missionary fire upon the Orthodox Church itself, much to the alarm of the latter. The way was cleared by the split within the orthodox fold and, paradoxically enough, by the anti-religious propaganda of the Communists.

Anti-religious speakers entering a community would find ready listeners. When they left, more often than not the priests were driven from the villages and the Orthodox Church building turned into a club. But sooner or later an itinerant missionary, Baptist or one of some similar belief, would appear with his message of salvation, his preaching of the " True Gospel," and within a few months a community, apparently safely atheized from the Communist standpoint, would be shouting the Slavic version of our familiar gospel hymns.

So effectively did these holy outriders prey upon the ranks of the orthodox that in 1925 the Synod of the Orthodox Church called a special conference to discuss the distressing situation. The conference gave a number of reasons for the success of the Evangelicals, chief among them the disorganization of the Orthodox Church. It set up a Home Mission Department to look into the matter more closely and study the methods of the Evangelicals. It is significant that one of the reasons suggested by the Orthodox conference for the acceptance of Evangelistic teachings by the masses, was that the Baptists, Adventists, etc., used " social and political slogans which are akin to the Communistic ideas, for which they were formerly prosecuted but which now are looked on with tolerance by the new regime."

For over a decade the Evangelical movement had progressed triumphantly with little or no resistance on the part of the Orthodox Church or the Soviet Government, till it was checked somewhat by restrictive legislation in 1929. It probably will continue for some time to grow at the expense of the Orthodox

Church, but not forever, and it must look forward to the training of the new generation which now is growing up in their midst. This is recognized by some of the leaders of the movement, but so far they are little prepared for the task.

The Baptist movement in Russia was unable, however, to maintain its unity, and it split into two larger bodies. One of its former leaders, I. S. Prokhanov, a converted *Molokan*, felt that the name " Baptist " was foreign and its doctrines and organization were not so well suited to Russian psychology; he therefore broke away from the main body and organized an independent movement now known as the *Union of Evangelical Christians*. During the years of unlimited freedom for religious propaganda (1917-1929) the movement spread very rapidly and built up an efficient organization with a publishing department, a training school, and many regional organizations. The main body of Baptists also improved its organization and both branches are now about even in numbers. The *Molokans*, once numerically strongest, did not come up to the demands of the time. They had lost their youthful ardour and suffered also from the lack of organization and leadership.

Besides these main Evangelical sects there are congregations of Seventh Day Adventists, the New Israel, and other groups. All these rapidly increased their numbers under the favourable conditions after the fall of Tsarism. The reasons for favouring the sectarians on the part of the Soviet Government are quite clear. Under the old regime the sectarians were severely persecuted; many of them were imprisoned or exiled to remote places, together with those revolutionists who at present are governing the country. In exile the Communists learned to appreciate these revolutionists of the spirit, and when the old regime collapsed and the Communists came to power they naturally could not but be sympathetic toward the sectarians and, in turn, expected their support.

Moreover, some sects had Communistic tendencies and the Government favoured them for this reason. An early declaration of the Soviet Department of Justice says: " These sects adapt themselves quite readily to the common civil Soviet laws and regulations and organically unite as agricultural nuclei into the Soviet organizations, in spite of the religious form which their communistic tendencies, by force of historical conditions, have adopted. The task of the Soviet organs in regard to these organizations consists pre-eminently in seeing that these Communistic organizations, developed and fortified with the aid of science and superior technic, continue in their adopted habits and modes of Communistic organization as industrial agricultural groups. Raised to a superior form, they will serve as practical examples of the possibility and advantage of Communism for the toiling population."

Since then the favourable attitude towards the sectarians has greatly changed. The rapid spread of the Evangelical movement jeopardized in some places the hegemony of the Communist Party and Youth Organization. Moreover, the sectarians were not very enthusiastic and in some places even hostile to, the rural collectivization schemes of the Government. The reasons for this can be easily understood. Most of them were much more prosperous than the neighbouring peasants who did not belong to their religious community, and so, to give up their individual farms and join the collectives was to the sectarians a material loss. They opposed the Government's plan of collectivization and, when pressed, advanced the theory that their religious convictions prohibited them from sitting in Council with the " ungodly," quoting the First Psalm as a proof-text. They finally agreed to form collectives consisting only of members of their own religious organization, but the Government could not permit this and insisted upon non-sectarian collectives open to all toiling peasants. On these grounds the sectarians clashed with the Soviets, and in some places repressive measures were used against them. These facts and the alarm about their rapid growth prompted the Government to change its policy of tolerance towards religious propaganda. In April, 1929, an Amendment [1] to the Constitution was adopted, which provides freedom of religious worship but not freedom of religious

[1] See Appendix II, B and C.

propaganda. The Amendment also prohibits special organizations within the Church for educational and social service purposes.

During this period of changing policy the organization centres of the Evangelical sects were closed, their publications suspended, and their training schools closed. Now their administrative organs have resumed functioning on a somewhat modified but greatly centralized basis. They now have small but powerful administrative boards in the capital and no regional organizations. The Evangelicals no longer enjoy the freedom of open-air preaching and extensive travel as they were used before the change of the Constitution, but in their chapel services Evangelistic preaching and Baptism of converts continues and, so far as observation goes, their meetings are very well attended. There are, at present, some three thousand registered groups and congregations of Baptists and Evangelical Christians and their sphere of influence continues to spread throughout the whole country.

One of the problems of the Government in dealing with the sectarians is the attitude of the latter towards military training and service in the Red Army. The pacifist sects under the old regime were treated with little concern and frequently brutally persecuted. During the civil war the Soviet Government had to face the problem of the conscientious objector. Its legislation is quite definite on the problem. In principle all citizens are subject to military service, the exemptions can be made by decision of the People's Court. When trying cases of conscientious objection the courts pay due attention to the denominational affiliation of the objector, and only those are considered entitled to exemption who belong to denominations which before the World War stood upon a non-resistance platform. Thus a considerable number of Baptists have been refused exemptions on the ground that the Baptist Church did not advise its members to refuse service in the World War and hence should have no scruples in rendering service to the Red Army. In recent years the attitude of the Government toward conscientious objectors has been less and less lenient; there have been cases where members of sects formerly exempt are now compelled to render military service, even though without arms. The Government fears that by favouring certain religious groups it will encourage others who are not traditionally pacifist.

The central problem which the Evangelicals in Russia, as everywhere else in the world, have now to contend with, is the adjustment of the old-time religion to the workings of the machine-age and to the impact of modern natural science. They have no educational facilities with which to train a leadership able to cope with the skilled propagandists of the Soviets, despite the fact of their temporary emotional successes. It is necessary to remember that in Soviet Russia to-day every school child of twelve is taught the most advanced doctrines of evolutionary science. Naturally such teaching is in relentless opposition to the archaic doctrines of the sectarian theologians. The Evangelicals have so far ignored this menace. They have no men who can satisfactorily reconcile the teachings of the "Simon Pure" Gospel with the scientific demands of the industrial age. If coming generations of Evangelical Christians are to continue to flourish, somehow they must work out this difficult formula. It seems as though they were to pass through an even more painful readjustment of opinions than is the apparent fate of their fellow Fundamentalists in Western countries.

CHAPTER V

THE BEGINNINGS OF THE ANTI-RELIGIOUS TRADITION

RELIGION in Russia has a long unbroken tradition ; so, also, has atheism. In the past the latter did not speak out so clearly and so definitely as it now does under Communism. For a long time it was careful not to call itself atheism and paraded as " enlightment," " free thought," Deism, and Humanism. But essentially all these movements and doctrines were denying the old gods and replacing them by Reason, Humanity, or the ideals of the social revolution.

While Russian orthodox religion has its sources in the Orient and in the old pagan traditions of the Slavic tribes, atheism is entirely an Occidental product and its adepts in Russia were commonly called Westernites. Russian atheist thought may be traced to English Deism and French materialism. In Russia these teachings, due to the social-political peculiarities of the native scene, were carried to their logical conclusion. The Russian temper does not stop half-way ; it avoids compromise and dislikes the method of harmonizing old and obsolete with newly acquired ideals as, for example, is the habit of the Anglo-Saxon mind. The Russian is more apt to destroy the old even before he has given a fair test to the new ; he is temperamentally iconoclastic, though not so impulsive as the Frenchman.

The Bolshevik movement against religion has all the peculiarities of the Russian character in spite of the foreign origin of its philosophy and the international associations in its organization. It frankly calls itself " Bezbozhnik," i.e. " Godless," and Communists despise Western half-heartedness

THE BEGINNINGS OF THE ANTI-RELIGIOUS TRADITION

in its disguise of atheism under " free thought," agnosticism, humanism, and such descriptions.

The concept of atheism has also its history. Not every heresy which has been branded as atheism would be considered such to-day. Thus was Socrates charged with atheism and condemned to die for denying the old gods ; yet we know that his efforts were directed towards arousing in his people a conscious reflection upon life and its moral purpose and that he became the founder of the classic idealist philosophy so brilliantly developed by his pupil Plato. As an idealist philosopher he can by no means be considered an atheist, for atheism, according to Communist theory, means not only the denial of a personal God or gods in control of the universe, but it means the rejection of everything supernatural, including every idealistic philosophy from Socrates to Bergson.

If atheism meant only the denial of gods, then adherence to such great religions as the Sankya system in Hinduism, and Buddhism, should be considered atheist, since these religions emphasize self-discipline and deny a God superior to nature. But we should hardly call the adherent of any religion an atheist, even were his metaphysics as materialistic as that of the Sankya, or as pantheistic as the philosophy of Brahminism and Buddhism.

FOREIGN SOURCES OF RUSSIAN ATHEISM

Open militant atheism made its appearance first in France during the second half of the 18th century, heralding the great French Revolution. It was preceded by the more cautious English Deism which ruled God out of direct contact with the universe, of which he was considered to be nothing but the " first cause." In Deism theological thought followed in the footsteps of political philosophy. The Deist relation to God is not unlike the relation of British democracy to its king after the constitutional limitations of the throne were firmly established in England during the 17th and 18th centuries. As the king ceded his prerogatives of direct autocratic rule to Parliament, thus the Deist thought of God as a creator who permitted his creation to administer itself by natural law. Deism is also an attempt to put faith in God upon a scientific basis by discovering in humanity tenets of a so-called natural religion, independent of any cult, the necessity of miracles and revelation.

Thomas Hobbes advanced a purely materialist interpretation of religion, tracing its origin to the primitive fear of nature, from which arose anthropomorphic conceptions of natural forces. The worship of the Deity thus created was a part of the social life of the group, so that in its more highly developed forms religion became a phase of political life and hence was to be controlled in the interest of the state. Hobbes' materialistic interpretation of religion was much harsher than Lord Herbert's of Cherbury, who is credited with having given Deism its first systematic formulation, which he expressed in five fundamentals: the existence of God; the duty of worship; the need of repentance from sin; rewards and punishments. Charles Blount, a Deist theologian of the latter part of the 17th century, still further developed the compromising tendencies of English Deism toward the orthodox point of view by conceding the possibility of miracles. Yet he minimized the supernatural as an essential element of religion and sought to give Christianity and its teachings a logical justification as a product of social evolution and a universal reaction to natural laws.

The English Deistic movement had considerable influence on the 18th century French philosophers of enlightenment. The different social background of pre-revolutionary France with its powerful feudal Church made French Deism a weapon against organized religion instead of an apologetic system to meet the demands of Newtonian physics and modern science generally, as was the case in England.

The greatest interpreter of English Deism in France was Voltaire (1694–1778), the recognized patriarch of bourgeois free thought. His influence went far beyond the boundaries of his own country. He found access into Prussia where Frederick II permitted his court to be contaminated with Voltairian ideas, and as we shall observe later, Voltairianism became a regular cult among the upper classes in Russia.

THE BEGINNINGS OF THE ANTI-RELIGIOUS TRADITION

The French revolutionaries honoured Voltaire as the leader of progressive thought in his century. They transferred his remains to the Pantheon and upon his tombstone engraved the words: " He fought against atheists and fanatics; he advanced tolerance; he declared the rights of man in the face of slavery and feudalism; he prepared us for liberty." While this emphasized that Voltaire fought atheism it would have been more true to say that he prepared the way for it. History knows hardly another big mind who poured so much sarcasm, so much destructive criticism, upon organized religion and the hypocrisy of the clergy, " the pen in his hands was the sword of Mohammed of the West." Joseph de Maistre, one of the able critics of the revolutionary period of France, blames Voltaire with poisoning the mind of the French people with sacrilegious ideas. " Never," he says, " was the weapon of derision directed against truth with such shamelessness and success. Before him blasphemy found its limitations in the disgust of the people and was but killing the blasphemer himself. From the lips of this most vicious of men it became infectious, even charming." Thus, if Voltaire was opposed to open atheism and defended the necessity of a " first cause," this was due not only to the Newtonian and Lockian philosophies, which he uniquely interpreted, but also because he feared removing the restraints that the idea of God had upon untutored minds.

Voltaire took God for granted as a convenient though unknowable hypothesis and moral necessity. He says: " It would be almost folly to deny the eternal geometer. But where is the eternal geometer? In one place or everywhere, without occupying space? I know nothing. Has he created everything out of his own substance? I don't know. Is he immense without quantity and quality? I don't know. All I do know is that it is necessary to bow before him and be just." While granting this much he actually retreated to the Spinozian position of identifying God with nature. According to this theory the world runs its course by inner necessity of which man is but an eternally determined agent. In his *Philosophic*

Dictionary he calls free will an invention of theologians. He says : " People are essentially machines, moving in such a way as is preordained by the unchangeable laws and by the iron chains of necessary cause and effect."

In Voltaire's voluminous writings throughout a long and active life one may find quite a variety of ideas ranging between pragmatic Theism and a vague Pantheism. A child of his age and representative of the interests of the Third Estate, whose ideologist he was, he fought the feudal Roman Catholic Church, calling it the " l'Infâme," yet, at the same time, seeking to preserve religion as a bridle against the tyranny of the governing classes and against the anarchy of the mob which, as a man of wealth, he feared most of all. This explains his saying : " If there be no God, he should have been invented."

Not all of the French philosophers of enlightenment agreed with Voltaire in recognizing God for reasons of moral control. Thus Lamettrie (1709–1751), also a favourite of Frederick II of Prussia, altogether denied the necessity of religion for the happiness of man. In his famous work, *The Man Machine* and in the *Natural History of the Soul*, Lamettrie followed Descartes' observation that the animal is a machine and by analogy he carries it to the logical conclusion that man, being also an animal, must be equally a machine. Said Lamettrie : " Precisely this strong analogy compels all scientists and true judges to acknowledge that the proud and vain creatures, which differ not so much by the name of man as by their pride, are essentially but perpendicularly moving animal machines." In diagnosing the " soul " to which most theologians ascribe divine origin and immortality, he concluded that the soul, i.e. the function of reflective thought, is but a peculiar quality of matter, of the same nature as electricity, the power of movement, attraction, and so on. The " first cause " of things, i.e. the " Deist God," if there be such a god, Lamettrie considered altogether inaccessible to knowledge and outside the realm of positive science which alone can give trustworthy information. Atheism, he argued, could contribute to the happiness of man : " If atheism was a general phenomenon, then all the growths of religion would be destroyed and eradicated. There would no longer be theological wars, the soldiers of religion would disappear—those terrible soldiers ! Nature, now infested with holy poison, would reclaim its rights and purity." Lamettrie placed his trust in natural morality which he opposed to religious taboos. He was much bolder than Voltaire and as a result was persecuted by the clergy and was compelled to flee in fear of his life ; finding refuge at the court of Frederick II, he remained there till his death.

In the constellation of brilliant minds of pre-revolutionary France, Denis Diderot (1733–1784) holds a leading position, and his influence on Russian thought is particularly significant. He was the editor-in-chief of the famous French Encyclopedia and gave his life and talents to this huge undertaking. The son of an artisan it is said of him that " he bore the 18th century upon his shoulders as the Atlas of antiquity bore the world." He is also considered to be the first herald of the French Revolution. While many of his able contemporaries, like Voltaire, lived for their own intellectual satisfaction, Diderot denied himself for the sake of a big common cause—the Encyclopedia, which became the intellectual battering ram of the French Revolution. By its steady persistent strokes of criticism and its advancement of positive knowledge it broke down the Bastille of medieval feudalism and ecclesiastical tyranny. Diderot's fortunes were closely knit with Russia. Catherine II, in the prime of liberalism, lent him her powerful support, and when the Encyclopedia was prohibited in France she proposed the transference of its publication to Russia and endowed Diderot with a high pension so as to permit him to continue the work as its editor. The wrath of the Church against the Encyclopedia had its good reasons. Directly or by implication the articles of the Encyclopedia aimed at the teachings of the Church and its institutions. Many of these articles were written by Diderot and many more were inspired and edited by him. It is difficult to find the limitations of Diderot's mind. It was truly encyclopedic in range. In his thinking he felt the defects of mechanistic materialism and in his *Conversations with D'Alembert* he pointed toward the dialectic solution of the problem of materialism which was actually undertaken by the Marxian school a century later.

Diderot, trained by Jesuits in the fundamentals of the Christian dogma, ended as an atheist, but not a militant, enthusiastic atheist, for he feared the masses were not prepared for it. " The majority of the nation," he said, " will always remain ignorant, infested by fear, and hence superstitious; atheism will remain the teaching of a small school, but will never be the accepted doctrine of a large number of citizens, nor will it become the heritage of a low-cultured people. Faith in the existence of God or its old roots will always remain, and if free growth be permitted to these roots, no one can say what monstrous sprouts will issue from them." This is not the opinion of Communist atheists who broadcast to the masses their atheistic message without the fear that it will unbridle their morale.

Amongst the French atheists who still have their influence on Communist thought was Baron P. A. d'Holbach (1723–1789), close friend and, in a way, a disciple of Diderot. From a Voltairian Deist, Holbach, with the aid of Diderot, thought his way through to outright atheism which he propagated with great enthusiasm, erudition and literary skill. His principal work, *Système de la Nature* (1770), may be considered the matured product of French materialist thought. It has been called " The Gospel of Materialism " and " The Red Cap of Philosophy." In this epoch-making work, which roused the animosity and fear of the Roman Church, is collected and systematized the whole argument of the 18th century based on the materialist hypothesis of the universe. Its criticism extends not only against feudal religion and the Church, but equally against the whole system of the old regime. Morley characterized Holbach's work as a collection of all the explosives which were scattered by critics throughout the century, united into a monstrous machine of revolt and destruction. It is generally agreed that there is hardly another book which had so great a revolutionary effect upon the minds of the people and its influence has lasted till our own days. Lenin suggested its translation into Russian for use as a weapon of anti-religious propaganda in the Soviet Union.

The book has two parts. It first establishes the position of materialism on the principle of eternal uncreated substance of the universe as a mechanism of matter in motion, and the second part is devoted to an exposition of the atheist ideas of the author and the critique of contemporary religious philosophical teachings. In Holbach's *Système* man is a part of nature, though more highly organized. There is no God, no immortal soul and hence no divine right of kings and rulers. Nature must provide the remedy against all evil which error and fraud have created and which is exploited by tyrants and the clergy who keep the masses in fear and superstition. The book appeals to courage and faith in human reason to establish life on a rational basis of social utility and service. This is Holbach's message which in his later works he popularized so as to make it accessible to the widest possible public. This effort to democratize the materialist and atheist philosophy aroused not only the fear and enmity of ecclesiastical and State authorities, it even frightened many philosophers of enlightenment, who thought that the still popular author of the *Système de la Nature* had gone too far. Voltaire undertook writing a criticism of the book, but all this concern only added to its popularity. Diderot, who closely followed the developing conflict, wrote in 1771:

" The flames were steadily fanned, the principles of liberty and independence, once hidden away in the hearts of a few thinking people, now established themselves and are openly proclaimed. Each age is characterized by its peculiar spirit. The spirit of our era is the spirit of freedom. The first attack upon superstition was greatly turbulent. But as soon as people dared to attack the foundations of religion, the most terrible and most venerated of institutions, no stops were possible. Turning their threatening vision against the majesty of heaven, inevitably, in a short time, they direct it also upon terrestial powers. The cable which holds up and chokes humanity is braided of these two ropes. One cannot break without also breaking the other."

Besides Holbach, various others of a particular circle of friends contributed to the undermining of the old faith and authority. In their ideals they ranged between Deism, Pantheism, and open atheism. Their contributions include the two great books of Helvetius, *On the Spirit* and *On Man*; but none of these works were as bold and as frank as the writings of Holbach.

This survey of the philosophy of French enlightenment has been made because of its tremendous influence on the development of the anti-religious tradition in Russia, an influence which continues to this day in spite of the fact that its mechanistic theories of the universe and of religion are no longer tenable in the light of modern science, which has been fully recognized by Communist philosophy. Nevertheless, many of the arguments, particularly those in criticism of the institutions of religion, and its militant spirit, are appreciated by the Communist atheist movement.

THE BEGINNINGS OF RUSSIAN ENLIGHTENMENT

Voltaire's slogan, " Ecrasez l'infâme," directed against the Church was re-echoed not only in Western Europe, where antiquated orthodoxy and ecclesiasticism oppressed the masses and fettered free thought, it was heard also in far-off Russia and, for a while, flourished at the Court of Catherine II. But already, during the reign of Peter I, there had been some active minds and free spirits who felt and embraced the influence of the West.

The religious traditions of Russia were not suited to vigorous intellectual activity, and the ecclesiastical reforms introduced by Peter I reduced the Church altogether to a department of State with the express purpose of keeping the masses in servile obedience to the governing class. Peter himself was no particular devotee of orthodox Christianity; his unruly character and unrestrained passions frequently ended in drunken orgies in which were masqueraded religious ceremonies with himself as the " princely Pope " and his officers as his " clerical retinue." This hilarious company " celebrated holy mass," burning tobacco in place of incense and carrying, as the " holy cross," long smoking pipes tied together ; the Eucharist was celebrated by the dispensing of liquor, and the " holy gospels " were represented by a cask of vodka. Such blasphemous behaviour on the part of the Tsar increased the belief of his pious subjects that he was the " Anti-Christ," and it added zeal to the Old Believers movement which spread rapidly during his reign.

Disregarding popular protest, Peter I was determined to modernize Russia. Generally he favoured religious toleration and sympathized with Western rationalized Protestantism. At the same time he was quite ignorant of philosophical and theological questions and he let himself be guided by his advisers, frequently in most contradictory ways. A striking example of this ignorance was his attitude toward Huygens' book on astronomy and physics, the first scientific work ever translated into the Russian language. It was recommended to the Tsar for publication by General Jacob Bruce, in charge of Peter's artillery school and actual translator of this book. The Tsar ordered a certain Abramov, one of his trusted supporters in charge of the State printing establishment, to have 1,200 copies of the book printed. Later this Abramov, a former participator in Peter's blasphemous orgies, becoming somewhat conscience-stricken, drew the attention of the Tsar to the heretical contents of the book, recommending that it should be burned, together with its translator. Peter withdrew his order for the printing of the book, but graciously pardoned the translator for his heretical interests.

In spite of the Tsar's frequent changeability on questions of religion, his dislike of the old traditions made possible the development of free thought in Russia. To leadership in the Church he attracted such enlightened men as Theophan Prokopovitch, a Ukrainian, trained in a Jesuit College in Rome, but for some reason abandoning Roman Catholicism for the service of Peter who entrusted him with carrying through his ecclesiastical reforms and schemes of modernisation. Nominally Prokopovitch seems to have been loyal to the Orthodox Church. His criticism was directed against the Roman Church, its superstitions, and persecution of modern scientific thought. In the controversy over the publication of Huygens' astronomy he took Bruce's part : " If the pupils of Copernicus and scientists who defend the movement of the earth can present as proofs of their opinion reliable physical and mathematical data, then the text of Holy Scripture in which the movement of the sun is mentioned cannot be taken as a refutation, and the text must be understood not in the literal but in the allegorical sense." In one of his Latin poems, he denounces the Roman Inquisition over Galileo :

Why, oh infamous Pope, do you torture the industrious Servant of nature ?
Oh, cruel tyrant ! Why deserves the sage such persecution ?
Pope, thou art raging ! He does not touch thy worlds.
He does not invade with evil designs thy sacred premises,
Where the flaming Styx purges the souls of the dead,
Where abide the gods and goddesses of thy invention.
His earth is genuine and thine is false ;
His stars are creations of God, and thine are fraud.
" But," says the Pope, " our duty is to see that
Similar names (of different meaning),
Should not tempt the common people."
Oh, barbarian stupidity, abysmal dregs of a blind world !
Is it for thee to judge the luminous thought of Galileo ?
Is it for thee to accuse as criminal a penetrating mind vigilant as a lynx ?
Apparently the vile mole-warp sees better than the lynx.

Much of this criticism hurled as it was against the Roman Church hit the Russian Orthodox Church equally hard, for its obscurantism and intellectual backwardness was not less, but rather greater, than that of the Roman Church, as we have seen in the case of Huygens' book on astronomy. Prokopovitch's criticism must therefore be understood as a disguised attack upon superstition and reaction in his own Church. This he proved by his efforts to introduce popular education and the study of modern philosophy. He was well read in the works of Francis Bacon, Descartes and in all that was considered advanced thinking in his time. His library contained 30,000 volumes and was undoubtedly a great contribution to the cultural advancement of his people. We may justly consider Prokopovitch as the pioneer of Russian enlightenment.

Another outstanding personality of this period was *Vassily Tatischev* (1686–1750), a Russian nobleman with some Western education and profound critical abilities. He was well-versed in the philosophy of Hobbes, Locke, and Pierre Bayle. His chief work, *The History of Russia from the Earliest Times*, was considered too radical and could be published only some time after his death by the gracious permission of Catherine II. Tatischev must be considered also as the first Russian Biblical critic. He rejected Solomon's Song of Songs as a religious book, considering it simply a love song. Peter, who valued Tatischev's learning, could not agree with his criticism of religion and when his limited knowledge failed him in argument, to convince the obstinate Tatischev, he " beat him with his own royal fists " (so reports the chronicler)—a frequent habit of Peter's in argument with his statesmen and generals.

Tatischev's history shows that the clergy played no laudable part in the history of the Russian people. It did nothing for their education and, says Tatischev, " to accumulate great income and power the clergy found it profitable to keep the people in darkest ignorance and superstition." Tatischev sympathized with the Deists and held " natural law " and " reason " to be sufficient to direct man in his behaviour. Thus morality depends not on religion but is the product of enlightenment and of the understanding of natural law. " In every transgression of the laws of nature God has placed its own punishment." Sin is not that which contradicts the decrees of the Church but that which is harmful to humanity ! This was advanced thinking for the Russia of the early 18th century. Tatischev was as yet not a confessed atheist but he was an open sceptic and prepared the ground for the " Golden Age " of Russian free thought which flourished under Catherine II.

Before describing this " Golden Age " we have yet to mention a further contemporary of Prokopovitch and Tatischev, Antioch Kantemir (1708–1744), who gained the reputation of being wise, honest and kind, was one of the first students of the newly-organized Petersburg Academy of Science and was chosen for diplomatic service, representing his country in London and Paris. These contacts with the West, together with his natural abilities, made him very critical of the Church and particularly of its higher clergy. He satirized them in his verse, which had little poetic value, but was full of shrewd observation and exposure of the intellectual backwardness and moral degradation of the servants of the Church.

Under the influence of English Deism and French Rationalism he turned from theology to philosophy. The Holy Scriptures, he argued, are no proof of scientific truth, and revelation has no authority over reason. Kantemir made some of the first translations of the French philosophers of enlightenment, particularly Fontenelle and Montesquieu, and corresponded with Voltaire. The reaction which set in after the death of Peter I, in 1726, was not favourable to free thought, and Kantemir had great difficulty in publishing his works. His early death prevented him from fully unfolding his abilities.

Prokopovitch, Tatischev and Kantemir, the pioneers of Russian enlightenment, were all Westerners in their education and sympathies. They fully realized the horrible backwardness of their people, particularly of their Church, and their aim was to reform their country upon West European lines. While favouring education, they were not strong enough morally to proclaim against their country's greatest evil, that feudal servitude under which groaned millions of Russian peasants, nor did they dare to attack the autocracy of the Russian throne. They were enlightened but still loyal members of their class, the feudal nobility. As yet there was no strong bourgeoisie in Russia and no proletariat to exert pressure on them, and there could be none, so long as the peasants were tied to the soil, since from the peasant class was to come necessary free labour for capitalistic development. Prokopovitch, Tatischev and Kantemir must therefore be taken as mild reformers and not as revolutionists, yet they were the first to shake the foundations of Russian orthodoxy which itself was the foundation of the autocratic power of the Tsar and of the feudal aristocracy. In this respect these men must be considered the early forerunners of the great Russian Revolution of two centuries later. It must always be remembered that the weakening of ecclesiastical authority and religious faith is the beginning of revolution.

THE RUSSIAN VOLTAIRIANS

The process of Westernizing the Russian nobility which began during Peter's reign was continued and flourished under Catherine II. She considered herself an enlightened autocrat, rivalling Frederick II of Prussia and Joseph I of Austria in making her Court a radiant centre of intellectual life, where the artist and philosopher replaced the court jesters of an earlier age. France not only supplied the fashions and follies of European courts ; at this time she was equally rich in ideas and her philosophers were welcome guests at the courts of enlightened autocrats. Frederick II induced Voltaire and Lamettrie to settle in Potsdam ; Catherine II prided herself in inducing Denis Diderot to her court, and in her steady correspondence with Voltaire, D'Alembert and Grimm, who at the time was considered the travelling salesman of modern French philosophy at the court of Europe, finally settling at Catherine's court to end his days.

The popularity of Voltaire under Catherine's protection took the form of a regular movement among the educated Russians of the time. His writings were widely read and not only in the original, for during the later 18th and the beginning of the 19th centuries one hundred and forty editions in all of his various works were published in Russian translation. The importance of this number becomes still more evident when we learn that during the same period a total of only eight thousand titles was published in the country. In addition to Voltaire, Montesquieu, Rousseau, Helvetius, and the French Encyclopedists generally, were widely studied.

French enlightenment had not the same effect upon its many adepts. To the majority it meant simply freedom from the old religious traditions and produced a widespread disregard of the Church and a general laxity of respect for taboos and customs. This alarmed many of the more serious and conservative-minded Russian statesmen and hierarchs. Prince Shcherbatov (1733–1790), a contemporary of Catherine, described the disintegration of the older moral traditions in a book entitled *On the Depravity of Morals in Russia*. He complained that the situation had reached a point where " faith in Divine Law has disappeared from the heart and the divine mysteries (sacraments) are held in contempt." Shcherbatov blamed Peter I who, while striving to purge the people's faith of its many superstitions, went too far in his zeal. He compared Peter to an inexperienced gardener who applied to a weak tree the same pruning as to a strong one. Whilst in order to enlighten the people, it was very useful to remove superstition, in Russia such pruning had damaged the fundamentals of the faith. " Superstitions had decreased, but faith also had diminished; the slavish fear of Hell had disappeared, but so also had vanished love for God and for His holy law; and morals, for the lack of other enlightenment and uncorrected by faith, had lost their supports and turned into vice."[1] What was commenced by Peter was brought to its logical conclusion by Catherine. By her measures, complained Shcherbatov, she entirely destroyed the faith, " that eternal support of conscience and virtue." He accused her of having abandoned " the rock of God's law " and built her politics and her personal morals on the shifting sands of modern philosophy.

[1] Shcherbatov, *On the Depravity of Morals in Russia*, p. 28.

The moral depravity at Catherine's Court, as a result of the badly understood French enlightenment, may be seen from the complaints and invectives of one of the priests of the court chapel who had the moral courage to say in a sermon : " The Christian dogma on which depends eternal salvation has been turned into fables and into naught ; the solicitor of our salvation, the vigilant Christian helper, the shelter and shield (i.e. the Holy Virgin) is not called upon for aid ; the holy saints of God are not respected ; no regard is paid to the holy ikons ; the sign of the Cross, before which even Devils tremble, is despised ; the traditions of the Apostles and the Holy Fathers are rejected ; good deeds, for which there is eternal reward, are swept away ; meat is during the holy fasts devoured, and of the mortification of the flesh no one wishes to hear ; prayer for the dead is derided, themselves children and heirs of Hell, they believe it not."

Whilst the majority described in these priestly invectives unquestionably understood the new philosophy as a license to live each according to his desire, it would be wrong to denounce the Voltairian movement of Catherine's day as wholesale licentiousness and Godlessness. Neither Catherine nor her court was in theory atheistic. In her youth Catherine was brought up a Protestant, but when she married the fool-hearted Peter III, to comply with the traditions of the Russian Church, she nominally accepted Greek Orthodoxy. Eager for knowledge, she sincerely wished to be an enlightened monarch. Of this she assured Voltaire and other philosophers with whom she corresponded and who flattered her as the hope of the new age. Unquestionably, she did much to lighten the burdens of Russian womanhood and free it from its age-long Asiatic seclusion. She organized the first schools for women in Russia and built homes for unmarried mothers and maternity hospitals.

In 1767 she attempted to carry out some drastic reforms in the Church. She outlined her ideas in a memorandum placed before the Holy Synod. Her recommendations were : to give toleration and to permit open divine service to all dissenters; to shorten the length of the fasting seasons; to purge the Church of superstition and of fraudulent miracles; to stop the visitation of houses by ikons; to cut down the number of Church feast days; to simplify the church ceremonies and to introduce, instead of the long vigils, short services with prayer and exortations; to permit bishops to marry; to introduce a simpler respectable dress for the clergy; to make divorce easier; to permit marriage between distant relatives and between persons of different faith; to abolish prayer for the dead; and other similar reforms. These much-needed reforms were ignored by the Synod, which gave her to understand that any attack upon the traditions of the Church would produce another schism and jeopardize the security of her throne. Her " Grand Instructions," which she prepared as a general guide for a reconstitution of the country, had the same fate. They reflected the principles contained in Montesquieu's *Spirit of the Laws*, and other advanced ideas which she had learned from her French philosopher friends. These " Grand Instructions " she later banned when frightened by the rumours of the French Revolution. She began to realize the danger to her autocratic power of free ideas, and we see her enlightened liberalism rapidly fade into darkest reaction, with a corresponding development of piety in which she loved to pose as " Holy Catherine."

The French philosophers, now banned, she turned her attention to the Masonic Order, which was also suppressed. This could hardly be otherwise, for the chief evil of Russia, the fate of the peasants, was not alleviated during her long reign, but on the contrary worsened. By this time half the peasants were under serfdom, a condition which did not differ much from slavery and against which the Cossack leader, Pugatchev, led his revolt. Catherine's brilliant court and the feudal nobility lived on the blood and sweat of the millions of enslaved peasants, and whilst the illiteracy and religious superstition of these peasants kept them in ignorance of the bourgeois enlightenment which inspired the French Revolution, nevertheless some of these ideas began slowly to penetrate into ever widening circles. Catherine made frantic efforts to undo the work of her own life. The young people, whom she once educated to scepticism and disrespect of the old traditions, she now tried to turn back to the obscure discarded faith. This proved impossible; there were already many apart from the nobility who held to the new ideas. While still relatively small in number, one may nevertheless speak of an intelligentsia developing in Russia. This new class claimed the right to independent thought and took the new revolutionary ideas seriously. There were also not a few amongst the higher nobility who had become confirmed atheists and some of them formed the nucleus of the Decembrist movement of a later date, which started the first organized revolt against the Russian autocracy. Thus we see that during the reign of Catherine a serious anti-religious movement made its start in Russia. It took a firm hold upon the newly-forming intellectual class and never left it despite every effort to eradicate it on the part of Catherine and her successors.

THE MASONIC REACTION

The reaction to French enlightenment and atheism showed itself in the spread of the Masonic gospel and of similar mystic cults to which the upper classes turned in preference to their own traditional faith. The Masonic movement in Russia had several sources: one trend came from Germany, another from England and a third from Sweden. The first Masonic lodges were established in Petersburg in the middle of the 18th century and were patronized chiefly by Catherine's officers of the guard, who took it as a new form of entertainment, attracted to it by the gorgeous ceremonies of initiation which at that time usually ended in wild orgies. A contemporary initiate characterized this first period of Russian Masonry as " a play in which the service of Minerva was transformed into a celebration of Bacchus." The Voltairian Deistic philosophy worked well in conjunction with the Masonic ideas which, however, were not taken seriously.

The French Revolution resulted in serious changes in the

Russian Masonic movement. The initiative was taken by a certain *Elagin* who, in 1750, as a young man joined the Freemasons but, disappointed by its vulgarities, drifted into French free thought and atheism, from which he finally recoiled when frightened by the French Revolution. Elagin met a distinguished English gentleman travelling in Russia, who revealed to him the tenets of British Masonry, which he interpreted to Elagin as a pious sacred science which did not share the ideas of the Godless French Encyclopedists even though many of the latter were members of Masonic lodges. Elagin learned that there were different trends in Masonry and he sought contact with the " great London Lodge " into which he was finally initiated and rose to " Provincial Grand Master of Russia." Elagin became an enthusiastic advocate of English Masonry in Russia and sought to adapt the new Creed to the peculiarities of the Greek Orthodox faith.

This conservative tendency of Russian Masonry still further increased under the influence of another Voltairian renegade, *I. V. Lopukhin* (1756–1816), a man of considerable erudition and literary ability. In his youth he translated some of Holbach's and Diderot's works, but later turned against their atheist teachings and sought solace in the mystic Masonic cult of the " Rose and the Cross," known in Russia after its German name the " Rosenkreuzer." Lopukhin became its fanatic interpreter and managed to unite it to the mysticism of the Greek Church. This former Voltairian was now an uncompromising enemy of the French Revolution, which he considered the result of the godless philosophy of the Encyclopedists. He appealed to his brother Masons : " As far as possible to counteract the wild and destructive system of pretended liberty and equality and seek to destroy it by every available means." He defended the system of Russian peasant servitude as being the best for the people and only asked the landlords to be humane masters and to be kind to their serfs. He himself set a fine example of humanitarianism and was ready to suffer persecution for his Masonic convictions. Catherine II mistrusting the secrecies of the Order, decided to make an end of Russian Masonry. On the whole she was mistaken in her suspicions, for the nobility, which made up the membership of the Lodges, was true to its class instincts and in time of crisis turned from French Revolutionary philosophy to the otherworldly mysticism of the " Rose and the Cross."

Another humanitarian Mason was *Nikolai Novikov*, a close collaborator of Lopukhin in the " Rose and the Cross." He was active as journalist, publisher of popular literature and organizer of schools and philanthropic agencies for the poor. His religious mysticism separated him from French atheistic enlightenment and like other leaders of Russian Masonry he remained loyal to his class and to the autocratic regime. But this did not save him from imprisonment when Catherine commenced her drive against the Masonry.

While on the whole the Russian Masonic movement was politically reactionary, there were individual Masons and a few Lodges which followed the French tradition, similar to the Lodge of the " Nine Sisters," founded in Paris by the atheist, Laland, and joined by such free and revolutionary minds as Franklin, Helvetius, Diderot, Voltaire, D'Alembert, Condorcet, and a number of others who became active republicans during the French Revolution. There was also the influence of the German progressive Masonic lodges of the " Illuminates," founded by the former Jesuit professor, *Adam Weisshaupt* of Anglestat, Bavaria, and the restless Baron *Adolf von Kniggen*, a close and enthusiastic associate of Weisshaupt. These lodges were promoting French enlightenment in Germany; their activities became known in Russia and their influence was felt by some of the more progressive and freer minds among the Masons.

A. N. RADISCHEV, FIRST MARTYR OF REVOLUTIONARY THOUGHT

An outstanding personality and revolutionary thinker in Russia at this period was *Alexander Nikolaevitch Radischev* (1749–1802), whose political and philosophic martyrdom and tragic end by suicide left a lasting impression upon the progressive intellectuals of later generations.

Of noble origin, Radischev was trained in Catherine's school of pages in St. Petersburg. At the age of seventeen he was honoured for his abilities and diligence and was sent, together with a dozen other worthy Russian young noblemen, to the University of Leipzig, which at that time had the reputation of being one of Germany's first institutions of learning, established by the brilliancy of the philosopher Leibnitz. French enlightenment was equally felt in Leipzig University circles and the young Russians had the opportunity of learning something of German profundity and French brilliancy.

At that time Catherine II was in the full flow of her liberal enthusiasms as patron of the French Encyclopedist philosophers. Young Radischev had enthusiastic faith in her serious intention of reconstituting Russia upon modern principles and making the Empire a constitutionally governed state. He studied Montesquieu and Mabli, whose *Thoughts on Greek History and on the Causes of the Welfare and Misfortunes of the Greeks* he translated. The study of this work helped him to the conclusion that autocracy is a most unfavourable state of human nature. He also studied Rousseau, who shaped his political theories, whilst from Helvetius he acquired ideas of naturalist ethics independent of supernatural revelation. His religious ideas passed through many vicissitudes. He wavered between Voltairian Deism and Orthodox mysticism according to the changing fortunes of his own life. He never became a real philosophic atheist; philosophic atheists, at the time, were rare even in France.

On his return to Russia in 1771, Radischev was gradually disillusioned as to the sincerity of his Empress with regard to reconstituting Russia upon modern lines. He realized that in Catherine the patron of philosophy differed radically from the ruler of the people. This blighted hope concerning the future of his country is reflected in his work. The events of the American Revolution inspired him to write an ode to " Freedom," considered the most revolutionary poetic pronouncement of the 18th century, not only of Russia but of all Western civilization. In this ode he attacks religion equally with autocratic government as an implement of oppression:

> " It was, and is, and ever will be
> The source of cruel shameless servitude."

The culmination of Radischev's revolt was his famous anonymously published book, *A Journey from Petersburg to Moscow*, appearing in the summer of 1790 when Catherine's reaction to the revolutionary developments in France was at its height. This book has been characterized as the Encyclopedia of the feelings and opinions of advanced Russian thought at the close of the 18th century. It describes the fearful backwardness, poverty and depression existent in Russia, unreservedly condemning feudal serfdom and the autocracy of the Russian throne. It advocates, though still in cautious terms, a democratic, republican social order. Its effect was tremendous; the friends of Russian freedom rallied to it as to a " declaration of independence," and it aroused the bitter wrath of all reactionaries, most of all of Catherine II. She personally undertook the prosecution of the author, ordering his immediate arrest. Her former contacts with French progressive thought made it easy for her to discover the real purpose of the book. Already after its first perusal, she wrote:

" The purpose of this book is seen upon every page; its author is filled and infected with the French error; he seeks and detects everything to minimize respect for the State and authorities, to rouse the people to indignation against chiefs and principalities." This was the first point of the indictment; the next was a charge of heresy:

" The author is an absolute Deist and (the corresponding pages of the book) are incompatible with the Orthodox Eastern teaching."

Catherine justly suspected Radischev of sympathy with the French Revolution and of advocating a similar revolt in Russia. She turned him over to the courts on the above indicated charges and the court, after a long and trying solitary confinement, pronounced the death sentence over him. This cruel decision broke the nerve of the bold thinker and in pleading mercy before the Empress he recanted his political and religious heresies. Seeing his spirit broken, Catherine "graciously" commuted the death sentence to ten years of Siberian exile in the Ilimen Prison. After her death in 1797, Radischev's lot was somewhat eased; he was permitted to return to his family estate but not allowed to live at the capital. But with the temporary wave of liberalism, which marked the ascent of the new Emperor, Alexander I, Radischev regained his civil rights and took an active part in designing a project for the reconstitution of the Russian state, which reforms it was hoped Alexander I would grant. Among other reforms Radischev proposed complete liberty of conscience, religious toleration and the separation of the Church from the State.

These noble hopes of a better day for Russia were too premature. The reactionary elements, who observed the revival of enthusiasm in Radischev, intimidated him, threatening to renew his Siberian exile. This was too much for his strained nerves and in 1802 he ended his unfortunate life by suicide. "Posterity will avenge me," were his last written words. Radischev, like many who came after him, fell victim to the despotism of his time, which could not bear the force of ideas and could resist it only by brute violence. Yet Radischev did not suffer in vain. His martyrdom inspired others to continue the struggle, nor was he the only revolutionist of his day. It is known that Russians even of the high nobility, like the two brothers Galitzen, who were living in Paris at the time when the French Revolution broke out, enthusiastically participated in the Storming of the Bastille. Another young Russian count, T. A. Stroganov, went so far as to reject his title and to join the Republican Jacobine Club of the "Friends of the Law." It is also known that P. P. Dubrovsky, secretary of the Russian Embassy in Paris, tried to organize a printing shop on the premises of the Embassy for the purpose of producing a Russian translation of the *Declaration of the Rights of Man and the Citizen*. All these facts frightened the Russian autocrats who, blessed and aided by the Church, suppressed the revolting spirits. Under the short reign of Emperor Paul I, who succeeded his much-hated mother, Catherine II, frantic efforts were made to erase every trace of liberal thought. Paul went so far as to prohibit printing such words as " society " and " citizen " because these, he explained, were republican expressions which should have no place in the Russian language.

Under such conditions, revolting minds in Russia, still impotent to attack enthroned autocracy on earth, turned against the autocracy of heaven by whose authority the terrestial despots pretended to rule. Later the same process was observed in Germany. Karl Marx expressed it in his famous words : " The critique of heaven was thus transformed into a critique of the earth, the critique of religion into a critique of law, the critique of theology into the critique of politics." [1]

In spite of the brute despotism of Emperor Paul I, there were some courageous men who continued to attack heavenly autocracies under the guise of literature. One of these was the young poet, *I. T. Pnin* (1773–1805). He continued the Radischev tradition with his friend, A. F. Bestuzhev, whose sons became leaders in the Decembrist Movement. In 1798 Pnin and Bestuzhev began to edit and publish the *St. Petersburg Journal*. In spite of rigid censorship, the editors managed to carry on articles on " nature," " education," and the like, whose gospel was to preach the nobility of mankind. Pnin is the author of the ode to " Man," a poem of revolt against the " Autocrat of Heaven," and against the idea of man as the " human worm." Crying out against this unworthy self-effacement, we read in Pnin's ode :

> " Away vile thought ! Thou art kin
> To wretched souls of slaves
> Whose darkened minds were never lit
> By thoughts with noble strains."

K. Marx and F. Engels Works, Vol. I, p. 366 (Russ. Ed.).

Man is the product of nature, this Pnin knows, but he is also its master, for by the power of his mind he can make order of its chaos. Pnin stakes his faith in man's intellect, his sense of justice, his solidarity, and he looks forward to the time when justice will :

> Unite all people
> Children of one nature.

In harmony with the idealism of his time he believes in abstract " justice," to which he dedicates the ode from which the above two lines were quoted. The ode bears the epigraph from the French arch-heretic Holbach : " Justice is the foundation of all social virtues." Pnin claims the right to think his own thought and he tries to impress this upon his censors in a fable about the " Riding Horse " whose master, fearing the horse's shyness, blindfolds it and as a result both fall into a pit filled with water. The moral of the fable is given in the closing verses :

> Oh, rulers of beast or men !
> Note from this experiment
> The folly of pretence
> Of shutting out the light
> Needed by the sight ;
> Like beast so man,
> When deprived of vision,
> Is difficult of supervision.

This might have been taken as a warning by the ecclesiastical and temporal rulers of the Russian people, but no regime, it is said, yields its power unless forced to do so by threat of revolution. Of this, Russia is a classic example. Like the foolish equestrian in the fable, Church and Throne tried to blindfold its people. This fomented revolt. The seed of the French enlightenment fell upon a fertile soil in Russia. In this chapter it has been shown how, under these conditions, there developed a small but resolute intellectual class, which

THE BEGINNINGS OF THE ANTI-RELIGIOUS TRADITION

took a critical attitude first toward ecclesiastical authority and dogma, developing an anti-religious tradition, and later towards the temporal powers. We shall now follow the vicissitudes of this tradition in the unfolding drama of the Russian revolutionary movement.

CHAPTER VI
RELIGION AND THE REVOLUTIONARY MOVEMENT

THE 19th century will go down in history as the age of bourgeois revolutions and the triumph of Capitalism. The modern French Revolutionary ideas which Catherine for a while permitted to flourish at her court could never be again eradicated in Russia. The ripples of free thought, first observed in the narrow circles of the court, began to widen and deepen, penetrating into ever increasing sections of the population and finally rising in the mighty wave of the Proletarian Revolution which finally swept away the throne and broke the power of the Church in Russia. We shall now sketch this process in relation to the institution of organized religion.

THE DECEMBRIST MOVEMENT

The first stage of the revolutionary movement of the 19th century in Russia is associated with the so-called Decembrist uprising in 1825 on the occasion of the ascent of Nicholas I to the throne. Its purpose was to overthrow autocracy and compel the Tsar to grant Russia a liberal constitution. The leaders of this movement were military men from the upper ranks of the nobility; true liberals following the tradition of English and French free thought. Some of them had participated in the campaigns against Napoleon and had had opportunity of seeing for themselves what Western Europe was like. The defeat of Napoleon and the " Holy Alliance " of the monarchs of Russia, Prussia and Austria, vowing to preserve the institutions of autocracy and orthodoxy, signalized the beginning of dark reaction against liberalism in every form. It was particularly felt in Russia, where the old traditions of feudalism and serfdom were still intact. The development of capitalist forms of production were for these reasons retarded in Russia, although the time for them was ripening. The Decembrist uprising signalized the general discontent which was felt by various classes in Russia.

The Voltairian tradition of the 18th century was naturally unable to flourish in an atmosphere created by the " Holy Alliance." The history of Russian higher education at this period records many heresy trials and the dismissal of many professors for failing to teach their science in the " spirit of the word of God." Geology was barred as incompatible with the teachings of the Bible and strict censorship was exercised over the instruction of philosophy, so that none of the ideas of the French enlightenment might reach the students.

In this atmosphere of reaction and terrorism against independent thinking the young Russian intellectual class was curtailed in its development. This resulted in producing most grotesque forms of servile submission on the part of the weaklings and a most radical protest on the part of the stouter spirits against the religious and temporal authorities. This period has produced some martyrs. Russian revolutionists to this day honour the name of *S. M. Semenov*, a priest's son who became an atheist under the repressive influences of his training at a theological seminary. At the Moscow University this young man became a leader amongst the students and a tireless propagator of modern republican ideas. He also found his way into one of the Decembrists' secret societies, and after the debacle of the insurrection was exiled to Siberia.

At that time a large proportion of the students in all higher schools of learning, in spite of repressive measures, sympathized with the radicals and eagerly read the prohibited books, especially the works of the French Encyclopedist philosophers. Even such aristocratic schools as the Tsar's School of the Pages, to which were admitted only the sons of the upper nobility, did not escape the infection of free thought. It is known that a number of students from the School of Pages participated in the Decembrist Insurrection and that there were secret fraternities studying radical thought in practically every higher institution of learning. As in the pre-revolutionary periods in France, emancipation from traditional ideas began with a revolt against religious authority, later embracing radical political and social doctrines.

The leaders of the Decembrists, the Colonels N. M. Muroviev and P. I. Pestel, had quite definite ideas about the place of the Church in the future political order. They hoped to accomplish their revolution by means of an insurrection in the army which they were gradually preparing. Neither of the leaders favoured the separation of the Church from the State, nor did they want to deprive the Greek Orthodox Church of its favoured position as the religion of the State. Personally, Muroviev was a Deist free thinker, yet like Voltaire he thought that religion was necessary for the masses and should be put into the service of the State as an institution of moral control. Pestel was a Protestant of the Lutheran Confession, " with the heart of a materialist and a mind which refused to follow it," as he characterized himself. Nevertheless he favoured the Greek Church as the more suited to the character of the Russian people.

The Decembrist projected constitution for the new State had this provision in respect of religion : " The people's Vecha (Parliament) has no power to decree nor to prohibit any creed or sect. The beliefs, conscience and opinions of the citizens, as long as these do not result in unlawful action, are not within the jurisdiction of the people's Vecha. But sects based on vice and unnatural deeds are prosecuted on the basis of the Common Law." The project further guaranteed the hegemony of the Greek Orthodox Church and permitted no non-religious status ; that is, every citizen was to be compelled to register with some Church or sect. Thus we see that the leading Decembrists were quite conservative in their views on religion.

We have already observed that the majority of Decembrists were military men from the upper aristocracy. They were no democrats and had no trust in the creative abilities of the common man. They were rather paternal and believed that a State must do for the people what they really should and could do for themselves. Hence their propaganda was limited to a very narrow circle of the upper classes. It centred upon two societies; one in the north, and one in the south. These societies were known as the " Union of Benevolence," in addition to which were a number of Masonic lodges of the order of the " Illuminators," and others which had contact with the conspirators. Alexander I was himself a Mason, and during his reign the Masonic lodges, prohibited by Catherine, were revived and many others founded. Some of these proved convenient places for plotting the revolutionary coup against the autocratic regime, and most of the important Decembrists were members.

While the initiative in this first organized revolutionary movement was taken by the upper class of the nobility we observe, even at this time, a tendency towards the promotion of a wider, democratic, revolutionary movement. Such was the secret society of the " United Slavs " which had distinctly democratic aims. It was founded in the south by men who came from the lower ranks of Russian society, and its constitution demanded no discrimination against the lower classes. The leaders were convinced that their revolutionary purpose could only be achieved if people of all ranks and classes participated. The founder and leader of the " United Slavs " was *Peter Borisov*, a young officer with no relation to the nobility. He was a remarkable character, possessed of courage, a strong mind, kind heart and devotion to the cause of the common people. He imbibed the French enlightenment from the works of Voltaire, Helvetius and Holbach, learning French for this purpose without the aid of a teacher, being too poor to engage one. His contemporaries characterized him as " a man who, unknown to himself, was possessed of the true spirit of Christianity."

The idea of the " United Slavs " came to him through his friendship with the Polish revolutionist, *Julian Lublinsky*, who shared Borisov's plan that Russians and Poles should make a common cause in the overthrow of autocracy. These men put their trust in the common people and showed their willingness to fight with arms to gain their liberty. " It is unreasonable," says Borisov, " to expect that a man born for the throne and possessed of the lust of power should voluntarily reject what he considers to be his right." This Borisov was one of the few Decembrists who took his religious doubts seriously and who sought " to be virtuous while denying God," as he himself put the problem. Therefore he and his brother Andrew, in recruiting members of the " United Slav Society," demanded almost a puritanic attitude to life, a trait which became quite common among later revolutionists of lower rank in Russia.

The Decembrists from the upper classes, with few exceptions, generally followed the tradition of their social group, with its moral laxity and superficial attitude towards religion, considering it an institution still necessary for the mob but no longer binding to upper society. They did not mind using the religious convictions of the people for their revolutionary purpose and clothing their propaganda in religious phraseology and Bible texts. The use of the catechetical form of agitation was considered a good approach to the masses and Muraviev, the leader of the northern society, wrote the *Catechism of a Free Man*, in which were questions and answers in religious terminology with a liberal supply of proof texts. For example, the question : whence originates freedom ? Answer : Every good thing is from God ; having created man in his image and provided eternal rewards for good deeds, and eternal damnation for evil works, he endowed man with freedom ; otherwise it would be unjust to reward for the good done under compulsion or punish for involuntary evil. Stating further that not all people are free at present, since a minority exploits the majority, the catechism explains that : " Some have grasped the unjust idea of lording over others, and some have been willing to accept this mean idea and so resign the natural rights of man granted him by God." Then follows the question : Has not God himself established autocracy ?

Which is answered: God in his goodness never created evil. To the next question: Does it not say, " for there is no power but of God; the powers that be are ordained of God "—the answer is given: No evil power can be from God; " Even so every good tree bringeth forth good fruit. . . . Every tree that bringeth not forth good fruit is hewn down and cast into the fire. The same fate shall betake the clergy, who are as wolves in sheep's clothing, and of these the Lord shall say, ' Depart from me, for I have never known ye.' "

We see here how the Bible was used for undermining the faith of the common people in the authority of the Tsar and his clergy. The younger brother of the author of the *Catechism for a Free Man, Sergious Muraviev,* nicknamed the " Apostle," was very active in preparing the insurrection in some southern regiment. He wrote a similar tract which he called " The Orthodox Catechism." This " Apostle " was a unique personality who took his catechism seriously and gave his revolutionary propaganda a glowing prophetic interpretation.

After the collapse of the movement, when the chief instigators were executed and the rest exiled to Siberia, the hardships and loneliness of the exile made most of the men who formerly were indifferent or even opposed to religion turn back and seek its comforts. Thus this first stage of the revolutionary movement must be recorded as one which still preserved contact with religion and considered the Church a necessary institution of organized society.

THE NARODNIK MOVEMENT

The lesson of the Decembrist Movement was that no successful social revolution can be made from the top by any small group if there is no conscious support and vital co-operation on the part of the masses. These masses in Russia were the peasants, a good half of whom were still held in serfdom, tied down to the soil and owned by the nobility. The petty bourgeoisie of artisans and traders was relatively small in numbers, unintelligent and unorganized. The heavy industries and manufacture were but in their infancy. The first railway connecting Moscow and Petersburg was just being built and the long regime of Nicholas I was the most despotic and reactionary of 19th century Russia.

Under these conditions no organized revolutionary activity was possible. The dynamic forces of society were driven to a cloistered existence and there they were thinking over their problems, turning to philosophy for aid.

At this period, the second quarter of the 19th century, there developed two currents of thought stimulating the minds of intelligent Russians : one, the German idealist philosophy of Fichte, Schelling, and Hegel, the other, the French Utopian Socialism of Saint Simon and Fourier. These two currents of thought were revaluated and synthesised by Russians to satisfy their national consciousness and needs, and the product became generally known as the Narodnik or Populist social philosophy. There were two distinct trends in the movement, one orientating toward the west, and seeking to reform Russia along West-European lines by means of industrialization, education and the abolition or limitation of autocracy. These thinkers were known as the Westernists. The other trend, also pursuing the study of German idealist philosophy and French Utopian Socialism, did not believe that Russia must necessarily follow Western Europe, but that it could develop indigenously by improving its traditional national institutions of autocracy, religious orthodoxy and the peasant land commune which, it was thought, could be made the basis of a socialized economic order. This latter trend of thought was known as *Slavophilism*. From its ranks came a line of religious thinkers and philosophers who made strenuous efforts to revive the orthodox religious heritage and elevate the dignity of the Church. The outstanding leader of this school of thought was the poet-philosopher, A. S. Khomyakov.

The ideology of the Westernists, on the contrary, was in opposition to orthodoxy and autocracy and continued the anti-religious tradition under French influence. The outstanding thinkers in the camp of the Westernists of this period were V. Belinsky, A. Herzen, M. Bakunin, and M. Petroshevsky. All began as orthodox Hegelians and gradually moved leftwards, simultaneously becoming more and more hostile to the Church, as we shall see from the subsequent analysis of the views of these exceptional men.

V. G. Belinsky (1810–1848) is considered the Father of the revolutionary Narodnik philosophy. He came of a family of village priests and has no connection with the nobility. Expelled from the university for radical thought, he fought his way to leadership of Russia's newly-developing militant intellectual class, whose beloved idol he became. Unsurpassed as literary critic and publicist, a master of the Russian language, he is still read by Russian youth. Suspected and feared by the Tsar's secret police, he escaped imprisonment and exile to Siberia—the lot of Russia's intellectual leaders—only by his early death, at the age of 38. Belinsky is so typically a 19th-century Russian intellectual that we must make a closer analysis of the vicissitudes of his mind. Circumstances compelled these men to limit themselves to thinking, for it was quite impossible under the oppressive conditions of the time to do more than that.

Belinsky began to think independently very early. According to his own confession, made in a letter to his friend Bakunin, a still greater rebel than himself, he writes : " I suffer from a horrid education. I reasoned at the time when one is only supposed to feel ; I was an atheist and a blasphemer, not having been as yet religious ; I composed before I was able to write between the lines of a copybook ; I dreamed and fancied when others were learning their vocabularies." This is quite characteristic not only of Belinsky but of the whole impatient Russian intellectual youth of that period, who " like fools rushed in where angels feared to tread." In his youth we find Belinsky passionately embracing every new Western idea which penetrated the fissures of the intellectual *cordon sanitaire* established by the Tsar's censorship.

When expelled from the university in 1832, Belinsky continued his contact with modern thought in the circle of the noble Russian humanist, *S. Stankevitch*, a rare personality who enthused eager Russian youth to independent thinking and directed their minds and wills towards social ideals. The circle of Stankevitch may properly be considered the cradle of the Narodnik Movement, which popularized the philosophy later carried as revolutionary doctrine amongst the masses.

Belinsky in rapid succession embraced the idealistic and pantheistic philosophies of Schelling, Fichte, and Hegel. With exceptional literary skill and lucidity he popularized and reinterpreted their teachings for Russian readers. At this stage he expressed his philosophy of life in the following glowing terms :

" All of God's infinitely beautiful world is but the breath of the one eternal idea manifested in innumerable forms as a magnificent phenomenon of absolute unity and endless multiplicity. The flaming emotions of mortals in moments of enlightenment can only grasp the immensity of the body of this soul of the universe, the heart of which are the great suns, its sinews the milky way, its blood the pure ether. This idea knows no rest ; it lives forever ; it creates continually in order to destroy and destroys in order to create. It incarnates itself in the glowing sun, in a beautiful planet, in an wandering comet ; it lives and breathes in the ebb and flow of the tides of the sea, in the fierce hurricane of the desert, in the whisper of the leaves, in the murmur of the brook, in the roar of the lion, in the tears of an infant, in the smile of beauty, in the will of man and the mighty creations of genius. . . . Thus lives the idea. We see it with our own faint eyes. . . . Here is its wisdom, its physical light, but where is its love ? God created man, endowed him with reason and feelings to grasp this idea with his mind and knowledge, to embrace it with warm, vital sympathy, to share its life in the emotions of infinite creative love ! "

Then Belinsky appeals to proud and powerful man not to exalt himself :

" Deny yourself, suppress your egotism, scorn your selfish ' I ' ; breathe for the happiness of others, sacrifice for the good of your neighbour, your country and the happiness of mankind ; love truth and goodness not for the sake of reward, but for the sake of truth and beneficence ; suffer under the heavy cross to accomplish your unity with God, your immortality which lies in the destruction of your ' I,' in the emotions of infinite bliss. . . . Such is the moral life of the eternal idea."

Here we have the thoughts and aspirations of Belinsky, the idealist. For a decade he preached this gospel of submission and long-suffering : " Seek God not in temples made by man, but seek him in your own heart, seek him in your own love." Such were the admonitions to his readers. Christianity, which he considered formerly to be contemplation and faith, should now become a conscious truth, a philosophy. Belinsky disliked the French political enlightenment. He says : " To the devil the French ; their influence has never brought us anything but evil." And then he appeals to Russian youth, saying : " Let us be apostles of light, this is our calling ; let us imitate the disciples of Christ, who did not hatch conspiracies and did not form either secret or open political societies to spread the teachings of their divine master."

Now let us look at this " Apostle of light " a decade later. He still is the same tireless agitator of dynamic ideals, still carrying upon his heart the welfare of his people and of mankind generally, for Belinsky, like a true Russian, was never narrowly nationalistic. During a decade his ideas have passed through a dialectic process of negating absolutely that which he once so enthusiastically affirmed. The idealist had become a materialist, the fervent believer in God has become an open atheist. Now we hear him saying : " In me developed some vile, furious, fanatic love of freedom and independence of human personality which can exist only in a society based upon truth and valour. . . . I now understand the bloody love of Marat for freedom, his sanguine hate for everything which wanted to separate itself from brotherhood with mankind. . . . I am more and more a citizen of the universe ! I begin to love mankind in Marat's way ; to make happy the smallest part of it, I, it seems, could destroy with fire and sword the rest of it."

Belinsky is now an uncompromising revolutionist. "The millenium upon earth is not established by the sweet, enthusiastic phrases of the idealistic and noble Gironde (i.e. the moderate French revolutionist), but by the terrorists, by the two-edged sword of word and deed, of Robespierre and Saint Juste." In 1841 he calls himself a socialist. "The idea of socialism," he writes, "became for me the idea of ideas, the being of beings, the problem of problems, the alpha and omega of faith and knowledge." This socialism of his is still very sentimental and Utopian. It means to him a social order where there be no rich and no poor, no kings and no subjects, but where all shall be brothers. In his apocalyptic ecstasy he calls it the time when "Christ will resign his power to the Father, and the Father, Reason, will again reign but in a new heaven and over a new earth." Having declared himself for socialism he restlessly searches for the ways and means of its realization, and here he approaches the reasoning of Marx in the solution of the problem. He begins to understand the class nature of society and to see that the "new heaven and new earth" lie beyond the economic and social stage of capitalism, the stage which his country was only approaching. "I know," he says, "that Industry is the source of great evil, but I also know that it is the source of great good to society. It is the last of evils in the reign of capital, in its tyranny over labour."

In embracing socialism, Belinsky begins also to revaluate his cherished religious idea. Here, too, he dialectically negates that which he formerly affirmed. "For me," he writes at this period, "there is no way out to the *Jenseits*, into mysticism, into all that which is the escape of poorly-endowed natures and semi-depraved souls." He gave up the faith of his youth which once sustained his turbulent soul, but we see him return again and again to this old source of comfort. The question of immortality particularly disturbed his restless mind. Somehow he revolts against the idea of annihilation of personality which he lauded as the superb product of nature. The study of Feuerbach's *Wesen des Christentums* corroborated his growing belief in the anthropomorphic nature of religion.

Simultaneously he studied Comte's positive philosophy which deepened his materialist convictions in spite of Comte's *Neo-Christianity*. He says : " It is necessary to free science from the phantoms of transcendentalism and theology, to show the limitations of reason, in which its activity is fertile, to sever it forever from everything fantastic and mystical ; such will be the new philosophy, but this Comte will not do." In this he looked forward to dialectical materialism which at that time just received its first formulation by the genius of Marx and Engels.

Belinsky's dialectic negation of religion has been vividly expressed in his famous controversial letter to Gogol, in which he censures the great writer for his renegade attitude towards religion. Gogol, the bitter critic of Russian feudal society, turned at this time back to that religion, the escape from which Belinsky was just celebrating. His letter, written in 1847, is his last word and testament on the question of the Church and religion. It contains not a few prophetic statements as we shall presently see. Gogol at the eve of his life came to the conclusion that Russia's salvation lay in mystic pietism and in fidelity to the Greek Orthodox Church. Gogol, like Tolstoy and Dostoevsky later, believed the Russian people to be profoundly religious, to whom a rationalist civilisation would prove a dagger to the soul, and this reactionary opinion made Belinsky rage, turning upon Gogol all his revolutionary wrath :

" In your opinion, the Russian people are the most religious in the world. This is a lie ! The basis of religiousness is pietism, reverence, fear of God. But the Russian pronounces the name of God while scratching his . . . Look closer and you will see that it is by *nature a profoundly atheist people*. It is still possessed of many superstitions, but there is no trace of religiousness. Superstitions pass away with the achievements of civilization, but religiousness frequently accommodates itself thereto : France is a good example. Here are still many good Catholics among enlightened and educated people, and many who have severed from Christianity still believe in some kind of God. The Russian is not so. Mystic exaltation is not a part of his nature ; for this he possesses too much common sense, clearness and definiteness of mind, and in this is perhaps the immensity of his future historic destiny. . . . Religiousness appears among us only in the Nonconformist sects which are so different in spirit from the mass of the people and so insignificant in number."

These words give food for thought. Perhaps the present mass movement towards atheism among the Russian people is the fulfilment of Belinsky's prophecy. In any case, his own personality, with its extreme change from mystic religion to revolting atheism, is quite symbolic of the intellectualist movement which he inaugurated. We must now introduce some of his brilliant contemporaries and pupils who will even more corroborate our hypothesis that it was the abnormal conditions of Russia's development, with its overhanging heritage of sterile orthodoxy, despotic autocracy and feudal servitude, which produced such rebellious reactions as were witnessed in Belinsky and in his generation of intellectuals.

A. I. Herzen (1812–1870) belongs to this constellation of brilliant revolutionary thinkers and teachers of the Russian people. As son of a rich and easy-going Russian nobleman he received a liberal education. A French Jacobin immigrant was one of his tutors and from him he first learned the meaning of the French Revolution. He began early to read the French philosophers of enlightenment. His father apparently sympathized with free thought for he advised his son not to take religion too seriously. By nature Herzen was profoundly sensitive and serious in all that he did and therefore his break with religion had its dramatic side.

The events of the Decembrist uprising deeply stirred him. He writes : " The stories told about the insurrection, the trial, the horrors in Moscow greatly shocked me. A new world appeared before me which gripped my whole moral being. I don't know how this came about but, understanding little and very vaguely what it all meant, I felt that I am not on the side from which the cartridges were fired and victory proclaimed.

I could not be on the side of prisons and chains. The execution of Pestel and his comrades completely awakened my soul from its childish sleep." How deep these impressions were may be seen from another reference, which he makes thirty years later, to these Decembrist events : " The victory of Nicholas over the Decembrists was celebrated in Moscow, after the executions, by a solemn religious service in the centre of the Kremlin. In the service participated all the Tsar's family, the Senate, the ministers of State and the Guards. Cannons were fired from the Kremlin walls. A boy of fourteen, I was present at this divine service, and there, before the altar stained by the bloody prayers, I swore to revenge those executed men and give myself to fight this throne, this altar, these guns. I did not revenge ; the guards and the throne, the altar and the guns, all are still there, but after thirty years I stand under the same banner, which I have never deserted." Thus we see Herzen become a revolutionist while yet in his early teens. His hatred of the bloody Russian throne and its altars deepened as he grew older. At the age of sixteen we see him, with his equally ardent playmate and life-long comrade in the struggle, Nicholas Ogarev, swear a solemn oath to sacrifice their lives in the struggle for liberty. This solemn act took place on the occasion of a walk through the woods on the Sparrow Mountains, overlooking Moscow, where these noble boys in the sight of the city, symbolizing their country, could not but think of its woes, and swore to sacrifice themselves for its liberty. Such was the youthful Herzen.

Entering the Moscow University he soon became the leader of the revolutionary students. From France at that time began to penetrate the Utopian writings of Saint Simon and these Herzen and his friends embraced as their new gospel and became its ardent advocates.

Saint Simon was the author of the *Outline of the Science of Man* and of *The New Christianity*. In his analysis he came to the conclusion that it is impossible to equalize men who by nature are most differently endowed. Therefore society should be so organized as to give opportunity to all for developing their abilities, an opportunity quite impossible under conditions as they existed in modern civilization. Saint Simon proposed to reform the existing social order by abolishing hereditary political power and wealth, placing the government in the hands of the wise and talented. There should be three chambers: one of inventors, one of examination, and one for executive purposes. In the first two the sovereignty should be held by positivist philosophers, scientists, engineers and artists, to the exclusion of the clergy which it was feared might corrupt the sciences. The land, capital and the implements of production should be owned the State. Reward for toil should be differentiated with a view to stimulating initiative and production. Since people are not equal by nature the tie of solidarity between them must be a socialized religion, which would stimulate service and help to overcome the existing differences. Saint Simon was thoroughly convinced that religion was the only means of inspiring leadership and guaranteeing justice and honesty. In Christianity he believed are those ethical and human values which could awaken the nobler impulses in man and make him socially-minded. This was the message of his *New Christianity*, completed shortly before his death in 1825. His parting words were: " It was thought that religion must disappear because Catholicism had become enfeebled. This is a mistake: Religion cannot disappear out of the world, it will only be transformed. . . . Do not forget this . . . and remember that to do great things one must be inspired."

Saint Simon's appeal suited the temper of Herzen and his group. It removed many obstacles in the appreciation of religion, for which Herzen had constant longings, and it gave him a goal for which to struggle. Characterizing this new outlook opened to him by Saint Simon, Herzen wrote: " On the one hand it meant the liberation of woman, her enlistment into the common task, placing her faith in her own hands, uniting with her as with an equal. On the other it meant the justification of the flesh. Magnificient words embracing a whole world of new relations between people, a world of health, of spirituality, of beauty, a naturally moral world and therefore morally pure." Many mocked over the liberation of women, over the recognition of the rights of the flesh, attaching to these words a filthy and low meaning. This was due to the monastically depraved imagination, the fear of the flesh and the fear of women. " Good people understand," said Herzen, " that the purifying baptism of the flesh is a retreat of Christianity ; the religion of life came to replace the religion of death, the religion of beauty came to replace the religion of flagellation, of emaciation from fasting and prayer. The crucified flesh was resurrected and no longer ashamed of itself ; man attained a harmonious unity, he guessed that he was a unified being and not a mechanical composition, like a pendulum made of two different metals each resisting one another ; the enemy thus clinging to him disappeared."

Herzen became an enthusiastic neo-Christian socialist and republican, preaching against all violence and degradation. As a result, shortly after his graduation from the University, he was arrested and exiled to the town of Vyatka in a remote north-eastern province. The religious experience, which the contact with Saint Simon had given him, now deepened under the influence of isolation and loneliness. He gained the friendship of an exiled Evangelical mystic, the famous architect, A. L. Whitberg, designer of the original Cathedral of Christ the Saviour in Moscow. Influenced by this exceptional man, Herzen experienced his " second birth " into the life of the spirit. At this stage we find him reading the gospels, the works of Swedenborg and other mystical writers. His love for the gospels never left him, even when, devoting himself to revolutionary propaganda, he parted company with mystic religion. The religious experiences of this period are reflected in two unfinished dramatic plays written by Herzen in blank verse ; their subject is the conflict of two worlds. The first play shows decaying Rome in conflict with the regenerating power of Apostolic Christianity. Licinius, a rich young Patrician, realizes the decadence of his people and of the Roman nation ; he abhors his class with its conflicts and slave-exploitation ; he dies but is brought to life by the regenerating power of the Christian gospel. The other drama handles the same theme, but in the period of the industrial revolution in England ; it is called " William Penn " and tells the story of the regenerating power of the Quaker gospel in conflict with decaying feudalism. There is much of useful autobiographic value in these works of Herzen. He felt himself, like his heroes Licinius and William Penn, a preacher of the new regenerating gospel of Socialism. Herzen prophesied that it would be Russia that would realize his vision of Socialism, should Western Europe fail to do so. Driven into foreign exile by the persecutions of the Tsar, Herzen continued to preach his socialist gospel from abroad through two papers, *The Northern Star* and the *Bell*, which he published in London and which were smuggled into Russia in large numbers. Through these media Herzen hoped to cast the light of the social gospel into the darkness of his country and awaken his slumbering countrymen.

Under the influence of Feuerbach's famous *Wesen des Christentums*, the works of the German materialists, Moleschet and Buechner, the Comtian positivist philosophy and the Darwinian evolutionary doctrines, he rapidly outgrew his early pietistic mysticism. He became a severe critic of the Church and a confessed atheist, in this respect following Belinsky and other contemporary Russian revolutionists. Disappointed with the revolutions in the west and the inconsistency of bourgeois revolutionaries, who supported with one hand what they broke with the other—" because," says Herzen, " they are sorry for this feeble world, bewail and weep over it while the world of the future slips through their fingers, fearing the logical consequences, while others cannot understand it. Almost all of them still stand on that shore where are the palaces, the churches, the courts." Herzen hated these institutions and sent out the cry to Russian intellectuals : " To the people ! To the people ! "

The Church, at this time in servile obedience to the Tsarist regime, sought every possible means of diverting the attention of the masses from the revolutionary propaganda that aimed at their emancipation. Herzen attacked their treasonous behaviour to the people : " We cannot be silent witnesses," he writes, " seeing the dumb, down-trodden clergy sprinkle holy water over the institution of chattel slavery, over the militarized settlements and over every kind of execution, blessing for two and a half centuries compulsory marriage and burying, without protest, serfs who have been whipped to death by their masters." To maintain the superstition of the ignorant the Church announced new discoveries of miraculous " uncorrupted saints." Herzen, outraged by the fraud, asked why this idolatry and hypocrisy, since none believed in the miraculous powers of the newly-made saints, neither the Tsar, nor his ministers, neither the clergy nor the monks. Thus not for these was all this staged ; for whom, then, asked Herzen, and answered :

" The peasant with his childlike soul will believe in miracles. The poor, robbed by the nobility, cheated by the officials, deceived by the emancipation act, exhausted from endless labour, from inescapable poverty, the peasant will believe. He is too crushed, too unhappy not to be superstitious. Not knowing where to lay his head at heavy moments when human needs ask for rest and for hope ; surrounded by a pack of ferocious enemies, he will come to drop a hot tear to the dumb sarcophagous, to the dumb body of the saint, and by this relic, by this sarcophagous, he will be deceived, he will be comforted so as not to fall into other comforts. And you, the spoilers, who have robbed the unfortunate of his very shirt, you are not ashamed to use these means ! You want to make him a spiritual beggar, spiritually blind, pushing him into the darkness of superstition. What servants of darkness you are, what enemies of the people ! "

This protest against the Church as an implement of deceit illustrates best of all the position the honest revolutionary was inevitably compelled to take towards organized religion. Had he lived before the age of positive science, he would have become a religious reformer like George Fox and William Penn, whom he once made the heroes of his revolutionary drama. But no banner of revolt had been raised in Europe in the name of religion since the French Revolution. Organized religion was in the exclusive control of the governing classes and in conflict with modern science and therefore could not become the vehicle of the new revolutionary message to the masses.

M. A. Bakunin (1814-1876), a friend of Herzen and Belinsky, was in many respects the most dynamic personality in the gallery of Russian revolutionists at this period. He wrote a great deal on the question of religion in relation to revolution and his views have deeply ingrained themselves in the anti-religious tradition of the Russian revolutionary movement. Bakunin is therefore of exceptional interest for our special purpose.

Born of an old, wealthy, aristocratic family, Bakunin enjoyed a happy youth under the influence of an enlightened father whom he continued to love and honour long after their ways had parted. Bakunin was trained as an officer of artillery and graduated from a military school in Petersburg. Having no liking for the profession he resigned from the army, devoting himself to the study of science and music which, as he says himself, " always awakened in him religious emotions, a faith in life and a desire to live." Early he came under the influence of the same Stankevitch that had inspired Belinsky to his public mission. The remarkable character of this man turned Bakunin's heart to the serious problems of life. " It was impossible," writes Bakunin, " to live near him and not feel oneself in a certain sense better and ennobled. In his presence a low and trivial thought and base instinct seemed impossible. Under his influence the most ordinary people became significant." In the circle of Stankevitch, Bakunin pursued the study of history and of German idealist philosophy, particularly Schelling and later Fichte and Hegel. These awakened in Bakunin the agitator propagandist. He began to spread his newly-acquired philosophy with such skill and ardour and persuasion that soon a group of young people gathered about him who regarded him as their teacher, and even the brilliant Belinsky for a time fell under his spell.

The study of Fichte's *Anweisung zum seligen Leben* gripped Bakunin's sensitive soul. He was now about twenty-two years of age and readily responded to Fichte's appeal to the heroic, to service, sacrifice and love. In a letter to his sister, he writes under date of February, 1836: " I finally reached this goal, I recognized the emptiness of these desires, I became conscious that outside the spiritual world there is no true life, that it cannot have another goal. This path may not be an easy one, but it is worthy of man ! . . . And so for the world I am an insignificant creation, a zero, a teacher of mathematics, but for myself, for my friends who understand me, I became much more significant than before. I killed the petty egotism of self-preservation, I shook off its prejudices, I am a man ! " This religious experience left its lasting impression upon Bakunin's character. His biographer, J. Steklov, though himself an atheist, recognizes this. He says : " One must concede that this religious passion was not without influence upon his further development, although it passed over into its very opposite, becoming a militant atheism. In any case the interest which Bakunin always revealed in questions of religion, even when he made it his aim energetically to combat it, probably had its roots in this period of his Moscow life."

To satisfy his craving for spiritual truth and freedom, Bakunin decided to go to the Berlin University where Hegel and his great contemporaries had taught. This was in 1839, at the time when the despotism of Nicholas I was strangling every free idea in Russia and widespread discontent prevailed among the oppressed peasants and shackled intellectuals. Bakunin's seismographic soul registered all this social unrest and he left his country to find a weapon by which to combat the evils of which he was becoming increasingly conscious.

In Berlin at this time the revolutionary wing of the young Hegelians, of whom Ludwig Feuerbach was the moving spirit, was shaping itself, and Bakunin joined them with great enthusiasm. He surprised his teachers and fellow-students by the daring of his mind and his courage in drawing the most revolutionary consequences out of the philosophic premises of Feuerbach's teaching. Writing of this transition, he says: " I sought God in Man, in his freedom, and now I seek God in revolution. I am blessed, if I shall be able even in part to contribute to the emancipation of the Slavs, the emancipation of my country; blessed am I if I shall be able to die for the freedom of the Poles and the Russians." [1]

Under the influence of the 1848 Revolution, Bakunin developed into a militant anarchist. His theory of society calls for the negation of all authority and on this ground he comes into conflict with the idea of God as the source of all authority. From this premise developes his atheist doctrine: " The Church and the State, these two are my *bêtes noires*." Not that he spared any other institution which was controlled by or served the interests of the State. Thus he denounces the prostitution of science and learning: " Doctrinally learned vice is perhaps more dangerous than anything else. It penetrates, as gradual poison, every thought and emotion, the will, the heart and the mind of man, creating and authorizing, in the name of the false as well as boasting word ' civilization,' a theory of the most outrageous exploitation of the people."

" Religion is collective insanity, so much the more powerful because it is traditional and has penetrated into all the pores of the personal and social life of the people." [2] Bakunin frequently criticizes Voltaire's epigram: " If there were no God, He should be invented," which he inverts: " If there is a God, He should be destroyed." He traces man's progress to his spirit of revolt. This he finds in the meaning of the Biblical myth of the " Fall of Man " in the Garden of Eden. It was his desire to assert himself, to free himself from the damnation of real or imagined Gods or powers of nature, by which revolt man escaped the animal realm and became man. " By an act of disobedience and knowledge, i.e. by revolt and

---

[1] From a letter to the Pole, Iliodor Storchevsky, written about 1848.
[2] This and most of the following quotations are from Bakunin's *God and the State*, 1918, Russian edition.

by thought, he began his independent human history and his human development." If in spite of this man became possessed of the spirit of submission to deity, it was because of the burden of nature and its forces which he felt impotent to control. Then, when class stratification began, Religion was made the implement of control and of enforcing submission to the governing classes. To rid mankind of God it is necessary to free him of the factors which created God. Religion is the product of impotence against nature and against the organized despotic powers of society. "There is but one remedy, the social revolution."

Man has become a slave of God; hence, a slave of the Church and of the State, since the State is sanctified by Religion. "If God exists, then Man is a slave," concludes Bakunin. "But man can and must be free; then God does not exist. There is no escape from this dilemma, hence it is necessary to choose." Bakunin makes his choice and devotes himself to demonstrating in what way religion lowers and degrades the people; how it belittles the mind, which should be a mighty implement of power for their freedom; how it stimulates cowardice, the chief cause of slavery; how it depraves human toil, making it an attribute and a source of slavery; how it kills human pride and dignity by declaring submissiveness and meekness as virtues; finally, how it strangles the feeling of brotherhood by the cruel sacrifice of animals and man.

Bakunin opposes the efforts of idealist philosophy to ennoble God by attributing as divine all that which is worthy in man. To do this, he says, "is to agree without protest that mankind by itself is unable to create this, i.e. left to itself human nature is poor, unjust, low and ugly." For this very reason, religion is incompatible with true morality. Bakunin rejects God and places his trust in nature and man, nature's superb product. This he declares to be materialism and explains himself thus: "We call material everything that exists and takes place in the actual world, within man as well as without him; we call ideal exclusively the mental activity of man; but since the brain is but a purely material organization, its function is equally material as the action of all objects together. It appears therefore that what we call matter or the material world does not exclude, but on the contrary includes, the ideal."

It is interesting to note how Bakunin explains his metamorphosis from extreme idealism to equally extreme materialism and atheism. He reverts to the Hegelian dialectic logic and says: " Since the basis or the starting point of the materialist school is material, its negation must by all means be ideal. Departing from the essence of the real world or from that which in the abstract is called matter, materialism logically arrives at actual idealization, i.e. in respect to man, at a complete and final emancipation of society. Inversely, since the basis and starting point of the idealist school is the ideal, by force of the same cause, this teaching inevitably arrives at social materialism, the establishment of crude despotism and mean, unjust exploitation in the form of the Church and the State . . . in a word, in life you will always find idealists practically realizing the lowest of material aims, whereas the materialist you will find pursuing and realizing the most ideal aims and thoughts." Bakunin concludes: " Everywhere religious and philosophic idealism (in which the latter is but a more or less free interpretation of the former) serves in our day as the banner of material exploitation ; whereas, on the contrary, the banner of theoretic materialism, the red flag of economic equality and social justice is raised by the practical idealism of the exploited masses, dying from hunger but striving to realize the greatest freedom and the human rights of each in the brotherhood of all people on the earth. Who are then the real idealists ? Idealists not in the abstract but in life, not in heaven but on earth ? And who are the materialists ? " Bakunin put the cardinal question to the problem of Religion and Revolution and he has given a clear answer. His arguments against religion and the idealist philosophy have ever since been incorporated in the revolutionary anti-religious tradition and there is little that can be added to his line of thought. Bakunin, the arch-rebel and anarchist revolutionist, may equally be considered the major prophet of Russian militant atheism.

A CONSPIRACY OF IDEAS

The first half of the 19th century in Russia terminated in a widely-spread " conspiracy of ideas." This expression was used by one of the members of the prosecuting committee to which was referred the case of the *Petrashevtsy*, so-called after N. V. Petrashevsky the leader of a group for the propagation of radical ideas.

The revolutionary year 1848, that shook the thrones of the kings and princes of Western Europe, frightened Nicholas I and he undertook a search for the existence of any possible conspiracy in Russia. As a result, in 1849, took place the famous trial of the " Circle of Petrashevsky," charged with the propagation of radical ideas destined to overthrow the existing order in Russia. Sixty-three persons were tried and twenty-one of these were sentenced to death, clemency being granted to them by the Tsar a few moments before execution, when already they had passed through the ordeal of the expectation of death. The condemned men were driven to Siberian exile, among them also the famous novelist, F. Dostoievsky. In this manner Nicholas hoped to break the power of ideas in Russia.

Petrashevsky, like Stankevitch who inspired Belinsky and Bakunin, gathered friends and visitors into his house to discuss social philosophy and religion. The " Circle of Petrashevsky " was exceedingly democratic and in this lies its chief significance. A generation before, when the Decembrists plotted the overthrow of autocracy, they only admitted into their circles men of high rank amongst the nobility. Not so in the circle of Petrashevsky. Of the sixty-three persons arrested there was not one representative of the upper society ; they were teachers, writers, petty officials, students, a few landlords and even shopkeepers, in short a class of people who in the days of the Decembrists were considered quite unfit to occupy themselves with revolutionary ideas. In all it is estimated that the circle of Petrashevsky, through the years of its existence, must have brought some two thousand persons under its influence.

N. V. Petrashevsky (1821-1866), the son of a physician and grandson of a priest, was a graduate of the Faculty of Jurisprudence at the St. Petersburg University. Since 1841 and until his arrest in 1849 he held a position in the Ministry of Foreign Affairs, but his chief interest lay in the study and propagation of advanced ideas. He embraced the teachings of the French Utopian socialists, Saint Simon and Fourier, and his house soon became the centre for propagating these and other radical teachings. Petrashevsky was very eager to educate his countrymen for the revolutionary changes which were imminent and inevitable; he seized upon every opportunity to do so and was able to obviate the rigid censorship which at the time made circulation of printed matter almost impossible. Quite unique in this respect was his " Dictionary of Foreign Words," written by himself and his friends. It contained articles interpreting the various "isms" and also biographical notes concerning philosophers. Thus, in the article on the word *naturalism*, Petrashevsky interprets the naturalist philosophy of Feuerbach; in the article on *Neo-Christianity*, the teachings of Saint Simon; under the words *obscurantism*, *oracle*, etc., he criticizes the superstitions of religion; and under the word *optimism* he advances the materialistic teachings of the 18th century. In this manner, in the disguise of a reference book, radical ideas were spread into ever-widening circles of Russian society. Petrashevsky did not consider his mission to be political; he had no plans for a revolutionary coup like that of the Decembrists. He was above all a propagator of ideas and he believed that when the time became ripe the leaders would appear and set up the new social order.

He was, of course, critical of the Church and the institution of religion generally. This was lamented by F. Dostoievsky who could not so easily rid himself of his religious convictions, though this did not save him from the death sentence and the subsequent Siberian exile. The European revolutionary crisis of 1848 hastened the doom of the Petrashevsky circle. With it came to an end the epoch of the conspiracy of ideas which, as we have shown, persistently and continually existed throughout the second quarter of the 19th century, producing such brilliant and devoted personalities as Belinsky, Herzen, Bakunin, Petrashevsky and many others. In this period the anti-religious tradition firmly established itself and became more and more distinctly atheistic. With the crushing of the Petrashevsky circle Siberian and foreign exile swallowed up another generation of revolutionary thinkers, only to give way to a new, more numerous, more democratic and more widely appreciated group of intellectuals and political leaders. In the last quarter of the century the Narodnik movement split into several definite trends: the bourgeois-liberal, the anarcho-revolutionary and the Marxian movements. All these, while differing on questions of political and social programmes and tactics, were nevertheless unanimous in their opposition to autocracy and orthodoxy, and the anti-religious tradition of the 19th century became permanently established in Russia.

In following the development of the anti-religious tradition in Russia we saw, by example of such representative minds as Belinsky, Herzen and Bakunin, how their revolutionary anti-religious passion was but the antithesis of their former religious passion, and how their immense spiritual energies had been diverted from organized religion into the social channels of an organized revolutionary movement, inspired by a messianic and apocalyptic vision of an approaching cataclysm which was to give birth to a new and better social order. The essentially spiritual nature of the revolutionary movement is also the clue to the understanding of its anti-religious passion and of Communist atheism, as will become more and more evident in the course of this study.

CHAPTER VII

INTELLECTUALIST GOD-WRESTLERS AND SEEKERS AFTER GOD

The generation of Russian intellectuals inspired by the teachings of Herzen and Bakunin amongst others, went " amongst the people," preaching the gospel of liberation from the old traditions, the old religion and the old economic and political yoke. This movement attracted many young people and intellectuals who, leaving their homes and studies went amongst the common people with a gospel of liberation and found on the part of the masses some occasional enthusiasm, some curiosity, but on the whole, apathy, ignorance, gross superstition and, above all, that abject poverty of peasants and workers in spite of their continuous but inefficient toil. These facts cast gloom and disappointment upon the youthful enthusiasts.

What could be done? A mightier force than the verbal message of revolt seemed necessary to remove those mountains which pressed heavily upon the peasants. Those few intellectuals who had been abroad and had witnessed the revolutionary effect of industrialization and urbanization, and those who had studied Marx, favoured the coming of the machine into Russia, with its consequent proletarianisation of the peasants, the new class stratification of the village, and the rapid growth of the city bourgeoisie. Marxism became popular amongst the more sober-minded Russian intellectuals and there was considerable response also amongst industrial workers. Socialism was becoming a mass movement. Those of the intellectuals who did not grasp the logic of Marxism, who for sentimental reasons could not rid themselves of the romantic traditions of the Narodnik movement, became desperate and turned to terrorist action, plotting the assassination of the Tsar, his hated ministers, and his chiefs of police. The remnants of the Narodnik movement organized themselves into groups for political action, such as the " Peoples Liberty Party," which later developed into the large party of Socialist Revolutionaries, which was popular among many intellectuals, certain elements of the petty bourgeoisie and also found response among a limited number of peasants and workers.

Other intellectuals, whose class interests restrained them from joining the revolutionary movement, either settled down to the ordinary routine of life or sought comfort in religion, philosophy and art. This explains the popularity of such semi-religious and philosophic cults as advanced by the Tolstoyan Movement and the development of mystic and spiritual sects. The intellectualist God-Seekers were tragic figures; disappointed in the revolutionary movement, alienated from Church Orthodoxy, full of doubts and yet eager for a faith that might sustain them, they struggled desperately to find some satisfactory solution to the eternal problem of " the meaning and purpose of life." The outstanding figures amongst these God-Seekers were Tolstoy and Dostoievsky. The demand for a new, intellectually satisfactory religion, increased enormously after the debacle of the 1905 Revolution. At this period even a number of distinguished Marxists lost their scientific bearings and revolutionary hopes and sought escape in religion, finally reconciling themselves to the Church. Such renegades from Marxism were Sergius Bulgakov and Nicholas Berdyaev. Other Marxists and active revolutionists, like Lunacharsky and Maxim Gorky, sought to reconcile religion with their revolutionary aims; they became " God-builders," that is, they did not want to return to the old obscure orthodoxy but sought to create a new socialist religion which would preserve the values of religion without the necessity of accepting the dogmas of the Church.

THE CHURCH AND THE INTELLECTUALS

The estrangement from religion, which many of the intellectuals felt, found no sympathetic response on the part of the Church. It had no message for the modern age. This was bewailed by many of the intellectuals. True enough there was the Slavophil religious tradition with its idealization of the Church, which appealed to some of the nationalistically-minded Russians; but its feudal paternalism and its eulogy of autocracy were repulsive to most intellectuals who sought a more liberal regime for Russia. Nevertheless the contribution of the Slavophils to a reinterpretation of the Church must not be overlooked and we must briefly consider it here.

A. S. Khomyakov (1804–1860) was the leading mind of Slavophilism and its chief interpreter. He must not of course be considered a revolutionary nor even a liberal; on the contrary he wished to make revolution impossible in Russia by arousing the national consciousness of the Russian people. A representative of the feudal nobility, he was deeply rooted in his native soil and his relation to the common people was a kind of benevolent paternalism. As a student of German idealist philosophy he was faced with the problem : is Russia a nation and, if so, what is its individuality, what contribution has she to make to human values and national ideas ? The 18th century was a transitional epoch in Russian national life, symbolized in the removal of the capital from Moscow, the removal of the heart of the nation to Petersburg, an artificial city created on the outskirts of the nation and setting itself up in imitation of Western civilization. Only after the defeat of Napoleon did national consciousness awaken in educated Russians. The Slavophils made the first effort to formulate the still vague consciousness by giving it an independent ideology.

Where does Russia belong ; to Europe or to Asia ; or is it an independent cultural union ? This was a much debated question in Russia, and Khomyakov and his friends answered that Russia is the centre of the Slavic world and culture, destined to gather together the Slavic races, uniting them about a common language and religion and common social ideas. Russian thought, they insisted, is essentially religious, and the contribution of the Slavs will be to demonstrate to the world the nature of true Christianity. A. N. Berdyaev, a thorough student and contemporary ideologist, following the Slavophil tradition, thus characterizes this movement:

" Slavophilism brought to conscious ideological expression the eternal truth of the Orthodox East and the historical order of the Russian land, uniting these organically. The Russian land was for the Slavophils the bearer of Christian truth, and the Christian truth was in the Orthodox Church. Slavophilism meant the exposition of Orthodox Christianity as a special type of culture, as a special religious experience, differing from Western Catholicism and therefore creating another life." [1]

The Church was considered a voluntary association of brotherly love and of free common thought; the true society which is not political, not authoritative, and yet a unity. " Here says Berdyaev is a peculiar organic democracy, a thirst for Catholicity, a predominance of the unity of love over a single authority, a dislike of the State, of formalism, of outward guarantees, a predominance of inner freedom over the outer forms, a paternal populism, etc." [2] The Slavophil idealization of the Orthodox Church was of course a fiction; there never existed a Church like that anywhere. The best proof is that when Khomyakov wrote his famous treatise on the Orthodox Church, the leading hierarchy of his own Church forbade the publication of Khamyakov's book in Russia. It first appeared abroad in the French language and was tolerated by the authorities as good foreign propaganda, but was not to be known by the Russian people. There was too much emphasis on freedom, too little recognition of authority in Khomyakov's teachings. His was essentially an anarchistic doctrine, which suited perfectly the Slavic temperament of the time but could not be tolerated by the authorities. It was considered as dangerous as any French revolutionary doctrine. This will be clear from the following outline of Khomyakov's ideas.[3]

The Church is first of all a living organism, a unity of love

[1] N. Berdyaev, *A. S. Khomyakov*, 1912, Russian, p. 9.   [2] *Ibid.*, p. 13.
[3] From Vol. II of his collected works (Russian).

and truth, a faith impossible to rationalize. There is no head of the Church, neither spiritual nor secular. Christ is its only head and none other is recognized. The Church is no authority as God is no authority, as Christ is no authority, for authority is something alien. It is not authority but truth and the life of the Christian, his inner life, which matters. The Church knows only brotherhood, recognizes no subjects. The unity of the Church is voluntary ; more precisely, unity is freedom itself expressed in inner agreement. When this inner unity was rejected, the freedom of the Church was sacrificed to arbitrary artificial unity by outward means. In matters of faith any compulsion is false and any coersion to obedience is death. The mystery of moral freedom in Christ, and the unity of the Saviour with rational creation, could be worthily revealed only to free human reason and by the unity of mutual love. The unity of the Church is nothing but free personal agreement. Liberty and unity are the two forces to which is entrusted the mystery of human freedom in Christ. The people heard the preaching of love as a unity ; but they forgot that love is a divine gift by which the knowledge of unconditioned truth is warranted to the people. In Scripture we must see not a dead letter, not an external object, not an ecclesiastical or State document, but the testimony and the word of the whole Church. The Scripture is from us and therefore cannot be taken from us. The history of the New Testament is our history.

These thoughts all testify to the one cardinal idea of Khomyakov's teaching that in the Church there should be no external compulsion but that everything should be prompted by inner impulse. The Church is a unity in love and freedom. Such he imagined was the Russian National Church, as the expression of the genius of the Russian people. Social relations should be a correlative to this religious faith ; the relation between master and serf should be regulated by mutual voluntary recognition. Therefore Khomyakov favoured the election of landlords by the peasants, and prided himself that the peasants had chosen his father to be their landlord. The city of God on Earth was " Holy Russia " ; its traditions and its culture were sacred. The Russian people did not want authority, they wanted only freedom and love. They did not want a kingdom, they wanted only a Church.

This is pure anarchist doctrine. What the Slavophil social philosophy recognized was not a dead State mechanism, but a living social organism; it emphasized the people and ignored the State. The Slavophils embraced the idea of autocracy, not because they idolised the State but because they hated political power and rejected it by turning it over to the Tsar as a burden they themselves had no wish to bear. Autocracy was to them an escape from political responsibility. The Russian people, in the opinion of the Slavophils, refused any guarantees by law, they had no need for them; State responsibilities are contrary to their natural inclinations. Constitutions, laws, etc., are needed only in conditions where the people are ruled by conquerors and not where they have chosen their own ruler, as the Russian people have in electing Michael Romanov autocrat of all Russia. Political parties, parliaments, and bureaucracies, all these institutions of government they considered alien and unnecessary in Russia, which wanted to live its own life unconcerned of any such responsibility. In this manner they hoped Russia would become free from political strife and the economic class struggle and would demonstrate to the rest of the world what true Christianity should be.

The Slavophil theocracy proved to be an Utopia. Russia did not follow and could not follow its precepts. It did not avoid the political and the class struggles. Rather it intensified them, since the Tsarist regime made use of the Slavophil ideology for its own selfish purposes and the Church, which was idealized as an organism of love and freedom, was degraded to a department for the policing of the conscience of the people and keeping them in subjection to an outworn and obscure economic, political and social system.

Half a century after the death of Khomyakov the Church was further away from the Slavophil idea than ever before. The Russian religious modernists who sympathized with

Khomyakov's idea of the Church as a free organism of love and truth could see nothing like it in the existing Church. Their grievances briefly stated were: that the Church had an ascetic view of life; that it despised the "flesh" as intrinsically evil and opposed to the spiritual man. It split man in two, and taught that in order to save the soul the body must be sacrificed. "Sinning," under this theory, meant the abuse of the body in lustful unrestrained living, and "saving the soul" meant "despising the world and mortifying the flesh." Either way meant some hurt to the body.

One of the able contemporary apologists [1] of the Russian orthodox point of view says:

"Asceticism is the foundation of historical Christianity. It is its principal peculiarity, it is its pillar of truth, and in Russia it has received a particular emphasis. . . . In asceticism, in the merging of the body into the mystery of Christ, in this beautiful sorrow lies the true life of a Christian; besides such mode of life he desires no other, for his kingdom is not of this world. Death and the Russian soul are inseparable. . . . Christianity, particularly contemporary Christianity, is exclusively construed upon the idea of death, and if there were no death, there would be no Christianity. *The Church could not receive the intellectuals and unite with them, for this would have meant to betray its eternal traditions, it would have meant paying tribute to the prince of this world.*" [2] This frank statement of the position of the Church lifts the curtain upon the religious tragedy of Russia's intellectual class.

The Russian religious thinkers—who could not accept the traditional asceticism of the Church, but who craved a religion of abundant life, a religion of joy and harmony, a religion of the unity of man—were hopelessly at odds with a Church which at its best was willing to wink at the flesh and graciously forgive it, but never sanctify, never harmonize it with the spirit.

A further grievance of the intellectuals was that the Church discouraged the efforts of the social reformer who wished to see Christ's Kingdom established on earth. The Russian

[1] Zakrzhevsky's *Religion*, Russian, 1913. [2] The italics are mine.

Church regarded the world as hopelessly lost; its message was to flee the world, save one's soul, and prepare for the kingdom in heaven. Because of this it frowned on worldly learning, art and science as anti-Christian and thus deepened the gulf between the intellectuals and the Christian Church.

What is the meaning and purpose of life? This was the great issue before thinking Russians. It became the pivot around which questions of theism and atheism, individualism and socialism turned. The young men and women of the universities sought a field of service, of sacrifice, of self-expression. To a certain extent the successive revolutionary movements in Russia were somewhat analogous to the religious revival movements in England and America. Young men and women, often of noble and wealthy families, broke away from home ties and society privileges and went among the common people, suffering persecution from State and Church and the ingratitude of the ignorant and superstitious peasants whom they sought to benefit.

These revolutionary revivals were regularly condemned by the Church and crushed by the brute force of the Russian autocratic regime until it finally destroyed itself during the World War and the great Revolution.

Each defeat of the revolutionists was followed by spiritual depression and general disappointment and expressed itself in all kinds of religious and moral perversion. The more mystically inclined drifted into extreme religious individualism and mysticism; others turned cynic, despising the world and their own spiritual consciousness. These periods of depression were also characterized by moral decadence and general social disintegration.[1]

The moral decadence of the Russian intellectuals reached its climax after the failure of the revolution in 1905, following

---

[1] The spiritual loneliness and moral despair after the failure of the 1905 revolution showed itself in the increase of suicides amongst university students: in 1902 there were 10 cases; in 1904 (the year of revolution), 20 cases; in 1906 (the beginning of reaction) there were 71 cases; in 1907 (the growth of reaction) there were 160 cases; and in 1908 (the climax of reaction) there were 237 cases.

the debacle of the Russo-Japanese War. Feeling themselves impotent to obtain political and economic freedom, Russian youth rose in revolt against the moral law. The philosophy of this revolt was given them by Artsybashev in his sensational novel *Sanine*, which appeared in 1907. Artsybashev, speaking through *Sanine*, ridiculed the struggle for political rights and advocated individual happiness through unrestrained gratification of desire. He considered it superfluous to have any theory of life, or to be guided by any principle, or to ask about God, or to have any regrets or twinges of conscience. Drunkenness and adultery were nothing to be ashamed of, and there was no such thing as sin. Love of strong drink and the lust for women were manly and natural passions, and being natural could not be wrong. Christianity, he claimed, teaches that man must live contrary to his natural instincts, and therefore " Christianity has played an abominable role in history, and the name of Jesus Christ will for some time yet oppress humanity like a curse." This immoral anarchism was immediately put into practice by the intellectual youth. Certain young men and women were invited into societies for " unrestrained gratification of natural desires," and speakers in the Duma alluded to this situation as " sanine-morality," which the Government did not suppress because *Sanineism* was not politically dangerous. Few only remained faithful during these years of trial, and upon these faithful lay the obligation of becoming the leaders of a new religious revival which repeated itself with every new generation.

In defeat the intellectuals turned to self-analysis, to self-abnegation and despair, or to the messianic-apocalyptical hope of a better world to come.

The Church in Russia either stood aside or was openly hostile to these successive romantic awakenings amongst its intellectual youth, which was destined to provide the future leadership of the New Russia. No wonder that when finally the Revolution succeeded, little sympathy was shown to the Church by the leaders of the Revolution. During this period of the prostitution of the Church by the State there were but

INTELLECTUALIST GOD-WRESTLERS AND SEEKERS AFTER GOD

few priests who lifted their voices in warning, and these were quickly silenced by the all-powerful hierarchy, so the Church remained deaf to the spiritual need of the age.

Among the few prophetic personalities of the Church it is no more than just to mention Father *Gregory Petrov*, a remarkable man with a clear prophetic vision. He entered the priesthood out of conviction, not belonging to the clerical caste, from which the Russian priesthood was generally recruited. His parish was in a Petrograd manufacturing district. Moved with compassion for his poor parishioners he commenced to preach a social gospel, and the common people and some intellectuals flocked to hear him. He was powerful and fearless as a speaker and a writer, and his religious tracts and periodicals were widely read. Some of the courtiers took an interest in him and called him as instructor to certain members of the Imperial family. He did his utmost to convice those in power of the need of thorough reform, but found no response.

Then he returned to the people, but the hierarchy of the Church had already decided to silence him. He was to be tried for heresy and disloyalty to the Church. Knowing that he could expect no justice from the clerical court, he wrote an open letter to his Archbishop, a remarkable document which gives in brief the message he had fearlessly proclaimed, a message which has not lost its significance to the Church even to this day:

" We have to-day, after nineteen centuries of preaching," he wrote, " individual Christians, separate persons, but no Christianity; there is no Christian legislation; our customs and morals are no longer Christian; there exists no Christian government. It is strange to speak of the Christian world. The mutual relations of the various people are altogether contrary to the spirit of the gospel; the most Christian States maintain millions of men for mass butcheries, sometimes of their neighbours and sometimes of their own citizens.

" To justify these monstrous butcheries the very soul of the mystified population is sapped away. The same butcheries are erected into a science. They are the object of the military art, the art of killing. In what way are these relations of Christian people distinct from the relations of the people of pagan antiquity. . . .

" The ruling regular clergy, with its cold, heartless, bony fingers, has stifled the Russian Church, killed its creative spirit, chained the Gospel itself, and sold the Church to the Government. There is no outrage, no crime, no perfidy of the State authorities which the monks who rule the Church would not cover with the mantle of the Church, would not bless, would not seal with their own hands. What power would the voice of the Church possess were it raised in genuine Christian words, it if should speak them to the rulers and to the people, to revolutionists and to reactionaries, if it should speak to the whole country ! Such words would become the voice of the eternal Gospel truths addressed to the conscience of the country. They would chime above the thunders of revolution, above the clamour of execution, like the voice of a church bell above the howling of the tempest. . . .

" In the Church the creative power of truth became withered, dried and anæmic ; separated from life, the thought of the Church was condemned to turn about in a world of abstract dogma and theological discussions. . . . God was reasoned about without being introduced into life itself. A sort of special atheism was created, practical atheism. Certainly in words and thoughts the existence of God was recognized, but live activity went forward as if it was not so, as if God was only an abstract word, a sound without meaning." . . .

The religious tragedy of the Russian intellectual class has been understood by its best literary geniuses and philosophers : Gogol, Dostoievsky, Tolstoy, Soloviev, Merezhkovsky, Berdyaev, Rosanov, Alexander Block and many others, who were deeply religious men. Their literary works tell the story of their spiritual struggles and of their almost desperate search for God and for the meaning and purpose of life. They were called at times the " God-wrestlers and Seekers after God." Few reconciled themselves to the historical Church. The majority looked either towards a social theocracy which would follow some world cataclysm, or towards the invisible Church of a universal Christian civilization.

F. Dostoievsky is without question the most dramatic personality in this company of God-seekers. He found God by way of Gethsemane. As previously mentioned he was condemned to death for associating with a secret society of liberal men of letters, and actually lived through the agonies of death, the sentence being commuted to Siberian exile only a few moments before execution. He knew how to appreciate the religion of sorrow, the mystery of the death of Christ, and the crucifixion of self for the sake of the kingdom of heaven. He knew this aspect of the Russian religion and he loved it. But he also knew the other side. The struggles of the Russian soul for the fullness and joy of life were not alien to him. He himself lived through the fearful conflict of the flesh and the spirit. He knew the intellectual difficulties of the Russian student, the aspirations of his mind and the cravings of his heart. The heroes of his great novels are all God-seekers and God-wrestlers; they speak his mind, and at the same time introduce to us the various religious and intellectual types of the Russian people.

There is Kirilov (hero of the novel, *The Possessed*), a typical God-wrestler in revolt against God and the established order because life is pain and fear and the Christian God is a God of pain and death. Kirilov cannot accept this and strikes at this god and this life for the sake of freedom and the life of joy: " Life is pain, life is terror, and man is unhappy," he cries. " Now all is pain and terror. Now man loves life, because he loves pain and terror, and so they have done according. Life is given now for pain and terror, and that's the deception. Now man is not yet what he will be. There will be a new man, happy and proud. For whom it will be the same to live or not to live, he will be the new man. He who will conquer pain and fear, will himself be a god." Yet Kirilov is not anti-religious and not a blasphemer, as may appear on the surface. He says when questioned about prayer : " I worship everything. Do you see that spider creeping on the wall? I look at him and am thankful to him that he creeps." His religion was something of a homotheism, a deification of man, of the abundant life. It was a protest against the humiliation of sickness and death, rather than be subject to which he kills himself. Kirilov is not an imaginary nor isolated character among the Russians; we shall recognize some of his characteristics among such Russian " Neo-Christians " as Merezhkovsky, Berdyaev and Rosanov.

Religion to Dostoievsky was a necessity of life, a supernatural power which gave to life a meaning, in spite of its contradictions, its sufferings and death. Dostoievsky did not trust reason, he trusted the heart, and no one could read the secrets of the human soul so well as he.

In his *Brothers Karamazov* he portrays the principal characteristics of his people. The Karamazov family is symbolic of the moral and religious history of the Russian people. The father Karamazov is a carnal brutish fellow; his sons are typical of the Russia previous to the Revolution. Dmitry the eldest is reckless, passionate, yet repentant at heart. Ivan, the second son, is thoughtful, sceptical, knows much but is inactive; he is always asking the eternal question of the meaning of life, but finds no answer, a typical pre-revolutionary intellectual. He has reasoned himself out of religion and out of morality, turning the God-man into a man-God. Dostoievsky shows how this pure intellectualism may become amoralism among his people. Ivan takes great pleasure in teaching his atheistic ideas to his valet, Smerdyakov, which finally lead the latter to crime. Smerdyakov, following the reasoning of his master, says: " Since there is no God and no immortality, it behoves modern man to take the place . . . and, if it be in his interest, light-heartedly to leap over the former moral barriers of the former man-slave; for God there exists no law! Where God is, he owns the place. Hence where I am, I am first. . . . All is permitted. That is the end of it." And he light-heartedly kills his old master who stood in the way of his interests.

Dostoievsky firmly believed that the Russian people were unable to live without God, that no reasoning, no sin, no crime, could crush their religious sentiment. The characters in his novels who profess atheism are always unhappy creatures, and either end their lives by suicide or insanity, or repent and are reconciled to God.

Dmitry, the elder of the brothers Karamazov, when innocently accused of the murder of his father and sentenced to go in chains to the horrible prisons of Siberia, cries out : " Oh, yes, we shall be in chains and there will be no freedom, but then, in our great sorrow, we shall rise again to joy, without which man cannot live nor God exist, for God gives joy : it's His great privilege—a grand one. . . . What should I be underground there without God ? . . . If they drive God from the earth, we shall shelter Him underground. One cannot exist in prison without God ; it's even more impossible than out of prison. And then we men underground will sing from the bowels of the earth a glorious hymn to God, with Whom is joy. Hail to God and His joy ! I love Him ! "

The youngest of the brothers, Aloesha, is healthy in body and in mind. He loves the Church and its sages. He wavers between the monastic vow and the life of action. Finally he abandons the gloomy atmosphere of the monastery, his instinct tells him that the future is not in denying life, but in asserting it. He leaves, but Dostoievsky does not tell what becomes of him. With his artistic instinct he sensed that a new era was opening in the history of Russia, in which the dominant type will be men like Aloesha, healthy in body and in mind, with an iron will creating their own destiny by building the kingdom of God here on earth and not by seeking it in dank cloisters behind the walls of medieval monasteries. One could continue the Karamazov story and, without violence to Aloesha's character, develop him into a representative type of contemporary young Russia. Dostoievsky did not and could not do this, therefore he left Aloesha's story unfinished.

It is futile to ask how Dostoievsky would have reacted to the social revolution. One thing is certain, that many of the things for which he strove the revolution has accomplished. He sought justice for the down-trodden and insulted people ; the social revolution has established this justice. It broke down the humiliating class barriers ; it abolished the filthy slums, breeding-ground of crime and poverty ; it made toil honourable and the workers masters of their own destiny. On the other hand, the revolution exposed the myth of the Russian people as the " God-bearers " bowing in servile submission and looking for relief in an unknown beyond, as Dostoievsky seems to have expected them to do. On the contrary the people smashed their old gods and revolted against submission to any master here or beyond.

Dostoievsky's ideal Christian is his Idiot ; an epileptic, like Dostoievsky himself ; sweet-tempered, an incarnation of beauty and holiness. " Just as a mother is happy when she sees the first smile of her nursling, so God experiences joy every time when, from the light of heaven, He sees a sinner raise to Him a fervent prayer." Such language is peculiar to his Idiot. Folks who came to be amused by him and to scoff at him, departed in a mood of prayer. His simple life without pride, deceit, revenge, or ambition, was a wonderful synthesis of beauty and prayer. Russia is no place now to breed such saintly idiots. But it does remove the conditions which necessitated people living a life of deceit and revenge. Dostoievsky felt deeply the corruption within the Church, yet he realized an imperative need for it as a bond of the spiritually-minded and as a means of saving the State and Society from disintegration. The Church and the common people were to Dostoievsky almost synonymous. He believed that they had the kingdom of God within them and would keep alive an unsophisticated idea of God. In this also he was largely mistaken. There are no signs that the Russian masses are so God-conscious. At least not in this generation, bred in the struggle of the Revolution.

Dostoievsky abhorred dogmatism and clericalism. He clung to Christ not because of any categorical imperative or necessary principle in a system of thought. Christ was to him the giver of life, the great liberator from sin, and the founder of the Church as a spiritual kingdom. In a letter to a friend he says: " If somebody should prove to me that Christ is outside the Truth, if it actually should appear that the Truth is outside Christ, nevertheless, I should prefer to stay with Christ rather than with the Truth." No common revolutionary would agree with him, unless he substituted the word " Communism " for the word " Christ."

To-day, Dostoievsky is above all the spokesman of that remnant of the old Russian intellectual class which lives either in exile in various parts of the world and feel that they are atoning for the historical sins of their class, or live under the proletarian dictatorship deprived of their former privileges. Of these many have accepted the social revolution and see in it an opportunity for unselfish service to the toiling people. They do not mourn the loss of their wealth and privileges, and, like their teacher, Dostoievsky, they have reconciled themselves to the Revolution through suffering. Many also have returned to the Church, and to-day the old enmity between the Church and the non-communist intellectuals has ceased.

THE NEO-CHRISTIANS

The religious tragedy of the intellectual class, which Dostoievsky experienced in his own life and which was reflected in the lives of the heroes of his great novels, manifested itself at the beginning of this century in an open religious movement, which some of its critics labelled the " Neo-Christian " movement. It had two distinct trends: (1) individualistic, culminating in religious anarchism, and (2) apologetic, developing finally into religious socialism.

Merezhkovsky, Berdyaev and Rosanov are the brilliant representatives of the individualistic trend. S. Bulgakov was the sole Christian socialist amongst these intellectualist seekers after God. A former Marxian professor of political economy, under pressure of the disillusionments of the 1905 Revolution, he painfully retraced his way from Marxism to idealism, seeking to reconcile the aims of socialism with the Christian gospel.

At the same time Bulgakov advocated the separation of the Church from the State and, when this was finally accomplished through the Bolshevik revolutionary decree, he signified his welcome of the Church's emancipation by entering its service as a priest, since when Bulgakov has become more mystical in his outlook and seems to have abandoned his one-time dream of a Christian socialist movement in Russia.

D. S. Merezhkovsky [1] is a typical pre-revolutionary Russian intellectual, a poet and an individualist, abhoring the utilitarianism of modern industry, science and art as much as the commonness and mediocrity of the social democratic movement, the asceticism and spiritual dullness of the Church, and the moral and religious nihilism of his own intellectual class. In utter despair at the spiritual and cultural bankruptcy of modern civilization he leaps into the unknown and becomes an ardent seeker after God, a maker of a new religious philosophy.

In telling the story of his spiritual bankruptcy, he says: " We come to the end of the historical highway ; to go further is impossible, but we know that when history ends then religion begins. At the edge of an abyss we naturally and inevitably acquire thoughts of wings, of flight, of a super-historical way, religion." He is conscious that his search for God, for a religion, is as yet a part of his egotism, a supreme desire to save himself from a life of despair and eternal death. He knows it and fervently prays to God to give him a heart of love for all mankind. During this period of struggle for a new life he wrote a number of lyrics, heart-rending prayers all of them. To quote one stanza :

> " I am frightened for I have loved no one all my life ;
> Is it possible that my heart shall be dead forever ?
> Give me strength, O Lord, to love my brother ! "

[1] To the English reader he is known through his critical character-study, *Tolstoy and Dostoievsky*, a book which has received considerable attention among students of Russian character and literature ; other works in Russian from which I quote are : *Revolution and Religion, Not Peace but the Sword, The Last Saint, The Coming Serf, The Struggle for Doctrine, About the New Religious Functionings*, etc. He now lives abroad, having been unable to reconcile himself to the Soviet regime.

In his desperate struggle for a way out of his spiritual darkness he knocks at the door of the Church. In 1902 he initiated the founding of the Religious and Philosophical Society. He called upon his fellow intellectuals to be reconciled to the Church, to come and learn from it. But these efforts failed. He complained that the Church did not understand them, that it had no message for them. When the teachers and prelates of the Church and the God-hungry intellectuals met, they talked in languages strange to one another. Says Merezhkovsky: " From old habit the Church saw in us, people from the world, only unbelievers whom they needed to convert. But we, or at least some of us, believed not less than all these monks and priests. For us faith was a wonder, to them almost wearisome; to us a depth of mysticism, to them a positive standard; to us a holy feast, to them a week-day; to us a holy vestment which we did not dare to wear, to them an old everyday robe. The words of the Holy Scriptures, which sound to us like the thunders of the holy mountain, were to them at best mechanically learned texts of the catechism, with a meaning like the rattling of a counting board or hammerings upon a soundless keyboard. We desired that the face of Christ should be like the shining sun in its full power, and they were contented with a tarnished old ikon in which none could detect real features. . . . They could not understand that we did not wish the Church to pardon the sinful flesh but instead to bless and sanctify the body." Thus the historical Church proved a disappointment to Merezhkovsky's intellectuals. It had no actual contact with real life and seemed surrounded by a Chinese wall of the past. Its pretended asceticism, which considered sex at its best as a necessary evil and not as a revelation of God, was particularly repulsive to the intellectuals. They knew from experience how degrading an influence it had upon morality, and so Merezhkovsky set out to formulate his own religious doctrine. He felt the need of doctrine, which may seem strange to Western intellectuals, who are accustomed to a non-dogmatic point of view in religion. But Merezhkovsky is a Russian intellectual, and as a Russian intellectual he cannot act unless he is guided by a clearly-defined principle. He called doctrine a diamond-edged sword.

Present-day Russian Christianity seemed to him something like a tomb of Christ. He called it a sterile religion. He abhorred asceticism, which he believed incompatible with the Christian message. Christ had risen not only in the spirit but in the body. Hence the ultimate mystery of Christianity is not the separation of body and soul, but the union of the body and the soul into sacred harmony. "If the flesh," argues Merezhkovsky, "is the absolute impurity, a negation of God and the pure spirit, why then was Christ, the Word, manifested in the flesh? Why the resurrection of the body? Why the sacrament of the body and the blood? ... The Word which was made flesh and dwelt amongst us is a revelation of the very essence of God, incarnated in the world, and becoming immanent in the world." He believes that the conflict between the flesh and the spirit, between individualism and socialism, can be solved through the Christian idea of the Trinity. To him the Trinity corresponds to three Kingdoms, the Kingdom of the Father, the Kingdom of the Son (New Testament), and the Kingdom of the Spirit, which unites these three kingdoms into one. In the Kingdom of the Father, truth was revealed as the power of God, in the Kingdom of the Son truth was revealed as love, in the coming Kingdom of the Spirit love is revealed as liberty. He believes this doctrine of the Trinity solves the unbelievable metaphysical dualism of flesh and spirit, of heaven and earth, of the world and God. The opposites become one through the metaphysical interpretation of the Trinity. Merezhkovsky looks forward toward an apocalyptical Church, a Church which Christ will gather round himself at his second coming, which may appear outwardly anarchistic, inwardly socialistic, but in its synthesis will be the unlimited liberty of the individual held together in the congregation by the unlimited ties of love. By the aid of this dogma Merezhkovsky hoped to give the intellectuals a metaphysical working hypothesis for religious action and social expression.

When Merezhkovsky took the thorny path and went forth

" seeking God," he believed that there existed two truths : a Christian truth about heaven and a pagan truth about the earth. The ideal religion of the future, he thought, would unite these two truths. But before he had gone very far he began to realize that the hope for unity of Christ and Antichrist was a blasphemous lie. " I learned," he says, " that both truths, that of heaven and that of earth, have been already united in Christ Jesus, the only-begotten Son of God, in the same Christ witnessed by Catholic Christendom, that in Him alone is not only the perfect, but the ever-growing truth, and that there shall be no other except in Him." . . . His voluminous works which, he believes, in spite of their seeming variety, are but links in one chain and have but one purpose, he dedicates to that generation of Russians " who will understand that Christianity is not only a thing of the past, but that it exists now and will exist in the future ; that Christ is not only the truth of the past and the present, but an endlessly growing truth ; that the liberation of Russia and the liberation of the world cannot be realized except in the name of Christ."

N. Berdyaev[1] is another of the leading " Neo-Christians " of modern Russia. Like Merezhkovsky he turned to religion because in life, in the whirlpool of modern civilization, he could find no sense. Science and the materialistic philosophy which dominated the minds of the intellectuals at the beginning of this century could not satisfy the religious cravings of his sensitive, self-conscious soul. " I need religion," he confessed, " because I want to live eternally, I want to assert my personality in the common life. I want to identify myself with the world unrestrained, and not by fatal necessity."

Like Merezhkovsky, he became disappointed in historical Christianity which, by its ascetic view of life, has disrupted the harmony of body and spirit, of the individual and society. His hope is riveted on the second coming of Christ, which, unlike

[1] N. Berdyaev's principal works are : *The Philosophy of Liberty, Sub specie aeternitatis, The Spiritual Crisis of the Intellectual Class, The Metaphysics of Sex and Love, Christ and the World, The New Medievalism, The Russian Revolution.* He lives abroad and is actively engaged in anti-Soviet propaganda.

Merezhkovsky, he understands mystically. The spirit of Christ, he believes, will establish the harmony of body and spirit, of the individual and society. It will also emancipate the creative impulses in man which now are fettered by a false materialistic determinism and a wrong social order. As much as the democratization of society he wishes to see the aristocratization of the individual. He says: " I believe that a spiritual aristocracy is possible in a democratic society, and it will have little in common with the trend of political and social standardization. It must be an aristocracy which raises itself above all class and group morality and will give new impulses for further progress; without such a class there would be stagnation and the rule of the herd."

There can be no spiritual aristocracy, however, as long as the mind of man is fettered by philosophical, ecclesiastical and moral tradition. Ethical ideals, he contends, must be free from ecclesiastical social control. The first condition of spiritual and ethical progress is profound respect for the spiritual man; it is liberty. The common, everyday morality must be overcome by a new religious regeneration, which by its very nature is above every code of morals.

The new religious consciousness is attracted as much by Calvary as by Olympus. " We are drawn," he says, " not only by the suffering God who died at the cross, but also by the God Pan, the God of earthly elements, the God of the joys of life, by the old Goddess Aphrodite, the Goddess of plastic beauty and earthly love." The new religious consciousness craves for a synthesis of Olympus and Calvary; it desires the fullness of life; it wishes to unite the opposing poles of the religion of suffering and the religion of joy and beauty.

This synthesis Berdyaev hopes to see realized in the messianic Church, which is to be a free theocracy headed by the returned Christ. " We seek a Church," he concludes, " which will embrace the fullness of life, all of the world's experience which has proved of actual value in history. Outside the walls of this Church should be left nothing except non-existence. Inside the Church should be all our values, all that we have gained by suffering in the world, all our love, all our thoughts and poetry, all our creativeness which so far has been excluded by the historical Church ; all our great men, all our elevating impulses and visions, and all which heretofore was thought of as only transcendental."

In this connection, Berdyaev's relation to Communism is of particular interest. He concedes that in Communism there are many truths and " only one untruth," which, however, he thinks " outweighs all the truths and spoils them." [1] Now what are the many truths and what is the one untruth ? Berdyaev we must remember was once a Marxist and hence knows something of the Communist theoretic background, and we must give him justice in that, for all his dislike of the Bolsheviks, he credits them with some very important verities. He first indicates some negative traits such as the Communist criticism of the falsehood of bourgeois capitalist civilization with its profound contradictions, its degenerate pseudo-Christianity, its miseries, exploitation of weaker nations, wars, etc.

Among its positive truths he emphasizes :

1. That of their new social order the Communists are making a working society with equal opportunity for the toilers to participate in cultural life ;
2. That the Communists emphasize that man should not exploit man, nor class exploit class, and " if any man will not work, neither let him eat " ;
3. That the political machinery of the Communists represents man's real economic needs and interests and therefore is arranged on a basis of profession and labour ;
4. That their political life goes hand in hand with a complete, consistent philosophy of life : " for politics without a soul, without some great idea, cannot enliven the souls of men " ;
5. That their theory and practice are being united in some all-embracing, complete type of culture and life ;
6. That the elite are serving the social whole ;

[1] N. Berdyaev, *The Russian Revolution*, English edition, p. 54, c.f. pp. 77-79.

7. That the Communist organization is a supernational organization overcoming national selfishness, isolation and war.

Thus Communism has " a complete design for reconstructing the world's life, in which theory and practice, thought and will, are at one." In short, it has that which organized religion and western bourgeois society have so far been unable to produce.

On the debit side of Bolshevism, Berdyaev records but one accusation which he considers outweighs all the above indicated credits . . . it is their *rejection of God* : " the social collective which receives divine honours steps into the place of both God and man."[1] This Berdyaev considers an unpardonable sin since, " in reality Communism is highly spiritual and idealist,"[2] but it sacrifices the individual for the group. Worst of all : " Communists do practise their truth and that fact they can always oppose to Christians." This sacrifice of the individual to " social collectivity," Communism's " new divinity," Berdyaev asserts is a denial of the " living God," and is a sin that cannot be forgiven. . . . Therefore he rejects Communism.

He proposes to oppose it by an integral renascent Christianity which would " abandon the support of capitalism and social injustice." It would seem that he pleads for a Christian Communism ; actually he does not. His social ideal is feudal, medieval, aristocratic, and his plea for the individual in the name of Christianity is the plea of an æsthete, and aristocrat abhoring the democracy of Communism. He says : " Christianity is the only basis on which a solution can be found for the painful conflict between personality and society, which Communism resolves in favour of society, completely crushing personality. And it is also the only basis on which a solution can be found for the no less painful conflict between the aristocratic and democratic principles in culture, resolved by Communism in favour of completely overthrowing the aristocratic principle."[3]

The aristocratic individualism of Berdyaev forces him to

[1] *Ibid.*, p. 83. [2] *Ibid.*, p. 85. [3] *Ibid.*, p. 94.

turn against the spiritual and cultural mediocrity of bourgeois society; in this respect he sympathizes with the proletarian revolution which has made an end of capitalism. Nevertheless he cannot reconcile himself to the Communist ideal which denies the individual for the good of the group. Erroneously Berdyaev considers the Communist attitude to the individual as anti-Christian. Christianity above all means to him the liberation of the individual. Berdyaev seems to forget the conditions upon which this emancipation is promised: " Who shall lose his life shall find it." Self-effacement for the good of the group is the first step and condition for finding one's real individuality. The goal, also, of the Communist teaching is complete freedom of the individual in a *classless* society, and to attain this classless society it is first necessary to abandon individualism It implies losing one's life in the proletarian class struggle in order to find it anew in the classless Communist society. This dialectic process is not understood by Berdyaev. To him a classless society means the denial of individuality and not its emancipation.

Berdyaev's aristocratic individualism, in the New Testament sense, is feudal and not Christian. His argument for condemning Communism is equally applicable to the teachings of Jesus concerning the individual and the group. The anti-Christian position of Communism must be sought therefore on other grounds and not in its teachings regarding the relationship of the real individual to his group. Berdyaev's personal tragedy is also that of the elimination of his class as a factor in modern life; he and his class seek to assert themselves in escaping to an imaginary concept of the Church, hoping for a miraculous regeneration of those social relations which in reality have already lost their basis of existence.

In analyzing the individualistic trend of the " Neo-Christian " Movement among Russian intellectuals, one must mention also *V. V. Rosanov*,[1] who in many ways is the most original

[1] V. V. Rosanov was a conservative in politics. His principal works on the religious question are *Near the Walls of the Church, The Dark Image,*

of the modern religious thinkers of Russia. Like Merezhkovsky and Berdyaev, he struggled to find a solution to the conflict of body and spirit, of individual and society. But unlike them he opposes dogmatism: "Why surrender the wonderful words of the Gospel to the relatively rotten words of dogmatism? Dogma is something deadening. Christianity, during the period of the 'Church fathers' and the construction of creeds, has lost its simplicity, its charm, its affection, and its power of attraction." . . .

Like Merezhkovsky and Berdyaev, Rosanov revolted against the asceticism of the Church. To him all that is human, all that appears to be a source of life, is sacred. Religion to him is a joyful wedlock of God and man. He considers sex the greatest and perhaps the only existing miracle. It is the great mystery. And yet, he complains, "historical Christianity is sexless." In Christ the world was embittered. Into the joyful life of the flesh Christianity injected the poison of death.

Rosanov believed that the solution of the religious tragedy of the Russian soul lay in the deification of sex. "There is no life outside sex." It may seem superficially that Rosanov is a materialist and a sensualist; but his materialism is different, it is mystical. The "flesh" becomes in his mind almost spiritual, and in this peculiarity lies the force of his appeal. Although Rosanov was considered by the official clergy as the most heretical among the "Neo-Christians," he himself, in spite of his bitter criticism, has alienated himself least from the Church. In his book, *Loneliness*, he says: "The Church is the only poetical, the only profound thing on the earth. My God, how could I for eleven years continually attack it? . . . How beautiful it is that in the Church we are all brothers."

That which was felt by Rosanov during the trials of the revolutionary period has become quite general with the remnants of his class. They have returned to the Church therein to spend their last days and to die. This is one aspect of the tragedy.

In the World of Obscurity and Indecision, The People of the Moonlight, Loneliness, About the Nondogmatism of Christianity.

The leaders of religious thought in pre-revolutionary Russia whom I have mentioned, whatever their deviations from orthodoxy may have been, expressed a positive and optimistic view upon religion and life and hoped for a regeneration of society through the divine power. The approach of others is altogether pessimistic and negative, but because of their incurable religiousness they have given their spirit of negation a religious interpretation in order to save themselves from inevitable despair.

Interesting in this respect is the religious nihilist, N. M. Minsky,[1] who was one of the first to revolt against the soullessness of the mechanistic philosophy adhered to by his generation of intellectuals. The truth he believed he had discovered was: " If there is any purpose in life, it is to be attained not in the interests of everyday life but in something deeper and mysterious, which is to be sought not outside of self but within oneself."

Minsky's philosophy is not a product of pure logic, it reflects the deep spiritual suffering of a sensitive soul and the despair of helplessness in the face of death. Turning his back on the utilitarianism and materialism of his age, he retreats into his own self and becomes an egocentric pessimist. He recognizes nothing as real but his own unhappy self. He subjects all existing values to destructive criticism, and rejects art, love, self-sacrifice, beauty, modern science, in short, all values, both good and evil. But when he faces the phenomenon of death he cannot reject it, and it hurts him as a painful and horrible reality. " Death is not only cruel, but it is unjust and revengeful." In his complaint, in his despair, in his ruthless spirit of negation, he grasps at the idea of God and constructs a peculiar religious philosophy which he believes does guarantee him inner liberty and peace of mind.

The " Neo-Christian " philosophers had considerable influence among the intellectuals until the Revolution upset their

[1] N. M. Minsky expressed his religious ideas in *The Religion of the Future ; In the Light of Conscience* and *Serenades*. All works are in Russian.

dreams. The Bolshevik appeared to them as the incarnation of Antichrist. Their æsthetic sense of life could not reconcile itself to the rough and ready ways of a proletarian revolution. They emigrated to Western Europe and thus shut themselves off from influencing directly the new generation of proletarian intellectuals, who hardly know them even by name.

In fact, one can no longer speak of an intellectual class in Soviet Russia. As a class it was broken up by the Revolution and a large part of it fled to Western Europe and America, where it lives like a plant which has been torn from its native ground. It does not feed on the joys and woes of its people from which it is severed, and it cannot make the fruit of its labours available to the people. This exile of the intellectual class from its native land is the culmination of its tragedy. In its foreign isolation a whole religious philosophic literature has grown which reflects the state of mind of the immigrant Russian intellectual. It is extremely nationalistic and theocratic, it idealizes the Church as the only institution which survived the revolutionary cyclone, and it condemns the proletarian revolution and the Soviet social order as anti-Christian. These exiled intellectuals live in apocalyptic expectation of the speedy downfall of the Soviets by divine interference. How long will they wait? A decade and a half has passed already. A new generation has grown up which has new ideas and new hopes. Sooner or later the old intellectuals may return or at least their literary works will become available to the new generation. But they will hardly be understood or appreciated. If there exists the possibility of a new religious revival among the intellectuals of Soviet Russia it will be inspired by prophets who will rise from the Soviet ranks, with a message which will reflect the needs of the new Soviet culture and not that of a past generation and of an epoch which has been relegated to the limbo of history.

CHAPTER VIII

TOLSTOY'S RELIGIOUS ANARCHISM

The life and teachings of Tolstoy present a separate chapter in the religious history of Russia. For a while they captured the imagination of certain sections of Russia's intelligenzia, whose class interests and temperament did not permit them to make common cause with the revolutionists. Some of the rationalistic and evangelical sects also felt his influence, but this was not lasting and soon gave place to the more orthodox evangelical doctrines. Since the Revolution some of his followers have made strenuous efforts to launch a movement which would carry out in practice his anarcho-Communist teachings. Vegetarian societies were established, his popular religious literature was circulated and there sprang into being a number of Tolstoyan agricultural communes conducted on Communistic principles.

The anarchist and pacifist agitation of the Tolstoyans was at first tolerated by the Soviet Government but, after Lenin's death and the general change of policy towards religious sects, the Tolstoyan movement practically ceased to be of importance in the Soviet Union, and for the present there is hardly any ground for its revival. On the other hand the Tolstoyan influence is much more felt in other countries where conditions are more favourable to the spread of his ideals. Thus Gandhi has incorporated Tolstoyan ideas in his movement and some of the pacifist elements in capitalist countries recognize Tolstoy as the prophet of their cause.

If we turn to the religious teachings of Tolstoy and search for their origins we find that they are very much a product of his time and of the personal experiences which went on in him throughout his conscious life. His chief work was done within the period of 1861–1905, the two important dates which mark the beginning and the end of an epoch. It began with the emancipation of serfs and ended with the 1905 Revolution, which marked the disintegration of the rural gentry and the advance of the city bourgeoisie with its accompanying transformation of the farmer peasant and former serf into a proletarian. Tolstoy felt deeply this transitional era. By birth, education and social position, he was of that class which was destined to go down with his generation. Herein lies his pessimism, his mystic restlessness, his desire to escape from the life of his class and merge into the life of the common people. His presentiments of the approaching cataclysm burst forth in vehement denunciations of the hypocrisy of the State, the Church, and the economic and social order of his time, which was based on the degradation and ruthless exploitation of the poorest and most helpless of the population in city and country. In this respect Tolstoy sided with the revolutionists, but he is unique in the artistic and tragic expression which he gives to his protest.

Lenin and other revolutionists who could neither share Tolstoy's mysticism nor agree with him in his tactics of non-resistance, nevertheless acknowledge Tolstoy's extraordinary power in exposing and denouncing their common enemy. Says Lenin : " Tolstoy's critique of his contemporary order differs from the critique of the same order by representatives of the labour movement in so far as Tolstoy stands on the ground of the paternalistic, naive peasantry. He transforms their psychology into his critique and into his teachings. For this reason Tolstoy's critique has such force of emotion, such passion, and is so convincing, fresh, sincere and fearless in getting at the root of things, discovering the real cause of the sufferings of the masses. His critique actually reflects the changes which were taking place in the views of millions of peasants, who only emerged from serfdom into a liberty which proved to be a new horror of ruin, of death from starvation, a homeless life among the city outcasts. Tolstoy reflects their feelings so genuinely that he incorporates into his teachings their unaffected simplicity, their estrangement from politics, their mysticism, their desire to flee the world, their non-resistance to evil, their helpless imprecations upon capitalism and the power of money. The protest of millions of peasants and their despair has merged in Tolstoy's teachings."

TOLSTOY'S RELIGIOUS DEVELOPMENT

Some critics speak of Tolstoy, the artist and the literary genius, and some of Tolstoy the religious philosopher and preacher. However, a closer study of his life shows that from early manhood he was religious, a dreamer and potentially a prophet of a new religion. Under the date of March 5, 1855, we read the following remarkable entry in his diary: "In conversing of God and of faith, I was led to a great and significant idea, for the realization of which I feel capable of devoting my life. My idea is to found a new religion which would correspond to the development of mankind, a religion of Christ, but purged from credulity and mystery, a practical religion with no promises of future bliss, but which would give bliss on earth. Its realisation, I understand, can be accomplished only by the work of generations, striving towards this goal. One generation will bequeath this idea to the next, and sooner or later fanaticism or reason will realize this idea. To work consciously toward uniting people by religion—this is the basic idea, which, I hope, will captivate me."

In a still earlier diary entry, referring to the year 1851, we learn something of Tolstoy's religious experience and mystic nature: "Last night," he writes, "I hardly slept at all; after writing in the diary, I commenced to pray to God. The sweet emotion which I experienced in prayer is impossible to relate. I recited the prayers which I was accustomed to repeat: The 'Our Father,' the prayer to the God Mother, to the Trinity, to the Door of Mercy, to the Protecting Angel, and then I remained in prayer. If one should define prayer as supplication or thanksgiving, then I did not pray. I desired something exulting and good, but what—I could not pronounce, although I clearly realized what I wanted. I wanted to unite with the Almighty being, I begged Him to forgive my sins, but no, I did not pray this, for I felt that since He has granted me this minute He has forgiven me. I prayed, and at the same time I felt that there is nothing for me to ask, and that I must not, and know not how. I thanked Him, but not with words or thoughts. In the same emotion I expressed all; supplication and thanksgiving. The feeling of fear disappeared altogether. None of the great emotions—faith, hope and love—could I separate from the total experience; no, what I felt yesterday, what I experienced, was love to God, sublime love, which unites in itself everything which is good, and rejects everything which is evil. How I resented viewing the mean and vain side of life. I could not realize how it could ever have attracted me. And now, with a purged heart, I asked God to take me to his bosom. I did not feel the flesh, I was . . . but no, the flesh, the mean side again came to its own; hardly one hour has passed and consciously I listened to the voice of evil, to the vain and empty side of life; I knew whence came this voice, I knew that it would destroy my bliss, I struggled, yet yielded. I went to sleep and dreamed of glory, of women, but I was not guilty, I could not do otherwise." Gorky, in his reminiscences of Tolstoy, observed that Tolstoy's mind and talk was continually occupied with two major subjects—God and women. " I asked God to take me to his bosom "—" I went to sleep and dreamed of women." There were never two Tolstoys. The converted Tolstoy was, psychologically speaking, long before his great crisis embryonically present, and his conversion was but a link in the chain of events that brought into the open that which long was hidden in the secret chambers of his heart.

Every close reader of Tolstoy's works, who knows also a little of his personal life will agree that, almost without exception, his novels are nothing but artistically worked out autobiographical sketches, which reflect clearly the development of his great soul. Already in his first works, *Childhood, Boyhood, Youth*, we read of his spiritual struggles and the attempts to draw up some rules of conduct which would make his young life godly and rich in meaning. These noble principles, however, were in constant conflict between his acute conscience, his keen, critical intellect and his physical passions. In a word, there seemed, as in Doctor Faust, " two souls within one bosom " contending with one another ; and as Goethe endowed his famous hero with all his own psychic strength of good and bad motives, so Tolstoy in a much more realistic manner reflected these, his own experiences, in the heroes of his novels. Volkonsky in *Anna Karenina*, Olennikoff in *The Cossacks*, Nikita in *The Powers of Darkness*, Pierre Besuchy in *War and Peace*, Nekhludoff in *Resurrection*, and especially Duke Kosatsky in *Father Sergius*—these and many others picture vividly the psychic turmoils and final victory of Tolstoy himself. These experiences, which for about thirty years he kept under the literary cloak, became known to the world with the appearance of his famous *Confession*. In this declaration Tolstoy opened his great passion-rent heart. He pictures his lost state by this parable :

" A wanderer, so goes the story, is surprised in a prairie and is pursued by a ferocious beast. He seeks refuge in an empty well which he happens to meet in his flight. But here he discovers, much to his horror, a fearful dragon which lives at the bottom of the well, ready to devour any victim that may enter his habitation. In despair, the unfortunate wanderer takes hold of a branch which hangs over the opening of the well, thus hovering between two dangers. But now, with still increasing terror, he beholds two mice, a black one and a white one, as they gnaw away the branch on which he is hanging. It becomes clear to him that he is doomed, that the branch before long will break and he will become a prey of the dragon. In this despairing situation he observes some honey dripping from the leaves of his branch and, for a moment forgetting his danger, he eagerly licks the sweet drops." " In such a manner," says Tolstoy, " I have hung on the branches of my life tree, knowing of the dragon of death which was waiting to devour me at any moment. I also licked the sweet honey of earthly joys, but they satisfied me not, for I was conscious of the white and the black mouse—each day and each night—which hastened my ruin."

Tolstoy, however, did not so easily yield to despair. He tells us how he sought for light out of the darkness which surrounded him. Thus exhausted, and at the very verge of suicide, he at last found the balm for his sick soul in the childlike faith of the unsophisticated mass of Russian peasantry. " I discovered the truth," he writes in his *Confession*, " which I later found confirmed by the Gospels, that men loved darkness rather than light, because their deeds were evil. For every one that doeth evil hateth the light, neither cometh to the light, lest his deeds should be reproved. I came to realize that in order to understand the purposes of life, it is necessary that one's life should, first of all, not be aimless and evil, and then that one should speculate about it to understand its philosophy."

With this testimony began Tolstoy's religious activity. It was, however, not a movement in the same sense as those inaugurated by Luther and Wesley, or Karl Marx and Morris, who called into existence new sects and political parties. It was rather an attempt at a reformation in the realm of ethical thought analogous to that of Rousseau, Fichte and Kant, and therefore its results were also rather indirect. Tolstoy co-operated but little with his contemporaries, who tried to solve the social and economic problems of Russia. On the contrary, he rather proved to be an opponent of the socialist-revolutionary movement, whose leaders accused him of pacifying the revolutionary spirit of the masses with his gospel of non-resistance.

This anti-revolutionary attitude does, however, not exclude him from the ranks of great reformers. He was working for the same end as other champions of the people, but he opposed his revolutionary contemporaries because he could not accept the methods by which they were trying to attain the commonly-desired end, the social and economic welfare of the masses. Tolstoy's principle was that evil can never produce good. Therefore to obtain good by murder and plunder (the natural by-products of revolutions) would mean to make things worse than they are.

TOLSTOY'S CONTACT WITH THE PEOPLE

In keeping aloof from the revolutionary leaders of his day, Tolstoy sought contact with the pacifist sectarians who influenced him as much as he influenced them.

Most remarkable in this respect is his acquaintance with the evangelically-minded rustic prophet, Ivan Sutayev, a peasant from the Government of Tver, who worked during the summer months in St. Petersburg as a stonecutter, and during the winter taught himself to read from a New Testament which somehow got into his possession. Unassisted, he sought for the truth in the Gospels. Each verse which he deciphered with great effort carved itself into his mind, and it assumed the importance of a new revelation which he believed was never conceived by anyone else. At the age of fifty, Sutayev returned to his native village and began with great ardour to preach the truth he had learned in the Gospels. He abandoned his Church, saying that "I have the Church within myself." With the Gospel in hand, he and his followers proclaimed : "We are new creatures, regenerate creatures. We lived in error. Now we know." Being charged by the police with forming a new sect, he replied : "We form no new sect. We merely wish to be true Christians—In what, then, consists true Christianity—In love." Love was the cornerstone of his religion. It was the fulfilment of all laws, it was the new life in Christ. Sutayev rejected the traditional asceticism of orthodoxy as the beginning of piety. The Gospels taught him that peace and justice among men will be attained only if men learn to love one another. When asked : "What is Truth ?" he replied : "Truth is love in common life." He repudiated the Sacraments because the Church traded in them and he buried his grandson in his garden, saying that "the whole earth is God's and therefore sacred." He performed the marriage ceremony of his daughter, entreating the couple to conform their lives to the Divine Law, and treat all men as brothers. When charged with failing to recognize lawful marriage, he replied: " I do not recognize the sort of marriage which is a lie. If I fight or quarrel with my wife, it is no marriage, because love is not there."

Sutayev preached: " The Kingdom of God must be brought here on earth." To realize this individual private property, which he believed begets envy, theft and hatred, was to be abolished. Community of goods, he believed, would destroy egotism and he asked the nobles and the rich to give back the land to those who tilled it and to whom therefore it rightfully belonged. He believed they would do it of their own accord as soon as the light of the Gospel illuminated their minds, and a little love touched their hearts. He divided his own possessions and burned the title to his property. He refused to pay taxes, and admonished his followers not to follow the call for military service. When his youngest son, Ivan, was summoned as recruit, and commanded to take the oath, he simply replied: " Thou shalt not swear at all." When he was handed a gun, he refused it, by saying: " It is written: ' Thou shalt not kill.' " He was thrown into prison and put on bread and water, but he took none of it. And, lest he starve himself to death, he was taken out of prison and sent to a disciplinary company. On his way he preached to his guard and convinced him of his error, who repented and became a convert. Sutayev believed that the Tsar was good, and if he only knew of the evil deeds of his officials he would reform Russia. He started for the capital to warn the monarch. In vain he begged to be admitted, and after persistent efforts he returned to his village.

What a striking similarity to Tolstoy there is in this simple, unlettered rustic prophet, who taught and practised the same doctrine which later the literary genius of Tolstoy interpreted to the world! Tolstoy confessed that he learned much from these unlettered people. And it strengthened him in his belief that the simple, but revolutionary teachings of Jesus were naturally fitted to the unsophisticated masses of common folk. Like Sutayev, he believed that if only a little of true

Gospel light could penetrate the darkened minds of the learned and a little love could touch the hearts of the mighty, they would do willingly what the revolutionists compelled them to do by force and the Kingdom of God would be established on earth. Tolstoy did not want to recognize the class nature of society, neither did he perceive the futility of such individual efforts as those of Sutayev and of his own followers. None of the Tolstoyan settlements, neither in Russia nor in other countries, survived. They were at their best tiny oases which gave weary wanderers in the wilderness of capitalist civilization an opportunity to rest a while, but these oases could not transform the desert. Sooner or later, when the springs of enthusiasm dried up, they themselves became part of the desert.

PRINCIPLES OF TOLSTOY'S RELIGIOUS PHILOSOPHY

1. *Life, its Meaning and Purpose.* Tolstoy raises the eternal question : what is the meaning of life, what is its purpose ? His answer is that neither exact science nor philosophic speculation gives a satisfactory answer. Only in faith can the meaning and the purpose of life be found. Ever since humanity existed faith gave the possibility to live. The principal features of every faith are the same. It attaches infinite meaning to a finite life, a meaning which is not destroyed by sufferings, privations and death. Therefore, religion always existed and must continue to exist. It is an indispensable condition of the life of every reasonable man and of reasonable humanity.

2. *The Necessity of a Universal Religion.* What originated religion with its belief in the supernatural ? Tolstoy rejects the rationalistic theories of animism, ancestor worship and fear of the forces of nature, as the origin of religion. Every religious experience is not the consequence of outworn natural phenomena, but of an inner condition which has nothing in common with fear of the incomprehensible forces of nature. Religion has developed out of man's consciousness of his insignificance, isolation and sinfulness. Therefore man may learn from observation and personal experience that religion is not a veneration of Deities called forth by superstitious fear

in face of unknown forces of nature, for such veneration is characteristic of man only at an early period of its development, whilst religion is something altogether independent of fear and of the degree of education of man, and cannot be destroyed by any kind of education, since man's consciousness of his finality within an infinite world and of his sinfulness, that is his omissions of duty, has been and will be as long as man will remain man. The assertion that science will replace religion is arbitrary and is based upon unjustified faith in the infallibility of science, which is just like faith in the infallibility of the Church. Religion, as in the past, will remain the chief dynamic, the heart of human society; and without it, as without a heart, there can be no reasonable life.

Whilst there exists a great variety of religious experience and a multiplicity of form, all religions are the same in their basic principles. These common principles of all religions are the true religion and prove to be acceptable to all. To formulate it in a definition: *True religion is a relation to infinite life, established by human reason and knowledge, and such a relation binds life to this infinity and guides man in his doings.*

The multiplicity of relations of man to the universe or to its first cause may be reduced to three basic modes: (1) Primitive-individual, (2) Pagan-social, (3) Christian or divine.

The first and most primitive consists in the desire for individual preservation and welfare, independent of the interests of others. The second, pagan relation of man to the world, is a social one in which individual interests are submitted to the interest of the group, the family, the clan, the nation, even of all humanity. The third relation of man to the universe, which is felt by every older person and into which humanity is now entering, consists in the recognition that the significance of life is comprehended not in the attainment of personal aims or the interest of the group but in serving the will which created Man and the Universe, and for attaining man's purpose he aims to do this will. Out of this relationship to the universe developes the highest known religious teachings, elements of which are found in all great religions.

3. *The Contradictions of Life and Their Solutions.* Life's instinctive desire for welfare is upset by contradictions, prompted by Reason, showing that suffering, death and annihilation is the lot of all men. The one I, that of personality, dictates life. The other I, Reason, asserts: "life is impossible." This split, this duality, torments men conscious of themselves. The escape from this unbearable condition may be found in the realization that the life of a separate being is but a temporary limitation, in reality it is a part of the divine life. This true life is present in every man, as life is present in the seed and in due time reveals itself. On this earth man passes through one of innumerable forms of life to do the will of Him who sent him into this life.

This truth cannot be established by observation of life in time and space. It will always remain a mystery and the life which has revealed itself to him in consciousness is subject to the law of Reason to attain this peculiar good. The emotion which solves all contradictions in human life and grants him the highest good is the emotion of love. Reason is that love to which, for its own good, must be subjected the animal in man. Love is therefore the only real activity in man. It must be always present. Who does not reveal love in the presence has none, and is still under the control of his animal individuality. True love is unselfish and directed towards the welfare of others. It is the very nature of love to embrace everything that exists. Love demands sacrifice. When man gives to others not only his time, his strength, but when he gives up his body, his life, then he really loves and finds his reward. There is such love and because of it the world remains.

4. *God the Supreme Will.* God is that which gives life to all, which exists and which reveals itself in man's desire for good. Thus God is love. Man learns of God directly through his consciousness. The Christian teaching states that the essence of life is not man's separate being but God who is in his being and becomes conscious in reason and love. Man says to himself: God is the unlimited form of that which I know in myself as limited: I am something limited, God is

something infinite; I am a being which lives for a period of years, God lives eternally; I am a being who reasons within the limits of my understanding, God reasons without limitations; I am a being who at times loves a little, God loves infinitely. I am part, He is all. I cannot think myself otherwise than as a part of him.

Man cannot help asking for what purpose has God, the one spiritual indivisible being, incarnated himself into separate bodies and man; why has the immortal united with the mortal? To these questions can be only one answer: there is a Supreme Will whose aims are not known to man. This Will has put man and all that exists into that position in which it finds itself. This cause, which for some reason unknown to man has incarnated itself into separate beings revealing love, is the same God whom man knows within and without himself; God is that towards which I aspire and in this consists my life. For this reason I cannot understand him, for should I have understood him there would be nothing to aspire to and there would be no life. I may approach him, come closer to him. In this is my life, but approaching does not increase knowledge.

Some say that God must be understood as person. This is a great misunderstanding: personality is limitation. Man knows himself as person only because he comes in contact with other persons. If man were alone he would not be a personality. We know God as one being but not in the arithmetic sense but as one which is All. Having faith in this, the religious man is conscious of God and has a firm concept of life. To know God and to live is one and the same thing. God is life. Live seeking God and there will be no life without God.

5. *Self-Perfection*. The ultimate purpose of life is hidden from man, but his proximate aims grow out of his love and desire of the good for all and consist in overcoming division and disagreement in the world. The inner growth in love is the means of contributing to unity and agreement, and in Christian teaching is called the establishment of the Kingdom of God. It is within us and without us.

The goal of life has been revealed to us by Christ in the words: " Be ye perfect, even as your Father in Heaven." This goal is reached not by ascetic practices but by a loving association with other people. Love generates love and hence awakens God in other men. This means building His kingdom.

Christ recognizes the existence of the two sides of the parallelogram of the two eternal indestructible forces which compose the life of man. The force of animal nature and the force of consciousness of sonship to God. The animal nature is always equal to itself and is outside the power of man, but the divine force may develop and free itself from the animal nature which handicaps it, a man who stands on a lower stage but moves towards perfection lives more ethically, according to the teachings of Christ, than a man who stands at a higher stage of perfection but does not move forward. To follow His teachings is to move from self to God.

6. *Sins, Temptations, Superstitions and How to Overcome Them.* Unity with God is growth of divine consciousness in man. This growth is hindered by sin, which consists in the indulgence of the desires of the flesh, prompted by temptations themselves false conceptions of good, and by superstition, which is false teaching justifying sin and temptation.

People who believe in God, the Creator, frequently ask why has God created man so that he must sin? Such a question is equivalent to asking why God has created mothers so that they must suffer in bearing, nursing and rearing their children? In such suffering and anxiety exists the secret joy of motherhood. The same is true of human life: the struggle and victory over sin, temptation and superstition, therein lies the meaning and the joy of human life. If there were no darkness we would not rejoice in the light of the sun. If there were no sin, man would not know the joy of righteousness. Sin, temptation and superstition constitute the soil which must cover the seeds of love in order that they may sprout. The worst sins are: excess, fornication, idleness, covetousness, anger.

Excess results from the false idea that the blessing of life is in serving the body; the aim should be a simple life so as to create the fewest handicaps for the spirit. *Fornication* is the sin of irrespect for woman, regarding her as an object of pleasure rather than as the temple of the spirit of God. *Idleness* is sin against the law of the bodily life, toil, in transgressing which man also transgresses the spiritual law of love. All men are brothers, hence equals; therefore it is essential that none should labour for us, but that each should work and earn the necessities of his own life. *Covetousness* consists in the acquisition of an increasing quantity of worldly goods and money, needed by other people; the only joy that wealth can give to man, is the joy in giving it away. *Anger* is the sin of ill-feeling, of the lack of love towards others; it provokes many evils.

The temptations which make it difficult to overcome sin are pride, inequality, violence, retribution, vanity. Nothing divides people so much as *pride*—personal, family, class or national. This leads to *inequality* and the temptation to do many evil things because of the belief that others are inferior and not equal. Equality is recognition of the equal rights of all people in the world to make use of the good of the common life and enjoy equal right to respect as human personalities. Inequality leads to violence and to retribution, the desire to compel people to submit to one's own ideas and punish them for not doing so. Any man who has done wrong is already punished by his conscience. Nothing so rejoices people as forgiveness for evil done. Goodness conquers and is itself unconquerable. *Vanity*, more than any other temptation, separates people and obscures their sense of genuine good; one must learn to live in such a way as to be fearless of the opinions of others, and to be guided only by the desire to do the will of God.

The superstitions which justify sin and temptation are those of the State, the Church and Science. The superstition of the *State* consists in the recognition that one is part only of one nation and an alien to all others, on the basis of which superstition, violence and murder take place. To free oneself from it man must recognize that he is of the same spiritual essence as any other man, and no human division can separate him from that which God has made one. Another superstition is that of the *Church*. The concept of the Church as the association of the elect, of the best, is not a Christian concept; it is proud and false; the Church has obscured the inner life of man and has turned it into darkness. The Christian Church has taken over and sanctified everything that was in the pagan world; she accepted and sanctioned divorce, slavery, the law court, and all the powers that be, wars and executions. The Church, whilst accepting in theory the teachings of Christ, actually in practice rejected them. Only in liberating oneself from the deceit of credulity man can be free from falsehood and temptation. It is necessary to remember that the only implement of knowledge is Reason, and all preaching which is contrary to Reason is fraud and aims at removing the sole implement of knowledge granted Man by his creator. Man needs no cults, no artificial means to know and associate with God, who reveals himself directly to the heart of man without intermediary. Truth is discovered gradually by those who seek it and cannot be transmitted by intermediaries who believe they themselves possess it. There are no infallible teachers and the search for truth must everywhere be checked by reason.

The third superstition is *science*. Its evils consist in pretensions of infallibility. Science to-day has replaced the Church of two or three hundred years ago. Its magicians are the professors, its councils and synods are the academies and universities, which expect that their opinions should be accepted uncritically as truth. Science clothes itself in a foreign terminology whose meaning remains a mystery to the many; but mystery is not an attribute of wisdom, and true wisdom speaks a language which all can understand. There is as much fraud in science as in religious beliefs and therefore it is just as harmful.

The chief evil of false science is that being unable to study everything, and not knowing without the aid of religion *what it should study*, it pursues knowledge which is pleasing to the men of science who do not live a proper life. One may know very much, without knowing that which is most necessary.

What must be done in order that people may live the good life? First of all, stop doing all the superfluous things with which most people are now occupied and which, in European countries, means 99 per cent. of their activities. It is more important that the people should *be* good, than that they do good. Don't strive to shine but strive to be pure; resist evil thoughts. Before there can be a change of feeling and doing, there must be a change of thought. As fruits grow out of seeds, so deeds grow out of thoughts.

Strive to free yourself from the flesh, be humble and truthful. Prayer can help to attain perfection. It is a test, by the soul, of past and present deeds. Pray, as Jesus taught you to pray, in secret. Pray always and you will conquer your animal nature.

7. *Non-Violent Resistance to Evil.* The chief evils among men result from the use of violence. Disguised as retribution it is used by some against others. The Christian teaching has not only shown its injustice but has demonstrated that to overcome evil it is necessary to suffer it without resistance. Violence should not be used under any provocation, and in no case under pretence of retribution. Only good can overcome evil and not be infected by it.

The law of non-violent resistance to evil is eternal. All progress in history against evil has been achieved through the agency of people who suffered evil and did not resist it by force. To overcome evil we must attack not its consequences, such as the invasion and loot of nations against their weaker neighbours, but its root—which lies in a false relation of a people to human authority. If a people recognizes human authority as higher than the law of God, that people will always remain in slavery. A people can only be free when it accepts the law of God to which all other laws must be subjected.

Any religious person who has accepted the divine law of non-violent resistance to evil should first cease for himself to act violently or prepare for violent action ; secondly he should not participate in any kind of violence which is done by other people, nor participate in any preparation for it ; thirdly, he should nerve approve of violence. Not to do violence means not to lay hands upon anyone, neither strike nor kill, neither in your own interests, nor in the interests of society ; not to participate in any kind of violence means, not only rejecting the function of the chief of police, of governor, judge, guard, tax collector, tsar, minister, soldier, but also in not applying to courts, nor appearing as attorney, guard or jury ; not to approve of violence means not to make use of violence for any personal benefit, neither in speech, writing, nor deed, neither to support or agree with violence nor anything founded upon violence.

This will probably result in persecution on the part of the authorities. By suffering this in loving kindness to the persecutors, the persecuted will open their persecutor's eyes and hasten the eradication of violence in society. It will come speedily if people who really believe in non-violent resistance are willing to put their belief into practice whatever the consequences. Those suffering to the end will be saved.

8. *The True Meaning of Life.* Efforts at self-denial, humility and truthfulness, destroy in man the hindrances for uniting the soul in love with God and other beings. This opens the way to a permanently good life, in which that which seemed evil disappears. This world is not a jest, not a vale of misery and a transition into a bitter, eternal world. The world in which we now live is one of the eternal worlds. It is beautiful, and by our own efforts we must make it more beautiful and more joyful for those who are with us, and for all those who will live after us. To be happy in this world we have only to live in accordance with the will of Him who sent us into this world.

The true reward of life is not in the remote future, it is now and within us in the perfection of our soul. In this is the reward and the incentive towards good.

Death exists only for people who fix their life in time. For those who understand life as it really is—as an effort to overcome the hindrances which separate man from God and other beings,—to those there can be no death. Fear of death is the consciousness of the unsolved contradictions of life. It is fear not of death but of a wrong life.

My body may be destroyed together with its temporary stage of consciousness, but that peculiar relation which composes my distinct ego cannot be destroyed. It cannot because it is the only thing which is. If it were not, I could not know my successive stages of consciousness, and I could not know my body, my life and the lives of others. Therefore the destruction of the body and consciousness cannot serve as a sign of destroying my peculiar relation to the world, which did not originate in this life. The more my carnal desires give place to spiritual interests, the less fearful death becomes. If my worldly passions be replaced by the one desire to give myself to God, then there is nothing but life, there is no death. Death becomes a superstition.

Christ revealed to men that the *eternal* is not the same as the *future*, but that the eternal is within us now, that we become eternal when we unite with God in the spirit, in which everything moves and lives. We attain eternity by love.

It is asked what will happen after death. There can be but one answer: the body will decay and turn into dust, this we know for certain. But what will become of that which we call the soul, we cannot say, because the question, " what will be ? " refers to time, but the soul is independent of time. The soul was not and will not be. It *is*. If it were not, nothing would be. Time cannot be the necessary condition of all that exists, since we are conscious of ourselves as something not subject to time. Death is the destruction of those organs through which we associated with the world. Death is the destruction of the glass through which we look and it is replaced by another. This life is one among a thousand lives into which we enter by escaping a previous life. And so it continues endlessly to the final life, which is the life of God.[1]

We have retold briefly the principles of Tolstoy's religious and ethical teachings. Much can be said in criticism of their many contradictions, from both the orthodox Christian point of view and from the point of view of the Communist theory of religion, and its social aims. Tolstoy's effort to outline a rational yet religious philosophy of life is unique in its sincerity and artistic form. While Russian revolutionary thinkers took a rigidly anti-religious position or became reactionary and drifted back into orthodoxy, Tolstoy strove to synthesize revolutionary criticism with religious faith, and while the Tolstoyan Movement, to propagate his ideas, does not show much vitality at the moment, it would be premature to say that Tolstoy is forgotten in Russia. The Revolution has solved most of the social problems he fought for, such as the question of land and property, of social equality, of the dignity of toil, the abolition of classes, and the consequent withering away of the State. Yet there are other problems still left unsolved, such as the subtler ethical experiences which Tolstoy considered particularly important. Finally the last word has not been said on the meaning of life and death; it is here that the inquiring mind will turn to Tolstoy to seek an answer to this eternal question.

[1] An excellent outline of Tolstoy's teaching may be found in *A. Bulgakov : Christian Ethics,* consisting of a symposium of thoughts from about 200 of Tolstoy's religious and ethical writings. This symposium was edited by Tolstoy himself. The outline of Tolstoy's principles, as presented in this chapter, generally follows that book.

CHAPTER IX
COMMUNIST THEORY OF RELIGION

THE Communist theory of religion is a product of the Communist philosophy of life and is generally in line with the anti-religious tradition of the Russian revolutionary movement.

We have previously shown how the materialist philosophy of the French Encyclopædists slowly undermined the religious tradition and faith of the Russian educated people, how it spread to ever-wider circles and how, finally, atheism became a tradition of the revolutionary intellectuals. German Hegelian philosophy merged with the French materialism through the influence of Feuerbach, who reinterpreted religion anthropologically and prepared the ground for the Marxian development of Dialectical Materialism.

Marx's attitude to religion was not emotional. He experienced no tragedy in breaking away from the faith of his fathers ; for, although a grandson of a Jewish Rabbi, he was not reared in the Hebrew religion. His father, a lawyer by profession, was a free-thinker, strongly influenced by the French enlightenment, and in breaking away from the faith of his people he became nominally a Protestant. Karl Marx approached religion as a philosopher and as a historian. He gave to it a social-economic interpretation, characterizing it as the " opiate of the people."

F. Engels, Marx's closest collaborator in creating the philosophy of Dialectical Materialism, had a much more tragic experience in breaking with the religion of his family. His father, a well-to-do manufacturer, was a strict Evangelical pietist, who did his utmost to make his son follow the traditions of his sect. Against this the young Engels revolted and, on joining the revolutionary movement, left his father's house.

These youthful experiences made Engels much more sensitive to religious and metaphysical problems than was the case with Marx.

In Marxian theory religion belongs to those social phenomena classified by him as ideological superstructures upon the social-economic basis of a given people. In their *German Ideology* Marx and Engels say : " The vague images in the brains of men are also necessary sublimations of their material life-processes empirically established and related to material conditions. In this manner, morals, religion, metaphysics and other types of ideology, together with their corresponding forms of consciousness, lose their apparent independence. They have no history at all, they have no development. They are only the developments of people in respect to their material production and their material relations ; as these activities change so change also the products of their thought." [1]

Religion thus is but a by-product of the basic factors of social life, which are economic. The classes which control the base are naturally also in control of its by-products, using them to their advantage. In the process of the class struggle, one ruling class is overthrown by a newly-rising class, as for example feudalism was overthrown by the town bourgeoisie and the proletariat. The struggle for democracy went on in the form of a struggle of one religious idea against another, as was the case of Nonconformity against the Established Church of England. With the development of social science there is apparently no further need to appeal to a religious ideology.

The conversion of Marx and Engels from Hegelian idealism

[1] This statement must not be interpreted, as it often is, that religion is not an active force in society. Engels took quite the contrary position, as may be seen from his correspondence with Mehring and others :
" Because we denied that the different ideological spheres, which play a part in history, have an independent historical development, we were supposed therewith to have denied that they have an *historical efficacy*. At the basis of this is the ordinary undialectical notion of cause and effect as fixed, mutually opposed, polar relations, and a complete disregard of reciprocity. These gentlemen forget, almost intentionally, that an historical factor, once it has been brought into the world by another, ultimately economic fact, is able to react upon its surroundings and even affect its own causes." . . . (From a letter of Engels to F. Mehring, July 14th, 1893.)

to Dialectical Materialism, which also determined their position in regard to religion, took place under the influence of Ludwig Feuerbach and his famous book, *The Essence of Christianity*. In this work Feuerbach showed that the contents and subject of religion are altogether human, that theology is a perverted anthropology, and that the mystery of divine essence is a human essence. Religion, however, is not conscious of its human content; it considers it rather the opposite and does not recognize its human origin—that Man was not created in the image of God, but God in the image of Man. The consciousness of God is nothing but the consciousness of human kind. Man can and must raise himself above the limitations of his individuality but he cannot raise himself above the laws and principal characteristics of his kind. Man can think, imagine, feel and love as an absolute divine being, which means as a human being.

Religion is Man's first self-consciousness. This makes it sacred; but what religion senses as the first (i.e. God) is actually the second. Since God is but the objectified essence of man, that which religion postulates as secondary (i.e. man) should be recognized as first. Love to man must not be derivative, it must be primary. Only then will love become the true, sacred and dependable force. If human essence is the highest essence of man, then love to man practically must be the supreme and first law of man. *Homo homini deus est*, such is the highest practical basis and the turning point of world history. Justice, truth, goodness have their sacred essence in themselves, in their quality. For man there is no being higher than man. These are the principal ideas of Feuerbach's theological anthropology. He did not intend it as a denial of religion. He wished to revaluate it and to raise it to a higher human synthesis. Feuerbach says: " My book has a negative tenet, but I beg you to note that it rejects only the non-human essence of religion and recognizes and asserts the human."

Feuerbach was therefore not opposed to religion; on the contrary he wanted to improve and to humanize it—" Religion," he says, " is a solemn revelation of the treasures hidden in man's nature. It is a recognition of his inmost thoughts, an open confession of the mysteries of his love." Feuerbach was convinced that his interpretation of religion was a progressive step towards a more profound self-realization. Not all of his pupils agreed with him. Marx and Engels in developing their dialectical philosophy saw no future for religion. For them, it was destined to disappear with human ignorance, misery and class exploitation. Marx writes: " The omnipotence of God is nothing but the fantastic reflection of the impotence of people before nature and the economic social relations created by themselves. . . . Such religious reflections of the real world will not disappear until the relations between human beings in their practical everyday life have assumed the aspect of perfectly intelligible and reasonable relations as between man and man, and as between man and nature. The life process of society, this meaning the material process of production, will not lose its veil of mystery until it becomes a process carried on by a free association of producers, under their conscious and purposive control." [1] Engels expressed himself similarly in *Anti-Duerig*: " If man not only expects to control but actually to master the social process, then disappears the last external force which until now has been reflected in religion, and with it will disappear religious reflection, for the simple reason that there will be nothing to reflect on."

Lenin, who was a thorough student of Feuerbach, Marx and Engels, takes the position of the latter two, and checks their point of view against the historic background of Russia, where he finds the fact corroborated that religion is the worst implement of class exploitation. With the disappearance of classes there will remain no reason for the existence of religion. Lenin was not a theologian; his approach to religion was that of a sociologist. His efforts were towards awakening the masses and spurring them on to revolutionary action, and here he continually came into conflict with the conservative tenets of religion. " All contemporary religions and churches, all and

[1] *Das Kapital*, Vol. I.

every kind of religious organization, Marxism has always viewed as organs of bourgeois reaction, serving as a defence of exploitation and the doping of the working class." But whilst an uncompromisingly enemy of every religion, Lenin understood that the sources of religion were deeply rooted in social economic conditions and he was therefore opposed to arguing about it on a merely intellectual plane. " The struggle with religion must not be limited to abstract ideological preaching. . . . This struggle must be in concrete practice with the class movement directed towards removing the social roots of religion."

Now what are these roots ? Lenin sees them in the social degradation of the toiling masses and their seeming impotence before the blind forces of capitalism. " Fear created the Gods ; fear, before the force of capitalism which is blind, for its actions cannot be foreseen by the mass of the people. On every step the life of the proletariat and that of the petty employer is threatened and leads to sudden, unexpected ruin, to calamities which turn them into beggars and prostitutes and end in death from starvation—these are the *roots* of contemporary religion." Religion feeds on the economic and social reactions of the mass. Religious beliefs are intensified by the blind forces of nature which man is impotent to control ; but religion serves chiefly as an opiate in which the slaves of Capital find temporary relief, at the cost, however, of losing their human worth.

Other roots of religion feed on the survivals of former social and political formations with their obscure ideologies, customs and traditions, themselves superstructures of past social-economic formations, and which now interpenetrate with the new. For example, the treatment of women in Moslem society, and the great religious festivities of Christmas and Easter which are rooted in the nature worship of ancient agricultural people antedating the Christian era. Finally there are the Epistemological roots of religion. These are also social because man can think only in association with actual experience. The splitting of man's consciousness into the abstract "idea," from which originated the idealist philosophy, is closely related to religion.

Lenin thought that the task of destroying religion really belonged to the bourgeoisie, as the class which carried through the industrial revolution and began to organize society on the principles of applied science. Writes Lenin: "The task of struggling with religion is the task of the revolutionary bourgeoisie, and in the West this task was accomplished to a considerable degree by bourgeois democracy during the epoch of its revolutions or its pressure upon feudalism or medievalism. Both France and Germany have a tradition of a bourgeois war against religion which commenced long before socialism." The bourgeoisie, however, lost its anti-religious ardour soon after it came to power, because it realized the value of organized religion as a power of control over the unruly masses. It sought and readily obtained the support of the Church. Even in France, the classical country of bourgeois militant atheism, the leaders of the Revolution came to a compromise with the Roman Catholic Church.

It was impossible for the leaders of the proletarians to do as the revolutionary bourgeoisie, and therefore it sought to formulate a new theory of life, giving the masses the assurance that religion is not necessary and that there can be a philosophy of life without a God. Such a theory of life will not demoralize the people but will make them more socially and ethically minded. To appreciate fully the impossibility of compromise between the Communist philosophy of life and the religious tradition, we must give a brief outline of the principles of Communist philosophy.

COMMUNIST PHILOSOPHY OF LIFE [1]

A philosophy of life is an attempt to establish man's relation to the universe in terms of rational concept. It thus follows that its first task is to arrive at a theory of being or ultimate reality which philosophers usually call the metaphysical or

[1] For a more exhaustive treatment of this subject, the reader is referred to my *Moscow Dialogues*, Chapman & Hall, London, 1933.

ontological problem. Then it must decide whether it can really trust its experience and its senses; this results in a theory of knowledge or epistemology. Finally there is the problem of the aims and modes of life; this includes a theory of development of the social life and of behaviour. The philosophy of religion differs from ordinary philosophy in so far as it takes for its working hypothesis the reality of religious experience and seeks to establish a reasoned interpretation of religion and relate it to the rest of experience. The philosophy of religion differs from the science of religion in so far as the latter seeks to establish *how* religion actually functions, whereas the philosophy of religion has for its chief task to determine how religion *should* ideally function. Hence it takes desirability of religion for granted and seeks to discover and justify the principles for furthering the development of religion and of life through religion. In this latter sense there can be no Communist philosophy of religion, for Communists reject the hypothesis of the desirability of religion; but there can be a Communist science of religion.

The Communist philosophy of life has developed upon a system of thought called Dialectical, Historical and Economic Materialism. The ontological and epistemological problems are dealt with in the theories of Dialectical Materialism and the sociological, religious and ethical problems in the theories of Historical Materialism. Problems of economics are treated in the theories of Economic Materialism, and the three together, Dialectical, Historical and Economic Materialisms, are also called the Marxo-Leninist Philosophy. The Communist theory of religion grows out of this philosophy.

Dialectical Materialism, as every other philosophy, is first confronted with the problem of defining its concept of reality, and the laws of its development. Contrary to popular ideas the " matter " or reality of Dialectical Materialism has little in common with the old Mechanistic or Atomistic Materialism. It considers this latter theory to be incompatible with modern natural science. The old Atomic Materialism with its indivisible " bricks " of the universe, is rejected by Dialectical Materialism. Life and mind are qualities which cannot be reduced to mechanical motion. The old Newtonian ideas of cause and effect as an unbroken continuity of motion are no longer tenable. They have been exploded by the modern theories of relativity, the quantum theory and the modern theories of heredity, the nature of the psychic life, and so on.

If we turn to the sources of Dialectical Materialism we find that it has a long genealogy. Already Engels has pointed out that Dialectical Materialism is a synthesis of French materialist and Utopian thought and the great philosophies from Spinoza to Hegel. Dialectical Materialism adheres to the monistic concept of nature or matter. Spinoza believed that there is but one substance or nature, which he also called God, which is real, existing independent of human consciousness and prior to it. It has many attributes of which two, those of extension and mind, are known in the experience of man. These two attributes are not the same but they are in inseparable unity. Dialectical Materialism also knows but one substance or nature, which is in constant movement but not in a mechanical motion. The movement which Dialectical Materialism emphasizes is one of opposites or of contradictions. The attribute of mind or spirit was potentially always present in nature but appeared as consciousness only at the higher stage of the organization of matter.

Lenin gave much thought to the ontological and epistemological problems. He drew sharp lines between the subjectivist or sensationalist philosophies and that of Dialectical Materialism. To have subjective knowledge of the world and ignore the possibility of knowing its objective stimulus was to him like having thoughts without brain. A materialist, he says, is one who " takes matter as the *prius*, regarding consciousness, reason and sensation as derivatives." Lenin asks whether the world would not exist independently of humanity and of human experience. His answer is that the world existed long before any human experience was possible. Hence reality is independent of human consciousness. According to Lenin, matter is that which, acting upon our sense organs, produces sensations.

It is some objective reality existing independently of the human mind and reflected by it.

The recognition of an objective world raises at once the question as to the reality of such categories as *space* and *time*. Kant, and philosophic idealists generally, accept these only as *forms* of human understanding with which the intellect is endowed. Dialectical Materialism on the other hand, while recognizing a certain relativity in these concepts, nevertheless holds that a philosophy which denies the objectivity of space and time is absurd.

THE LAWS OF DIALECTICS

Dialectics in the philosophic sense means self-movement, but not ordinary mechanical movement, which is replacement by outward force. It is movement prompted by an inner necessity which is the immanent law of existence of matter and the universe. Lenin defined Dialectics as a theory of knowledge, as the method by which the laws of the movement of the universe can be studied. He says : " Dialectics is a living, many-sided knowledge, with a continually increasing number of aspects, with an infinte number of shadings of every sort and approximations to reality." The Marxo-Leninist theory of Dialectics begins with Hegel, but unlike Hegel it applies its categories of thought to the study of a real world and not to an imaginary absolute spirit which was the object of Hegel's speculation. In Lenin's words : " It is the recognition of the mutually exclusive and opposite tendencies in all the phenomena and processes of nature." It is universally applicable to the study of nature, society and the workings of the human mind. Therefore, Marxo-Leninist theory insists that man *can know the objective world since it is controlled by the same laws as those operating in the human mind, since the latter is but a part of the same nature.*

The emphasis, in the dialectic process is on self-movement, in which occurs the interpenetration of opposite forces, approaching a unity and then again separating. In other words, in the evolutionary process of self-movement, there is continuity and there are spontaneous, periodic breaks. These breaks are a vital part of the process. They indicate also the beginning of a new synthesis and the resumption of continuity in the process of self-movement. Upon this law rests the Communist theory of revolution. It presupposes class differentiation and interpenetration of conflicting interests, as for example, those of the feudal aristocracy and the clergy which clashed with those of the peasant class and the town bourgeoisie as demonstrated in the great French Revolution.

In the field of biology the phenomena of *mutation*, by which appear sudden organic changes in the evolving species, are readily explained by the dialectic law of " sudden breaks " after a slow preparatory stage of minute evolutionary changes. These same sudden changes occur also in chemical reactions when interpenetrating elements suddenly break and again interpenetrate with other elements but in a different synthesis. The behaviour of the electron and the proton, according to the quantum theory, is also dialectic; there exists the phenomenon of continuity with sudden periodic breaks.

Engels who made a thorough study of natural science from the point of view of dialectics, points out that there are three principal laws in the dialectic process equally applicable to the study of nature as to the study of society and the workings of the human mind. They are: (1) the law of transition of quantity into quality and inversely; (2) the law of interpenetration of opposites; (3) the law of negation of negation. Marx used these laws as a hypothesis in his study of the development of capitalist society. He showed for example how the quantitative accumulation of capital is followed by qualitative changes in the economic class stratification, each stage showing a quality of its own, as for example the difference between the petty employer and the big capitalist on the one hand, and the artisan and the big factory worker on the other. The Marxian theory of class interpenetration and the class struggle is a brilliant exposition of the nature of the dialectic law. The unity of theory and practice, the interpenetration of thought and action, is basic in Communism.

DIALECTICS AND RELIGION

The question naturally arises as to whether the phenomena of religion are also subject to dialectical development. Hegel made extensive use of dialectics in his theology and there are signs of a return to his method which, under pressure of the crisis in the empiric sciences, promises to have an extensive revival. In Germany it is sponsored by the Hegelian society and philosophers like Kroner, who is also the head of the International Hegelian Union. At the centre of Hegelian theology stands the idea that God, the Absolute, realizes himself in an eternal thought process which includes all realities of time and space. These are essentially phases in the process of divine self-realization. This idea permits the acceptance of divine immanence without the sacrifice of man as a finite being. Hegel, who was concerned in preserving Protestant Orthodoxy, thought himself able to steer clear of Pantheism. He taught that man, possessed of conscious power of thought, shares in this thought process of God and realizes his life in the eternal absolute God. The Hegelian trilogy of thesis, antithesis and synthesis, lent itself to a logical interpretation of the Trinity in the 'Godhead. The Christian experience of conversion or regeneration follows accordingly the dialectic process of negation of the old, of the sinful self, and results in a conscious rebirth of the spirit to a new higher life. Finally the highest ethical precept of the Christian life, " who shall lose his life, shall find it," was quite in harmony with the law of negation of negations, conditioning the attainment of a higher synthesis of the spiritual life. Hegel had hoped to achieve a perfect religious system which in his opinion corroborated the doctrines of Orthodox Christianity. These pretensions of orthodoxy have severally been denied by those religious minds who see no advantage in a rationalized speculative religion and who cherish mystic experience as an intuitive knowledge of God.

The Hegelian dialectic interpretation of religion is not shared by Dialectical Materialists since religion is not considered to have an independent history; that is to say, it is relegated to a category of superstructures, which have no independent existence, but only reflect the social economic base of a given society. The Communist theory of religion does not take Deity for granted. In its hypothesis God is but a phantom, created by the splitting of man's consciousness during the stage of his rational immaturity; hence religion is destined to disappear with the growing maturity of the consciousness of man. A contemporary student of the Communist theory of religion, V. Ralcevitch, makes the sweeping statement: " Religion from beginning to end, in both its form and content, must be destroyed."[1] If we begin to inquire what are the reasons for this unreserved condemnation of religion, the answer is that " Religion in all its aspects, in its content, in its form and its social functions, is incompatible with the *movement* toward a classless society."[2] It is a dead body taking hold of the living and dragging them down. Religion is such a danger to future Communist Society because it is a reactionary social force. True enough, religion is not the only institution which Marxo-Leninist theory has sentenced to death and extinction. Social classes, the State and the institutions of law, all these are to disappear under Communism, but while the class struggle and the State as organized violence, with its institutions of law, are still useful and necessary implements in the transitional stage from Capitalism to Communism, organized religion is only a handicap and hence must be destroyed as quickly as possible.

This is the present position of the Communist Party, and it has outlined a definite plan for carrying out these intentions. What this plan is, we shall see in the subsequent chapters.

SOCIALIST GOD-BUILDERS

The Party's present uncompromising negation of religion has not always been shared by some of its distinguished thinkers and leaders. There was a time when it was thought possible to re-valuate religion and, while dropping its dogmatic and sacerdotal aspects, to preserve its emotional value. This

[1] V. Ralcevitch, *Marxism and Religion*, p. 3, 1929.   [2] *Ibid.*, p. 4.

opinion was held by the so-called Socialist "God-Builders," among whom Maxim Gorky and A. V. Lunacharsky, both old and distinguished members of the Communist Movement, were outstanding representatives.

Gorky, in opposing the efforts of Russian intellectualists to "find God" came out with the thesis: "Gods are not sought, they are created; life is not thought out, it is generated." According to Gorky, "God is a complex of ideas, produced by the tribe, the nation, by humanity, which awakens and organizes the social emotions, having for its purpose the binding of the individual to society and the control of his zoological individualism." Replying to a questionnaire of *Le Mercure de France* on the relation of Socialism to religion, Gorky stood by the belief that there is room for religion under Socialism: "The undeniable fact of progress must awaken in man a religious emotion, i.e. a complex creative feeling of faith in one's strength, hope in victory, love of life. . . . Socialism is an emulation of the past and the future in science and art . . . a feeling of relation to the past and to the future; this is religious emotion and it must grow." These remarks show no trace of a transcendental conception of God but they definitely advocate the development of religious values out of the emotional experiences of man.

A. Lunacharsky shared this position with Gorky and devoted himself to developing a Socialist religion. This "new religion," he says, "the religion of humanity, the religion of toil, has no guarantees, but I suppose that even without God and without guarantees, which are but masks of the same God, it remains a *religion*." This religion without a God, Lunacharsky defines as "such thinking about the world, such sensing of the world, as psychologically solves the contrast between the laws of life and the laws of nature." Lunacharsky keenly felt the contradictions between man's hopes and desires and the implacable laws of nature, with their inevitable suffering and death. Religion, he believed, could relate the ideas of life, born out of man's consciousness, to the hard facts of nature and make man fitter in the struggle for existence.

Lunacharsky explains his interest in religion by the leanings of his own character. From childhood on, he showed profound interest in the religious and artistic aspects of life. These interests ripened into a real life problem after his " glorious conversion to Marxism," as he characterized this experience of his youth. For ten years he studied the history and philosophy of religion and the results of his study he embodied in a two-volume work entitled *Socialism and Religion*.[1] His desire to create a new religion exposed him to severe criticism on the part of Lenin who could not share Gorky's and Lunacharsky's enthusiasms for religion and saw in it a dangerous deviation from the Marxian ideals of the Party. In a letter to Gorky (1913) he voiced his protest in most severe words:

" It is not true that God is a complex of ideals, awakening and organizing the social emotions. . . . God is (historically and in life) first of all a complex born of the dull suppression of man, due to surrounding nature and class oppression, it is an idea which affirms this suppression and which lulls the class struggle. . . . The idea of God always dulled and lulled the social emotions, replacing the vital with the deadening, it has always been an idea of slavery, the worst, inescapable slavery. Never has the idea of God bound the individual to society, it has always tied the oppressed classes to a faith in divine oppressors."

Lunacharsky tried to defend his position by explaining that not only the word " God " but such words as " ideal," " matter," and even " Socialism " have been discredited. He shares the opinion of Joseph Dietzgen that " words are pure on pure lips, and social democracy will only win through by saying— yes, I am a new, mighty religious force, I bear within me a religion which replaces all others and contains them in a higher degree."[2] This new religion is not a dream. " No," says he, " it is a hope, a hope which is better founded than any other religion." Lunacharsky felt that it is difficult to find a terminology to express religious values in a modern way. He suggested the term " Socialist culture " to replace the dis-

[1] First published in 1908. [2] *Ibid.*, p. 35.

credited word " religion," and this term he now generally uses. In his youth, however, the word " religion " awakened in him deep emotions : " Religion is enthusiasm and without enthusiasm people can create nothing great," [1] was his conclusion.

Lenin, who greatly disliked Lunacharsky's emotionalism, also thought that Lunacharsky exposed himself to abuse on the part of religious reactionaries, who might use his arguments not in the advancement of Socialism but in their own reactionary religious propaganda. In this he was, of course, right. Lunacharsky has been quoted more often in Russia by those who argued in favour of religion than any other Communist writer on the subject. For this reason, Lunacharsky now disavows his great work, *Socialism and Religion*, in spite of the fact that it is a very able exposition, from the modernist point of view, of this most important subject.

After the controversy with the " God-Builders " and the censure of their ideas by Lenin, there have been so far no other attempts on the part of Communists to re-valuate religion. This, however, does not mean that Communists have lost their ardour, their convictions, and their ethical principles, which outsiders have frequently characterized, psychologically speaking, as profound ethical religion. Some of its antagonists on the other hand consider it the very antithesis of Christianity. Thus Berdyaev, probably the ablest of the Russian counter-revolutionary philosophers, says : " Communism, both as a theory and as a practice, is not only a social phenomenon, but also a spiritual and religious phenomenon. And it is formidable precisely as a *religion*. It is as a religion that it opposes Christianity and aims at ousting it. . . . It takes possession of the whole soul and calls forth enthusiasm and self-sacrifice." [2] While the Communists object to calling their movement a religion, they do not deny their intentions of taking hold of the whole soul of man and wresting him from every religious influence.

[1] *Ibid.*, p. 228.
[2] Berdyaev, *The Russian Revolution*, English edition, pp. 59–60.

CHAPTER X

THE CONFLICT OF THE CHURCH WITH THE REVOLUTION

TOWARD the end of the last century, for the first time in Russia, enormous strikes occurred, beginning among the St. Petersburg textile workers and spreading rapidly to other industries and other cities. The Government was greatly alarmed at these events. The more far-sighted of the tzarist statesmen realized that a new era had commenced in the life of the toiling people of Russia. The chief of the Moscow secret police, Zubatov, sized up the situation in the following striking statement: " The working class is an aggregate of such power as revolutionists never before possessed as a weapon in their struggle. Neither in the Decembrist Movement, nor during the period of " going among the people," nor during the mass uprisings of students, were such forces available. Its magnitude is made still greater by the fact that the technique of the country is in their hands, and that the workers themselves are continually brought closer together by the very process of production. They root, at the bottom, in the peasant class, whose sons they are. On the top, due to the necessity of obtaining special knowledge, they come into contact with the intellectual strata of society. Stirred up by Socialist propaganda and agitation directed at destroying the existing political and social order, the working class becomes a serious threat to the existing order."

What was to be done to counteract the influence of the revolutionary agitators? Surely it was not enough to gaol them or exile them. Something more constructive was wanted. And here the Government thought of the Church with its enormous army of priests and monks who, they thought, could be of great service in diverting the minds of the workers from the influence of the revolutionists. Under the general direction of this same chief of the secret police, societies of mutual aid, and workers' associations for cultural and educational activities were started, similar to the welfare and social activities of the industrial Y.M.C.A.s in the United States. Priests possessing oratorical talent were sent to the factory districts. The line of agitation they carried through was to induce the unsophisticated workers to believe that the Tsar was their friend and supporter; that he would sustain them against the exploiting capitalists; that he possessed the power and that therefore the workers should be loyal to him and trust him.

During the years 1903-4 was produced a popular literature dealing with the social question, about 100,000 copies of which were freely distributed amongst the workers and their contents expounded. These pamphlets were written largely by the clergy and contained such titles as " Work and Property," " The Social-Economic Life and the Gospels," " To Rich and Poor," " The Supreme Power," " Christianity and Socialism," " The Wrong Way," " The Labour Problem," " The Future Social Order," and so on.

The line of thought throughout this literature was that: (1) Socialism is not synonymous with pure Christianity, as this is wrongly taught by the enemies of the Church; (2) Socialism is theoretically inconsistent and practically impossible; (3) The welfare of the workers may be attained without Socialism.

To appeal to the emotional life of the workers, a musical organization was set up with mass choruses organized of workers, and orchestras, with special performances.

One of the chief organizers and popular leaders of this anti-Socialist movement was the Priest Georgy Gapon who worked under the direction of the St. Petersburg Secret Police and who provoked the worker masses to march upon the palace of the Tsar. At the end of 1904 a strike broke out in the great Putilov Steel and Machine Works, which was joined by 150,000 workers. To avoid revolutionary outbreak Gapon proposed to present the grievances of the strikers to their much-advertised " friend " the Tsar, who would surely listen to them and help them.

Inspired by the agitations of this priest many thousands of the Putilov workers marched to the residence of the Tsar to present to him their petition. This was on Sunday, January 9, 1905. The workers carried sacred gonfalons, crosses, ikons, national flags, and portraits of the Tsar; they sang religious hymns and were convinced that the Tsar would hear them. Their petition began with these words:

" We, workers and inhabitants of St. Petersburg, our wives, children and our helpless old people, have come to you, our Lord, to seek truth and protection.

" We are impoverished, oppressed, burdened with unbearable toil, we are despised and not recognized as people, but are treated like slaves.

" We have suffered patiently but more and more we are thrust into the abyss of poverty, injustice and ignorance; we are strangled by despotism and arbitrariness, and we suffocate. We can bear it no longer, Lord, our patience has reached an end.

" We have reached that state when death is more welcome than continuing in these unbearable agonies."

Thereafter the petition states their immediate grievances in respect to hours of work, wages and conditions needing improvement, and is followed by a broader outlined programme of reforms, which they petition the Tsar to carry through and solve the nation's most urgent problems. The suggested measures of reform are listed under three headings. In its political aspect the programme asks for representative government, and then outlines

1. Measures against the poverty of the people;
2. Measures against the ignorance and lack of rights of the Russian people;
3. Measures against the oppression of Labour by Capital.

The petition concludes with the appeal:

"These O Lord, are the chief grievances with which we come to you; only in their satisfaction can our country be freed from slavery and poverty, and make progress. Only then will it be possible for the workers to organize themselves for the defence of their interests, from new exploitation by Capitalists and from the robbery and strangling of a bureaucratic government.

"Swear that you will order that they be carried out. In so doing you will make Russia happy and glorious and your name will impress itself upon our hearts and those of our progeny for ever; if you refuse we shall die here on the square before your palace. There is nowhere for us to go. There are but two ways, either to liberty and happiness, or to the grave. Order either of them, O Lord, we shall obey without murmur, even if it be the way to death. Let our lives be the sacrifice for our suffering Russia. We do not regret this sacrifice, we render it gladly."

The answer of the Tsar is well known. Thousands of dead and wounded were brought into sacrifice for Russia's dawning freedom and the myth of the benevolent Tsar was destroyed for ever in the hearts of the Russian people. How did the Church react to this hideous crime which it provoked through its own priests and agents? It did not voice one word of protest against the brutal massacre. It placed all the blame upon the workers and their revolutionary leaders and praised the Tsar for his firmness in maintaining the autocratic regime.

On January 16 the Holy Synod circulated a proclamation in which it censured the strikers and their daring to march to the palace of the Tsar. In this proclamation we read among other similar statements such words as these:

"In the capital and in other cities of Russia began strikes of workers and street riots. Russian orthodox people, from time immemorial stood for their faith, the Tsar and their fatherland, but now incited by evil-minded persons, enemies of their fatherland, at home and abroad, they have abandoned their peaceful occupation and decided as a mob and by force to obtain their rights, as if trampled down, causing much enmity and disturbance to peaceful inhabitants, leaving many without bread and leading others into useless death without repentance, with bitterness in their hearts and curses on their lips. . . .

"Our enemies wish to shake the foundation of our orthodox faith and autocratic power of the Tsars."

The proclamation exhorts to "fear God, honour the Tsar" (Peter i. 17) and "submit to every power ordained of God" (Rom. xiii. 1). . . . "To toil according to God's ordinance in the sweat of the brow," etc.

This proclamation was read in all the churches and widely circulated. It was followed by resolutions and telegrams on the part of assemblies of priests and bishops congratulating the Tsar on his firmness in resisting every attempt upon his autocratic sovereignity and assured him of the loyal support of the clergy.

In this spirit the Church continued to counteract the revolutionary activities of the masses and organized counter-revolutionary forces, known as the "Black Hundred," which were to crush the revolutionary movements by every possible means. Bishops published appeals to the faithful to resist the revolutionaries and to remain loyal to the Tsar and the existing social order. We shall quote from one of these written by Antoninus Krapovitzky, well known for his counter-revolutionary activities to this day; he writes:

"Brethren do not listen to those lunatics and liars who assure you that it is possible to have on earth a social order where there be no poor. . . . Sinful before God are the poor, who are full of covetousness and hatred against the rich, and murmurs against God. . . . We were sent to earth by God not for happiness. . . . Do not listen to those who have no faith in God, drive them from your homes that they may not corrupt your neighbours and children. . . .

"In their proclamations they have spread nothing but falsehood. God ordered to honour the Tsar (1 Peter ii. 17), but they incite the people against the Tsar. God ordered in the tenth Commandment not "to covet your neighbours' house, his village, his oxen and everything that is his "—but they incite the burning and robbing of the property of others. . . . Every printed sheet or book which is given you by a stranger of a suspicious spirit, show it to the priest and ask him whether what is written in it is good or evil." [1]

Many more such appeals one may find in the official press of the Church at that period, containing instructions as to how to organize the Churches to combat all revolutionary propaganda. Among other measures the Holy Synod decreed in 1908 the inclusion in the liturgy of the Church of the following prayer :

" God of power, Tsar of rulers, Lord over those who are masters ! In Thy hand is the heart of the Tsar, and power on earth. Thou placest the Tsars upon thrones and sayest of them : the Tsars rule through Me therefore do not touch those anointed by Me. Watch mercifully with Thine eye over our sorrowing country in which disorder and dissension have multiplied, threatened by intestine wars and resistance to our Tsar and to the power ordained by him."

These few examples of the methods of the Church to combat the revolution could be multiplied indefinitely. They leave no doubt where the leadership and the clergy of the Church stood in regard to the impending revolution in Russia, which was gaining in momentum from year to year.

The Orthodox Church at this time presented a very formidable force. According to the 1914 report of the Holy Synod there were on the territory of the former Russian Empire 57,173 churches and 23,593 chapels—with 112,629 priests and deacons —550 monasteries and 475 convents with 95,259 inmates. The property and wealth of the Church was enormous. It owned 7,000,000 desyatins [2] of land and many commercial enterprises and houses. Its annual income was estimated to be about 500 million roubles. At the time of the nationalisation of the banks its deposits were about 8 billion roubles.

This army of over 200,000 clerics, besides millions of armed forces, stood behind the tsarist regime and yet could not

[1] *Tserkovnye Vyedomosty*, No. 26, for 1905. [2] A desyatin equals 2.7 acres.

prevent its collapse. When in February, 1917, the Tsar abdicated the Church joined forces with the Kerensky regime to prevent the Bolsheviks from coming into power, and when this failed it fought them by every means, understanding very well that the triumph of Bolshevism meant death to the Church. In its official organ *Tserkovnye Vyedomosty* (No. 1, 1919), we read this frank statement:

" No class of society and no social group did prove so uncompromisingly and persistently an enemy of Bolshevism as the Church and its clergy."

This attitude the Church maintained even long after the White armies and the interventionists were defeated and the Bolsheviks had firmly established the Soviet Government. To the Communists, therefore, the Church in Russia, or what there is left of it, is still their most formidable enemy, which would seize every opportunity to overthrow the Soviet regime and turn the wheels of progress backward.

The record of the struggle of the Church against the Bolsheviks during the last fifteen years is a sad story, but it must be told, otherwise it will not be possible fully to understand the uncompromising enmity of Communism to organized religion.

THE 1917–18 COUNCIL OF THE CHURCH AND THE RE-ESTABLISHMENT OF THE PATRIACHATE

The mobilization of the forces of the Church to counteract the Revolution was begun at the Council (the so-called Sobor) of the Church which opened its sessions on August 16, 1917. It was preceded by an election of delegates from every part of the country consisting of 299 laymen and 270 clergymen, including the upper hierarchy of the Church. The classes represented among these delegates show where their sympathies lay in respect to the revolutionary events. There were 11 princes and counts, 10 generals and army officers, 132 former tsarist officials, 22 big landowners, 69 representatives of the bourgeois intellectuals, the rest being from the well-to-do peasants, manufacturers and the petty bourgeoisie. On the side of the clergy there were 10 metropolitans, 17 archbishops, 53 bishops, 15 archimandrites, 72 archpriests, etc.

In short the Council represented in a great majority laymen and clergy who by their social position could have no sympathy with the Revolution and considered it their task to counteract it with all the forces at their disposal.

The question which forcibly pressed itself upon the Sobor was " to be or not to be in politics." There was a group which favoured active participation in the elections and the formation of something like a clerical party. Others feared that this was a dangerous move to make and favoured remaining a non-partisan force.

When General Kornilov marched upon Moscow at the end of August, 1917, in order to establish a military dictatorship, he sent a message to the Sobor asking for its support. Many members of the Sobor welcomed his move and urged the Sobor to side with him. The question was debated in a closed and secret session. Only the prompt and inglorious failure of the coup prevented the Sobor from openly joining the General, and the incident was closed by a resolution of admonition to " unity and brotherly love " and a plea for mercy for the defeated usurpers.

One of the chief tasks of the Sobor was to devise a new form of Church government. The old Synod government had broken down completely, and even the most conservative elements of the Sobor did not desire its re-establishment. To remove the odious associations which were attached to the High Procurator of the Holy Synod, the Provisional Government abolished his office altogether and provisionally established a Ministry of Cult.

The debates on the question of the new Church government were naturally long and heated. There was one group, led by Archbishop Antonius (Khrapovitzky) of Kharkov, which stood for a strongly centralized government and was willing to vest much power in the office of the Patriarch, reducing the Synod to his advisory council. Another group was altogether against a Patriarchal Government and pointed out the danger of autocracy and centralization of power. This democratic opinion dominated the situation throughout October, but changed suddenly with the ascent of the Bolsheviks to power. It was an old tradition of the Church that when the throne was empty the Patriarch ruled interim.

Panic overcame the Sobor. They feared disbanding without accomplishing the purpose for which they had met. The debate for and against the Patriarchate had lasted for two weeks. Sixty speakers had expressed themselves on the question, and fifty more were registered to speak who were not heard. It was decided to terminate the discussion and proceed to elect a Patriarch. It was felt that the enemy was within the gates of the Church and that quick and drastic action was needed.

On November 17, 1917, the Sobor voted in favour of the resolution which should become the basis of the Constitution of the Church. This historic document in full is as follows : [1]

1. In the Orthodox Church of Russia the supreme power—legislative, administrative, judicial—belongs to the Territorial Sobor, which is called together periodically at definite dates and is constituted of bishops, clerics and laymen.

2. The Patriarchate is reconstituted and the administration of the Church is headed by the Patriarch.

3. The Patriarch is first among the bishops who are equal to him.

4. The Patriarch, jointly with the administrative organs of the Church, is responsible to the Sobor.

We see that this brief statement was definite as to the power vested in the Sobor, but it did not state the rights and responsibilities of the Patriarch except that he was to be *primus inter pares* among his colleagues in the episcopacy ; nor was any indication given as to the administrative organs of the Church. In the election the old custom was followed of choosing three candidates and then deciding by lot which of these three was to be Patriarch. The majority of the votes were given to Archbishop Antonius Khrapovitzky of Kharkov, who was the

[1] From the Sobor Definitions and Decisions Moscow, 1918.

main advocate of the patriarchal system of government of the Church, and who represented the right wing of the Sobor; next followed Archbishop Arsenius of Novgorod; and, as the third and apparently the least desirable candidate, Tikhon, then Metropolitan of Moscow. On November 8, while the city was still in panic over the fighting which went on for the possession of the Kremlin and the control of the city, the Sobor gathered at the Cathedral of the Saviour where the aged ninety-year-old monk Alexys drew the ballot which created Metropolitan Tikhon Patriarch of the Orthodox Church of Russia.

The election of Tikhon was a disappointment to the right wingers of the Sobor, particularly to the friends of Antonius Khrapovitzky, who had hoped to see him on the patriarchal throne. Not that Metropolitan Tikhon was a liberal; no one charged him with such heresy! It was thought, however, that he was not strong enough to cope with the situation, that the situation needed a ruthless fighter like Antonius. Tikhon was known as a kindly, not too aggressive, character, easily swayed by the men about him. The Sobor decided, therefore, to surround him with " strong " men by organizing a " Supreme Church Council " and a " Holy Synod," over which he was to preside and with whose aid he was to govern the Church.

Having thus organized itself, the Church felt confident of coping with the problems which the social revolution created. In spite of all difficulties, it expected to maintain its old privileges and hegemony in the nation. Anyway this was the hope of the old hierarchy created by the will of the Tsar, which by this time had the Sobor well under its control. By no means could it reconcile itself to the idea that, because of its former unholy alliance with the discredited Tsarist regime, it had lost the confidence of a large part of the population.

The old leadership of the Church was blind to the fact that the Church could not escape the logic of the social revolution, which authoritatively said: " Rights and privileges are granted for service to the people." This service the Church had yet to render and could do so only by reconstituting itself from the bottom up.

THE CONFLICT OF THE CHURCH WITH THE REVOLUTION

THE COUNTER-REVOLUTIONARY OFFENSIVE OF THE CHURCH

The re-establishment of the Patriarchate was a challenge to the Revolution; it showed the triumph of the right reactionary wing of the Sobor and the weakness, if not the absence, of a truly liberal trend in the Church. The Patriarchate was a challenge to revolutionary public opinion because it meant monarchy in the Church and would keep the monarchical idea before the people. The reactionaries, who by this time were in full control of the Sobor, hoped the Patriarchal throne would prepare the way for the re-establishment of the Tsarist throne. The Sobor could not read the signs of the time and had no faith in the triumph of the social revolution. The ascent to power of the Bolshevik Communist Party, which knew what it wanted and fearlessly carried out its revolutionary programme, intensified the counter-revolutionary aims of the Sobor which, blind to the actual situation, continued its work, totally misunderstanding the just claims of the workers.

There were two outstanding problems which the Revolution created in regard to the Church. First, there was the question of the separation of State and Church. Progressive public opinion demanded separation. The Church opposed it and presented a project which would free it from the unpleasant control by the State which it had experienced under the Tsarist regime and at the same time would safeguard all the privileges it enjoyed during that regime and even increase them. The Provisional Government favoured a gradual process of separation of State and Church, but left the issue to be decided by the Constitutional Assembly.

The other problem which called for immediate solution under pressure of public opinion was the separation of the school from the Church, to which the Sobor was uncompromisingly opposed. It must be remembered that education was not a natural function of the Russian Church, which never was a teaching Church. Rather it had opposed worldly learning, which it felt did not increase piety. In spite of its indifference and hostility to popular education, however, the Church could not, in the long run, prevent its spread. Modern life called for it. Russia could not maintain itself against the Western nations unless its people were educated. Thus the State undertook the organization of public schools which, in spite of all efforts on the part of the Church, were anti-clerical in spirit. To offset this and regain its authority among the masses, the Church, particularly after the 1905 Revolution, attempted to control public education by means of an extensive net of parochial schools. For this purpose it received abundant funds from the State. By 1917 there were 37,000 parochial schools for primary education, with buildings worth 170 million roubles. In addition the Church established many theological seminaries and several institutions of higher theological learning, the so-called Spiritual Academies.

The sudden coming into power of the Bolsheviks took the Sobor by surprise. Unwilling to give up the prerogatives of the Church without a fight, the Patriarch declared open war on the new revolutionary government and the new social order, and was determined to fight it out to the bitter end.

This was the meaning of the Patriarch's first message to the Church, issued on January 19, 1918. The document censures the excesses of the Revolution and the attacks against the Church. It threatens those who dare to harm the Church with hell fire and excommunication. We quote the salient statements of the message :

" That which you do is not only a cruel deed : it is verily a Satanic deed, for which you are condemned to hell fire in the future life and to awful curses by future generations in the present life.

" By the authority which is given us from God, we forbid you to approach the Sacraments of Christ, we anathematize you, if you still bear Christian names and even by your birth belong to the Orthodox Church.

" We also conjure all you faithful children of the Orthodox Church not to enter into any kind of association with these monsters of the human race; put away from yourselves that wicked person (I Cor. v. 13)."[1]

The message continues to enumerate the wickedness of "the monsters of the human race," the chief of which are: the secularization of marriage and the school, the nationalization of Church lands and buildings, the bombardment of the Kremlin churches during the taking of the city, and the desecration of the chapel of the Saviour in Petrograd. The appeal closes by entreating the faithful to support the Church by organizing sacred societies of defence. In demonstrating its spiritual strength it is " mindful that the gates of hell shall not prevail against it."

The message was enthusiastically received by the Sobor. One Sobor member hoped " that the first collision with the servants of Satan will serve as the beginning of saving the Nation and the Church from the enemy." Finally, he declared, " I would propose calling Bolshevism itself ' Satanism,' or ' Antichristianism.' "[2] The feelings of the Sobor were very frankly expressed in the speech of one of its influential members who said : " The only salvation of the Russian people is a wise orthodox Russian Tsar. Only through the election of an orthodox, wise, Russian Tsar is it possible to place Russia on the right historic track and establish good order. And as long as we have no wise orthodox Tsar there will be no order."[3] . . .

Such frank talking left no doubt on which side of the revolutionary struggle the Church had taken its stand. Both sides prepared for the battle, each side using the weapons which were at its disposal. The Church wielded its power of excommunication, not only against the members of the Government but against every Russian who in any way co-operated or rendered service to the revolutionary government. It organized mass demonstrations and appealed to the fanaticism of the ignorant masses. The Sobor appointed its special " general staff,"

[1] Quoted from the Acts of the Sobor, Book VI, p. 4.
[2] From the speech of the Priest I, V. Tzvetkoff, Acts of the Sobor, Book VI, p. 40.
[3] The Priest V.S. Vostokoff, *ibid.*, p. 43.

which was to work out an offensive-defensive plan and organize the forces of the Church for battle. Some generals and courtiers changed their military uniform and gilded dress suits for the cassock, and some became priests and even bishops.[1] The Sobor's " general staff " inspired every effort which was made for the overthrow of the new regime, and there were not a few priests and bishops who helped in the organization of the White armies. In the cities monster street demonstrations were set up and pilgrimages to the sacred shrines of the Church. The ringing of Church bells as alarm calls, special services and mass meetings, organization of brotherhoods for the " defence of the Faith" and every other mass propaganda measure was put into use to frighten off the revolutionary forces and compel the Bolsheviks to " come to Canossa." At first it looked as if the Church would get the better of the struggle and the revolutionary Government would have to abandon its plan of separating the Church from the State and nationalizing its property. It was this economic loss which fired the wrath of the Church and provoked its opposition. Occasional excesses and mob actions against unpopular monks and priests helped in an appeal for sympathy to the masses, but the cry of persecution concealed the real issue, which was economic and political, the diametrical differences in the religious and social philosophies adding zeal and idealism to the struggle.

THE COUNTER-OFFENSIVE OF THE REVOLUTIONISTS

A few days after the Patriarch's message of anathema, the Government replied with the publication of the famous decree " on freedom of conscience and religious societies "[2] (January 23, 1918), which broke the bonds of a thousand years of organic unity of the Russian State and the Orthodox Church and laid down a new basis for the existence of organized religion in the Soviet Republics.

[1] Thus Prince Oukhtomsky became Bishop Andrew of Ufa; Metropolitan Peter of Moscow, Patriarch Tikhon's chief adviser and temporary successor, was formerly secretary to the Grand Duchess Elizabeth, a sister of the late Tsarina.
[2] See Appendix II, A.

THE CONFLICT OF THE CHURCH WITH THE REVOLUTION

This law, if compared with the laws and practices of other countries where the Church is separated from the State, as in the United States and in France, is seen to have a number of new elements unique and revolutionary in character.

Like the United States it recognizes the equality before the law of all religious cults, with preference to none, and tolerates every form of religious custom and ceremony as long as it does not disturb the public peace and does not infringe upon the rights of other citizens. It is more thorough than the United States in its principle of secularizing the State, excluding from its functions every vestige of religious custom and practice. In that respect it is more similar to the practice of France. Its exclusion of religious teachings from every school, public and private, where secular subjects are taught, is a measure of secularizing education unparalleled in any other country.[1]

The real revolutionary significance of the law was, however, in its attitude towards the property of the Church. Here it must be noticed that in nationalizing the property of the Church, the State did not discriminate against it but treated it similarly to other institutions and private enterprizes, such as industrial corporations, banks, great land-holders and others whose properties were also nationalized.

In its practical sense it did not curtail the religious significance of the Church, since Church buildings used for worship were left to their congregations free of rent, and only revenue-producing property was taken from the Church for the benefit of the people. Those most affected were the monasteries, the upper hierarchy, and the central administrative apparatus of the Church which received its income from the revenues of these properties and from State subsidies.[2] Nationalization meant making the Church economically impotent and thus weakening its influence politically. Finally, the law not only

[1] In a later decree the admission to special schools of religion children under eighteen years of age was prohibited. An exception is made to Mohammedans, for whom the admission age is reduced to fourteen on the ground that they have to learn a different (Arabic) language to pursue their religious instructions.
[2] The Church received annually from the State a subsidy to the amount of 35,000,000 roubles.

stripped the Church of its wealth and State support, but it also made it impossible for the Church as a corporation to accumulate property. This is the meaning of the paragraph which deprived the Church of the rights of a juridic person.

In short, the revolutionary government proved itself as uncompromising towards the Church as it did towards the old economic and social order generally. To be consistent it could not do otherwise. It could not abolish private and corporation property generally and leave that of the Church untouched. Naturally, like every law, its application was left to expediency. Had the leadership of the Church recognized the justice and inevitability of the social revolution it could have adjusted its affairs much less painfully, by conferring with the Government and coming to an understanding. As matters stood, however, the gulf which divided the Church from the State was so wide that it could not be spanned by any bridge of compromise. Either one side or the other had to surrender its principles, and since neither side was willing to surrender the struggle continued.

After the publication of the Soviet decree separating Church and State, the Sobor expected drastic action on the part of the State in the application of the law. The Sobor General Staff issued orders and organized defence along two lines: non-co-operation with the civil authorities and mass agitation against the law. Wisely, however, the Government did not hurry with its programme of nationalization, except with regard to certain monasteries and particularly the monastic lands, which were appropriated eagerly by the local peasantry. The monks had little chance of finding sympathy and support on the part of the peasants in defending the property of the monasteries.[1]

The Churches, as such, did not feel any particular effect of the law upon their practices of worship. The property used for the purposes of the cult was at that time left to the congregations free of any charge, and all that the State demanded was that the congregations should organize themselves and select

[1] By 1920 the peasants had received 827,540 desyatins (a desyatin equals 2.7 acres) of monastic lands from 673 monasteries and convents.

a responsible body as trustees of the buildings so utilized. Against such arrangements nothing could be argued; therefore it was not easy to move the masses into action against something they did not feel as persecution of their religion. The fact that the central Church apparatus, the schools and publishing houses of the Church, were either closed or closing through lack of the financial support they formerly received from the State, was difficult to bring to the attention of the masses, who had no contact with these institutions and were not educated to appreciate their importance.

For a while there was a considerable stir regarding the discontinuance of religious instruction in the public schools, and efforts were made to continue it in spite of the decree. But here, too, the clergy was the first to lose its ardour when neither the State nor the Church had any funds to pay them for their work. Few priests had the will or the power to give their services as teachers without pay.

Then life itself demanded co-operation. No boycott of the Government could last without creating suffering among the populace. Moreover there were not a few clergymen who had suffered from the former princes of the Church. They were not so loyal to the Patriarchal regime as was desired. Frequent desertions and laxity of discipline threatened to weaken and undermine the resistance of the Church to the State. In April, 1918, but a few months after the decree of separation, the Sobor found it necessary to adopt repressive measures against "certain bishops, clerics, monks, and laymen who do not submit to, but rather resist, the authority of the Church, and turn hostile to the Church, in the relations of the Church to the civil authorities, thus bringing much trouble upon the Church, its servants, its members, and its possessions."[1] The resolution condemns them as "enemies of God" and threatens excommunication.

These rigid measures which the Sobor adopted show in themselves the difficulty which the rank and file of the clergy experienced in maintaining the uncompromising attitude of

[1] Resolution of the Sobor of April 19, 1918.

the Patriarch and the Sobor towards the laws of the State. Slowly the resistance of the Church began to waver.

The Soviet Government found rather unexpected support from exposing the frauds of which the Church was guilty in falsifying relics of " incorruptible saints." As previously described, the large monasteries of Russia, in order to attract pilgrims, sought to acquire some wonder-working relics, particularly in the form of the " incorruptible body " of a local saint, the idea prevailing that the body of a real saint should not see corruption. This idea had probably been developed among the cave-dwelling hermits in the Kiev-Pechora Monastery, where climatic and other conditions favoured the mummification of some of these self-immured fanatics. Other monasteries, who felt that their hermits were no less saintly than those of Kiev, sought for them the same popularity and went so far as substituting effigies made of wax and other materials for the bodies, leaving them in precious silver sarcophagi.

The frauds became known when an inventory was taken of the Alexander-Svirsky Monastery in the province of Olonetsk in October, 1918. It was discovered that the silver sarcophagus of Saint Alexander Svirsky contained, instead of an " incorruptible body," a wax effigy of the saint. The exposure caused indignation amongst large sections of the population, which demanded that all " incorruptible saints " be examined and the findings be published. The greatest scandal, however, was the exposure of the fraudulent relics of Tikhon Zadonsky and of Saint Sergius, whose shrine was one of the most popular pilgrimage places in Russia. The monastery of Sergievo, now a museum, was one of the richest in the country.

The revolutionary Government, of course, used these exposures to weaken the moral authority of the Church, not without success. The leaders of the Church and the Patriarch felt their defeat. Faint attempts were made to negotiate with the Government and to persuade a change of attitude towards the Church, but apparently these efforts were belated and no results were obtained. The last session of the Sobor, which reconvened on June 15, 1918, made no change in the situation. It prepared resolutions to rouse the sympathy of the masses in favour of the Church and resist the decree of separation, but its hopes of success were apparently on the wane. No longer trusting in themselves, they hoped more for the victory of allied intervention and the defeat of the Soviet Government in the civil war which was waged most intensively during the years 1919 and 1920.

THE CHURCH AND THE FAMINE OF 1921

The failure of the crops in 1921 and the approaching famine put the Soviet Government once more to a severe test of its vitality and again its enemies hoped for its fall. The Church shared these hopes, and the Patriarch listened to those advisers who wished to make political capital out of the national calamity.

As the horrors of the famine increased, certain priests and laymen began to agitate in the press for the realization of the many valuables used for decorative purposes in the churches. Soon the idea was taken up by the press throughout the country, and progressive public opinion favoured the idea of using the nationalized wealth of the churches in the help of the starving. This moved the Patriarch, and about the middle of February, in his message to the Church, he suggested that unnecessary objects such as trinkets, jewelry, and broken objects of gold and silver, which might be found in the churches, be given to the famine fund, with the consent of the congregation. This seemed to be the maximum that the Patriarch was willing to do and it did not promise large results. Then the Government took things into its own hands. By the end of February, at the session of the All-Russian Central Executive Committee, a law was passed stating : [1]

" In view of the pressing need of mobilizing all resources of the nation which might serve as means in the struggle with the famine in the Volga region and for seed for the fields, the V.C.I.K. (All-Russian Central Executive Committee), in

[1] Published in N46, *Izvestia*, February 26, 1922.

addition to its decree concerning the use of objects from museums, resolves :

> To instruct the local Soviets, within one month's time from the day of publication of the decree, to remove from Church property, given for use to various groups of believers of all religions, according to inventories and contracts, all precious articles of gold, silver and precious stones, the removal of which does not essentially infringe upon the interests of the cult, and surrender these to agents of the Commissariat of Finance, specially designating them for the fund of the central committee for famine aid."

The law further required that the removal of valuables from the churches should take place in the presence of representatives of believers to whose care the property had been intrusted, and that these valuables should be used exclusively for the famine fund and publicly accounted for.

To this law Patriarch Tikhon replied with a message to the Church (February 28) strikingly different in tenor from his previous declarations, which had been sympathetic to the idea of aiding the starving with the surplus wealth of the Church. The Patriarch branded the law as sacrilegious and non-canonical, and called upon the faithful to resist its realization with every available means. The agitation which began was carried on in much the same spirit as the previous agitation against the 1918 decree separating Church and State, but with the difference that the issue was now of an entirely humanitarian nature, thus giving the Soviet Government a moral backing which it did not have in 1918.

To argue the question on the basis of Church canons and State laws in a country just emerging from a state of war and revolution and struggling for the very life of starving millions, was a futile task. Even legally, religious groups could not refuse to return to the State that which they had received for use only and for which they had signed contracts to that effect.

Certainly the resistance of the Patriarch could not be justified from the humanitarian, not to speak of the Christian, point of view. Hence his policy was doomed to failure. The Government did not refrain from carrying out the decree, and crushed every resistance on the part of the leaders of the Church. The committees which were entrusted with the task of appropriating the valuables were instructed to use the greatest care in selecting the articles to be taken. No object should be removed which was needed for the cult, so that none could complain that his religious practices had been interfered with. The amount of surplus wealth taken from the churches was enormous,[1] and yet so much remains that the loss is hardly noticeable to the visitor.

The conflict which developed between the Church and the Government, because of the Patriarch's resistance, claimed not a few victims. There were riots with some bloodshed, followed by repressive measures on the part of the State. In Leningrad, for instance, many priests and laymen were tried and ten of them sentenced to death, among them the aged Metropolitan Benjamin. In Moscow, also, a number of priests and laymen were tried, of whom ten were executed and many imprisoned. In all were reported forty-five executions and two hundred and fifty long-term imprisonments. The Church throughout the country was in a state of anarchy. Large sections of it, particularly in the famine area, resented the Patriarch's stand. Priests and even bishops, who otherwise were loyal to the hierarchy, felt greatly distressed, and a few of the stout-hearted even dared openly to criticize the Patriarch's position. In Leningrad a group of liberal clergymen, under the leadership, amongst others, of the priests Vedensky and Belkoff, finally took the initiative. When it became known that the Patriarch was under house arrest and that many in Moscow had been condemned to death for their resistance to the State in turning over the valuables of the Church to the famine fund, they came to Moscow, where they were joined by the Priest Krasnitzky and Bishop Antonine. On May 12, the day before the

[1] The published reports state that the amount of gold taken was 442 kg.; silver, 336,227 kg.; other precious metals, 1,345 kg.; 33,456 diamonds weighing 13.13 carats; pearls, 4,414 gr.; other precious stones, 72,383 pieces weighing 28,140 gr.; 20,598 roubles in coins.

execution of the Moscow priests, they appeared before the Patriarch and remonstrated with him that he was chiefly responsible for the terror and anarchy in the Church and that with his name was associated the whole counter-revolutionary policy of the Church of recent years. They forced the retirement of the Patriarch and appealed to the Church to make peace with the new social order.

This appeal of influential clergymen of the Church, standing out for peace and co-operation with the State, and condemning unreservedly the old policy of the Church toward the Soviet State, marks the turning point in the warfare of the Church against the Revolution and the Soviet Government. For five years the Church had stood out solidly against the revolutionary State and the new social order, resisting it by every possible means and aiding its enemies. It proved to be the most powerful enemy of the Revolution and was the last to yield. But once its front was broken its surrender was inevitable. Those Church insurgents who finally refused to follow their hierarchial leaders, thus bringing about the capitulation of the Church before the Revolution, naturally became the objects of a most bitter hatred on the part of the defeated ecclesiastical leaders, considering them traitors and Bolsheviks, and branding them as " red " priests.

THE LIVING CHURCH MOVEMENT

The appeal of the progressive clergy against the policy of the Patriarch found ready response among the clergy, particularly the village clergy who for centuries had suffered from the heavy hand of those ecclesiastical feudal lords, the bishops. A veritable revolt took place throughout the Church. The clergy, who never before had had the right to organize and participate in the central administrative affairs of the Church, now began to organize. The initiators of the revolt were those progressive priests who now held the chief administrative centre of the Church which the Patriarch had allowed to slip out of his hands. This group was determined to use its power to carry out certain reforms. It took for its slogan the words a " Living Church," and began to publish under this name a periodical which was to carry its appeal to the masses. It organized itself into a union of white priests, also called the " Living Church," whose chief leader became the Leningrad priest, Vladimir Krasnitzky. Its first constitution, accepted on July 11, 1922, in Moscow, states as its purpose: " to guarantee to the orthodox parish clergy liberty in carrying on their pastoral duties and to free them from dependence upon the economic ruling elements of society."

At this stage the " Living Church " organization was not much more than a clerical trade union striving for the improvement of its rights as clergymen and for economic welfare. Its enemy it saw in the monastic episcopal order, and it called for the right of the white or married clergy to be eligible to the episcopate. If we remember the centuries-long subjection of the white clergy to their monastic overlords and the suppressed bitterness which existed among them against these black princes of the Church, this revolt is not difficult to understand. Then there was the fact that the majority of the bishops were giving sympathetic support to every counter-revolutionary move, whether undertaken by the Patriarch or the White armies or foreign interventionists, the consequences of which fell heavily on the rank and file of the parish clergy and added zeal to their desire to become independent of their ecclesiastical tyrants.

The " Living Church " group feared a reaction. It knew that the old monks and bishops would not surrender their privileges without a struggle, and signs of its coming were at hand. Metropolitan Benjamin of Petrograd excommunicated the leaders of the progressive clergy, among them the priests, Vedensky and Krasnitzky. Demonstrations against them were organized by the Conservatives, and they were branded as traitors and Bolsheviks. Fortunately there were among the old bishops a few who were sympathetic to the appeal of the " Living Church," and these agreed to create a new hierarchy of white, i.e. married, bishops, even before the meeting of the Sobor. On June 11, 1922, the Archbishops Leonid and Antonine ordained the first " white " bishops, the Moscow priest,

John Chancev, and the Petrograd priest, John Albinsky, and thus was broken the system of the " black " episcopate which had existed in Russia for over a thousand years. Soon other " white " bishops were ordained, and the progressives felt that they now could commence a " cleansing " from the Church of the reactionary episcopate and replace them by more trustworthy leaders. Scores of bishops were retired, so that on the occasion of the first conference of the " Living Church," in August, 1922, it was reported that of ninety-seven diocesan bishops, thirty-seven had accepted the " Living Church " platform, thirty-six were opposed to it, and twenty-four were undecided. Then and there it was decided to retire those who opposed the " Living Church " reforms and call upon the undecided to make their choice.

This first conference of the progressive orthodox clergy, which met in Moscow on August 6, 1922, was undoubtedly an event of great historical importance. Never before in the thousand year history of the Russian Orthodox Church had such a conference been called. There were present one hundred and fifty priest delegates from every part of the great Soviet Republic. Most of them had never seen each other and had never corresponded with each other, yet their common grievances and their common hopes gave them a sufficient tie of solidarity to commence far-reaching reforms in the administration of the Church.

The Sobor of 1923 confirmed the ecclesiastical and administrative reforms of the " Living Church." It also may be characterized as a peace conference of the Church with the revolutionary State. One may even say that it was a Versailles of the Church, where the victorious Revolution was dictating the terms upon which the Church was to be tolerated and permitted to continue its existence. The principal condition was that the Church abandon the monarchical system of government and become republican in form. A second condition was that the Church sever its contact with the counter-revolution and dismiss every prelate who was politically incriminated. With the dogmatic or religious interests of the Church the

State did not meddle, but upon these political aspects it was uncompromising.

The Sobor willingly accepted these terms and even went further. It assured the Government of its undivided sympathy and loyalty, declared capitalism a deadly sin, and pronounced the social revolution just. In this way it annulled the anathemas of the previous Sobor and recognized the decrees of separation of Church and State, of nationalization of Church property, and even those limitations on the rights of citizenship which were imposed upon the clergy and the Church as a punishment for counter-revolutionary activities.

The Sobor session of May 3 was planned to put into canonical law the state of peace between the Church and the revolutionary Government and open a new era in the history of the Church.

The resolutions of the Sobor condemned Patriarch Tikhon as " an apostate from the true commandments of Christ and a traitor to the Church." On the basis of the canons of the Church it declared him deprived of his office and of his monastic state and returned to his original state of layman.

With the passing of the resolution the leaders of the Sobor thought that they had cut off the Church from its inglorious past, and had opened the way for a brighter future.

This was not the case. The Patriarch, being informed of his removal, circumvented the decisions of the Sobor. To regain his freedom he paid the price of a most humiliating confession,[1] and when at liberty split the Church, thus still

---

[1] The confession says :

" In presenting this statement to the Supreme Court of the R.S.F.S.R., I consider it to be the duty of my pastoral conscience to state the following :

" Having been brought up in a monarchist society and having been until my arrest under the influence of anti-Soviet persons, I actually was hostile towards the Soviet power. This hostility at times passed from a passive state into active functions, such as the appeal regarding the peace at Brest in 1918, the anathematizing of the Government in the same year, and finally the appeal against the decree of appropriating the Church valuables in 1922. All my anti-Soviet actions, with the exception of a few minor errors, are summed up in the statement of accusation of the Supreme Court. Recognizing as correct the decision of the court to hold me responsible for anti-Soviet activity, according to the statutes of the Criminal Code indicated in the summary of accusation, I repent of these my trans-

further weakening its position before the State. After his death in 1925, the controversy between the various factions in the Church subsided. Under force of circumstances practically all the bishops and priests submitted to the regulations of the State and now they do their best to fit into the new social order. The introduction of the six-day week in the cities and the cancelling of the great Church feasts as legal holidays, together with the closing of about half of the churches throughout the Soviet Union, leaves the Church now rather unnoticed.

In 1929, when the persistent agitation of militant anti-religious propaganda had greatly weakened the Church, the Government by new legislation [1] still further weakened its position. The new law prohibits every social activity of the Church and in changing the former constitutional provision, permitting religious propaganda, it now tolerates only religious worship[2]; such are the results of the defeat of the Church in its struggle with the Revolution. Whatever influence the Church may still possess depends entirely on the service it is able to render the people and upon the personal merits of each individual priest and bishop. In its struggle with the Revolution the Church was completely defeated and now suffers the inevitable consequences.

gressions against the State order and ask the Supreme Court to end my isolation, i.e. to free me from arrest.

" Simultaneously I declare to the Supreme Court that I am from now on no enemy of the Soviet power. Permanently and definitely I reject the foreign as well as the inner monarchical white guard counter-revolution.

(Signed)   PATRIARCH TIKHON

June 16, 1923.   (Vassily Belavin)."

After the liberation of the Patriarch the author interviewed him to find out what was behind this " confession." To the question as to whether he had been coerced by agents of the Government to make the confession (this theory of coercion was much in circulation in Russia and abroad), he replied that he had not been coerced in anything and that in writing his confession he was following the dictates of his conscience. However, he added, suggestions were made to him of the advisability of this move to regain his liberty.

[1] See Appendix II, B and C.

[2] This decree handicaps chiefly the Nonconformist sects. The Orthodox Church rather welcomed it as a protection against the propaganda of the Evangelicals.

CHAPTER XI
THE ANTI-RELIGIOUS MOVEMENT

ANTI-RELIGIOUS propaganda in the Soviet Union commenced long before it received its present organized form in the Union of Militant Atheists. During the first years of the Revolution it was carried on by a few groups of convinced atheists who challenged religious propagandists to debate questions on the Church and the Revolution, Science and Religion, and so on. There were published also a number of books and pamphlets attacking religion, and the Department of Justice produced a magazine, *Revolution and the Church*, in which the State voiced its opinion on the Church and fought for the realization of the laws of its separation from the State, exposed fraud in the Church in the relics of saints, and the like.

Gradually voluntary societies for atheist propaganda were springing up in various parts of the country, but these were neither united by a common programme nor by organization. These early propagandists were zealous revolutionaries fighting for atheism as religious reformers would have fought against the abuses of the established Church. The first efforts at creating a mass organization for atheist propaganda was undertaken with the publication of the weekly paper the *Bezbozhnik* (The Godless), which began to appear towards the end of 1922 and was soon supplemented by an illustrated monthly, *The Godless at the Bench* (*Bezbozhnik oo Stanka*.) This effort to organize on a large scale an atheist movement found ready support from the large Party newspapers, such as the *Pravda*, and by 1924 a society was formed known as the *Friends of the Newspaper Bezbozhnik*. These *Friends* spread the paper *Bezbozhnik* and served as its correspondents. Locally, they also carried on propaganda against the Church and against religion generally.

In the spring of 1925 the *Friends* organized a conference in Moscow in which various projects of a wider organization were discussed and particularly the problem of aims and tactics. It appeared that in the atheist movement two separate trends in aims and methods of propaganda were developing. There were those who emphasized anti-clerical agitation, exposing the hostile class functions of the Church and ignoring questions of religious philosophy and culture; the others chiefly favoured cultural enlightenment, stressing science and the materialist philosophy of life. These two trends persist generally to this day, although it has been recognized by the conference and the Party that both aspects are of importance. In 1926 the Party adopted and published the theses on the basis of which anti-religious propaganda was to be carried on. These theses [1] present in very terse, distinct form the basic conditions of a correct approach and method of anti-religious propaganda. They deal with: (1) a correct understanding of the nature of religion; (2) a correct evaluation of the objective rôle and the subjective aspect of religion; (3) a correct grasp of conditions under which anti-religious propaganda is developed, relating it to the political and economic problems of the given period.

They censure the ignoring of the subjective subtleties of religion, the vulgarization and simplification of anti-religious propaganda, and they draw the striking conclusion that the drift from Religion is not due so much to the " enlightenment " of the masses as to the growing participation of the masses in Socialist construction, and that it is *Socialism* alone which will make an end to Religion and not atheist propaganda, and that the latter can only accelerate the process if the social-economic conditions are ripe for it.

These theses by their clearness and frankness are the most authoritative pronouncements of the Party and their basic principles are still accepted by Communist anti-religious workers as the platform of their movement.

On the basis of these principles the " Union of the Godless "

[1] For the full text of these theses see Appendix I, B.

developed its activities and in the years following spread its organization throughout the whole country. During this period public discussions upon religious questions were very popular and did as much to arouse and deepen the religious as the anti-religious interests. The religious forces in some places were even getting the better of the atheists; this was due to lack of experienced students of the problem in the anti-religious ranks and to the sentiment of the public which, under the revival of the N.E.P., was losing faith the in Socialist ideals. Since 1927, therefore, the " Union of the Godless " has changed its tactics and has devoted its efforts to more systematic education and training of the various organized groups in Soviet society: in the Red Army, in the Trade Unions, in Teachers' Associations, in schools, in young people's societies, in village reading-rooms and clubs.

At this period were organized the first anti-religious museums and exhibits, anti-religious " wall newspapers," films, plays and radio talks. To silence the religious forces as much as possible the anti-religious faction succeeded in 1929 in passing an amendment to the constitution, prohibiting religious and permitting only anti-religious propaganda. The advocates of the amendment justified these measures by the fact that religious propaganda was very often used as anti-Soviet propaganda. Coincidently a forcible drive was started to close the churches and 1929, on the whole, was the hardest year for organized religion. Many congregations could not withstand the pressure and liquidated their churches or united with other congregations in order to reduce expenses and escape the high taxes imposed on the churches.

This drive of 1929 coincided with the inauguration of the Five-Year-Plan of industrialization and agricultural collectivization and diverted the interests and enthusiasm of the population towards creative work, with a natural decline of interest in both religious and anti-religious propaganda. The introduction of the continuous week and the cancellation of all the Church holidays still more obliterated Religion in the life of the large cities and industrial centres. Church bells were heard no more, factory whistles and the noise of the street traffic drowned the last vestiges of the once-solemn tones of the Sunday and the religious holiday in Russia. This, it must be added, is limited to the cities; in rural communities the Sunday is still officially recognized as the day of rest.

In June, 1929, an All-Union Conference of Anti-Religious Societies was held. It renamed its organization *The Union of Militant Atheists*, and laid its plans of active participation in the realization of the Five-Year Plan. The atheist mass organization was to be henceforth the vanguard of constructive effort, fighting under the general direction of the Communist Party for the industrialization of the country and for the victory of Socialism in the villages. The local atheist associations were spurred on to organize collective farms, assist in the purchase of agricultural machinery and tractors and, by example of their life and work, attract others to abandon their religious superstitions.

The Central Council of the Union launched campaigns to collect a fund for the defence of the country, at which expense were built a battleplane, a tank and a submarine—all named *Bezbozhnik*.

Naturally such activities differed in no way from the work of many other Soviet social organizations and the atheist movement was rapidly losing its specific character and purpose as the advocate of a new atheist philosophy of life. This its leaders begin to realize and efforts are being made to revive the work of the Union and fit it for the present task of the Second Five-Year Plan aiming at the complete establishment of Socialism and the liquidation of class society.

NUMERICAL STRENGTH OF THE UNION

The official statistical data of the Union of Militant Atheists shows a mushroom growth since its organization in 1926. This is clearly seen from the following:

Years.	Number of local groups ("cells").	Number of members.	Growth per cent. in comparison to 1926.	
			Groups ("cells").	Members.
1926	2,421	87,033	100,0	100,0
1927	3,121	138,402	130,0	160,0
1929	8,928	465,498	370,0	535,0
1930	35,000	2,000,000	Increase 14 times	Increase 23 times
On 1.1.31	50,000	3,500,000	,, 20 ,,	,, 40 ,,
On 1.5.31	abt. 60,000	5,000,000	,, 25 ,,	,, 57 ,,
In 1932	65,000	5,500,000	,, 27 ,,	,, 69 ,,

In addition there are two million members in its junior organization, for children below the age of 14, about 48 per cent. girls and 52 per cent. boys. In the adult organization the percentage is about 30 per cent. for women and 70 per cent. for men.

The age grouping is seen from the following table:

14 to 22 yrs. of age . . . 45 per cent.
23 to 45 yrs. of age . . . 45 ,,
Over 46 yrs. of age . . . 10 ,,

According to occupation in the industrial districts about 50 per cent. are workers, about 30 per cent. students and the remaining 20 per cent. employees.

The number of non-party members is about 60 per cent. As to race and language there are about 100 different racial and language groups in the organization.

If we turn now to the qualitative analyses of this huge army of professed atheists, we find that only a very small percentage is actively engaged in any of the activities of the organization; not more than 10 per cent. at the most. The rest is satisfied simply in paying their annual dues, which are very small, about 5-10 cents. Nevertheless the huge membership does show that many millions, chiefly young people, have grown indifferent to religion and light-heartedly declare themselves atheist, which seems to them the proper and respectable thing to do. One may safely say, however, that the numbers who have become indifferent to religion are many times greater than actually recorded. At least half the population is already unchurched and more or less indifferent to the old religious taboos and traditions. This does not mean, as yet, that they are convinced atheists. They may become such, but they may also join some sect or, after a while, return to the old Church, which depends on their subjective experience and the opportunity to hear a message which may meet their conscious needs.

THE ATHEIST YOUTH MOVEMENT

The leaders of the atheist movement understand very well that the future of their movement depends largely on the proper training of the young. The Church is deprived by law [1] of the systematic teaching of children under 18 in Religion, and while religious instruction in the home is not prohibited, few parents avail themselves of this opportunity, nor is there a suitable literature for the purpose. True enough, attendance of Church services by the young is not prohibited and many children are seen there. Nevertheless the fact remains that in the Soviet Union there is no systematic religious instruction of children.

Some educators, sympathetic to the atheist movement, agitate for the introduction of systematic anti-religion training in the public schools. From the outset the Soviet educational system declared itself for a *non-religious* school. This means that the curriculum simply ignored religion as a subject, but it was expected that the teachers of the natural sciences, of history and of literature, would point out the anti-religious implications of their subject material. For example, in studying the origin of man, the teacher was to instruct that man was not created by God, as taught by the Church, but evolved from a lower

[1] See Appendix II, A.

animal species; a similar stand being taken with relation to all other natural phenomena. Into the study of history also might be introduced references to the evils of clericalism and the " holy inquisition." And so on. In 1927 atheist enthusiasts commenced an agitation against the non-religious school and demanded a definitely *anti*-religious school. The Commissariat of Education finally yielded, but in practice things remained very much as before. This at least is the general complaint of atheist enthusiasts—that the school does next to nothing to promote their cause.

The reasons for this neutrality are several. First of all, there exists the conviction among the Soviet educators that systematic instruction in " anti-religion " is too negative a subject to be appreciated by children. Further, the great majority of teachers have little sympathy in such teaching and above all are not trained for this work. Finally the curriculum of the schools is so full already with the study of the natural and social sciences, mathematics and languages and polytechnical training, that the introduction, it is felt, of a subject like " anti-religion " does not fit into the educational programme. The position of the school authorities is therefore that anti-religious propaganda should be carried on by implication as described above, and more systematically studied by voluntary societies, the so-called " cells of youthful atheists," a junior organization of the Union of Militant Atheists.

These " cells " normally exist in all schools but their work is not systematic and rarely enthusiastic. The reason for this apathy is again the lack of a trained leadership. The overworked teachers, even those who are members of the Party, show little enthusiasm for and understanding of this activity. Most of it is reduced to presenting two anti-religious programmes a year, at Christmas and at Easter, in which the children learn poems and produce a sketch or a play on an anti-religious tenet.

Further, there is the general feeling among many, even responsible Communist leaders, that religion is generally forgotten or in a lingering condition, and no longer dangerous to the young generation actively engaged in the constructive programme of the Party. In its leisure time youth prefers sport, or some scientific and artistic hobby. Questions of religion are generally forgotten and are not in evidence; to say, however, that they do not exist would not be true to the facts. If not life then death reminds them from time to time of the eternal question of the hereafter. Then there still exist Church and family traditions with their birth and name days, solemn Church services during the great annual feast days and the like events, all of which have a peculiar attraction and are witnessed by the crowds of people finding their way into the churches in spite of propaganda against it and even occasional disciplinary measures on the part of the various organizations.

The years 1927-28 were the most active on the anti-religious front, also in the schools. The junior sector of the Union of Militant Atheists has now about two million members and its own monthly periodical. The children are encouraged to organize campaigns against many evils and superstitions still prevalent in rural communities. Drunkenness on the great Church holidays is one of the worst evils and disgraces of the Church. The struggle against drink is naturally associated with the struggle against the Church and its feast days which, at times in the summer, become a real menace to the security of the harvest. The children agitate against these drunken feast days, and are the pioneers of temperance in the life of the village.

The Communist Youth Movement has grown to a membership of about three million. These young people, it is taken for granted, are all atheist, and as such should be actively engaged in anti-religious activity. As a matter of fact only 4 per cent. are members of the Union of Militant Atheists, and it is the general complaint of atheist agitators that the Communist Youth Movement has alienated itself from the anti-religious propaganda. The reason for this apathy to religion lies in the fact that the youth movement has been entirely absorbed by the constructive programme of the Five-Year Plan, and its interest in questions of religion and philosophy has waned correspondingly.

Efforts are now on foot to revive these interests in the Youth Movement and if a programme of vital interest should be presented the young people will respond. The more thoughtful are beginning to ask the eternal questions of " whence " and " whither," and have not received satisfactory answers. The old anti-clerical agitation does not appeal to them any more, they desire something more constructive and interesting, and in this respect the anti-religious movement has so far failed to meet the demand.

ATHEISM IN THE RED ARMY

The Red Army in the U.S.S.R. has become an active centre for disseminating atheism. The recruits are systematically trained in the Communist doctrines of atheism and at least 75 per cent. of them declare themselves against religion before they are dismissed from the army.

The Red Army was, from its very beginning, militantly anti-religious. During the civil war it fought an enemy which was in close alliance with the Church and which claimed that all the heavenly powers were on its side. These White armies carried crosses and ikons into battle against the Reds and had " Regiments of Jesus " and of the " Holy Virgin," organized by the clergy. In defeating these " holy " regiments of counter-revolutionists, the " Red Army " established an anti-religious tradition which is unique and is considered to add to its fighting quality.

After the civil war, in the years 1922–23, the educational programme of the Red Army training camps included frequent debates with the clergy on religious questions, which later developed into more regular courses carried on in special study circles. These courses more or less followed the line which the general Communist programme provides, emphasising the class nature of religion, the counter-revolutionary function of the Church and the anti-scientific position of orthodox theology with regard to the origins of the world, of man, etc.

With the inauguration of the Five-Year Plan, the Red Army undertook to train its best men for leadership, particularly for the collective farm movement and the cultural needs of the village community. Between the years 1928–30, 200,000 obtained their training in special subjects to fit them for the new tasks in the collective farms, the co-operatives, for cultural work, and as village Soviets functioning among them. 10,000 graduated as agitators in anti-religious propaganda and they spread throughout the country carrying with them a destructive message against the old gods.

The anti-religious training in the army pays special attention also to the sectarian pacifists who serve their term in divisions without arms. Efforts are made to convert the sectarians to atheism and persuade them to abandon their pacifism. These efforts are not without success, although it is not definitely known what percentage of the sectarians abandon their religious convictions.

ATHEISM AMONG THE MINOR NATIONALITIES

The Union of Soviet Republics is a huge international in which live about 200 different racial and linguistic groups. Some of these people, like the Ukrainians and the Tartars, number many millions, but there are others, particularly among the mountain races of the Caucasus, which do not exceed a few thousand persons. The Caucasus, lying between Asia Minor and Europe, was from time immemorial the refuge place of many races. Here scores of little remnants of defeated and pursued people hid themselves from their enemies and were able to survive, living in the narrow mountain valleys.

Most of the smaller and culturally backward racial and linguistic groups had no written language. The Soviet Government has undertaken to supply these, and during the last decade 32 new alphabets were devised to fit the demands of these languages; literature is produced in about 80 different languages. Over 70 of these nationalities have already a printing press into which anti-religious propaganda has been early incorporated. An important step forward has been the

Latinization of a number of the Turk languages which had their script in the difficult Arabic The native literature was almost exclusively of a religious nature. The introduction of the simple Latin script has radically changed the situation and now the anti-religious literature has the right of way. At present atheist papers in 14 different languages and anti-religious textbooks in 22 languages are published in the U.S.S.R.[1]

Work in the minor nationalities in the Soviet Union is considered highly important, for many of these racial groups are still exceedingly backward and their economic and cultural development is retarded by the tenacious hold of many pagan superstitions and taboos. In many of these groups religion and nationality have become synonymous, and whatever culture these peoples possessed was religious, their leaders being often also their priests and medicine men. This makes anti-religious propaganda among the minor nationalities much more complicated. To abandon their religion often means to these people the abandonment of their nationality. All these errors have to be combated. The Soviet Government is selecting the best active elements among the youth of these nationalities and training them for leadership in special schools organized for this purpose. It is unnecessary to say that this training is definitely anti-religious and that Soviet intellectual leadership of the minority nationalities has become altogether atheistic.

The industrialization of some of these minor national republics is rapidly increasing. The great Turksib Railway, connecting Siberia and Turkestan, has cut through large areas rich in oil, coal and non-ferrous metals, which wealth is now rapidly being developed. The Five-Year Plan has increased the industrial output of Kasakstan and Dagestan by over 500 per cent. and similar growth has been recorded in the other republics. This fact alone means a revolution in the thought and habits of the nomads of yesterday and this transition

---

[1] While it is estimated that there are 200, languages actually on record are 186 in the U.S.S.R. But scores of others exist which so far have not been studied.

naturally cannot occur without a struggle on the part of the conservative and former ruling classes among these people. The collective farm movement, which is successfully carried through among many of the minor nationalities, has similar effects as industrialization. To many of these primitive people to enter the collectives means, at the same time, to abandon their religion; on this ground there is opposition and, at times, bitter struggle.

The spread of atheism among the minor nationalities may best be seen in the records of the recent All Union Conference of the Atheist Movement. At the first conference in 1926 there were but six nationalities represented. By 1931 their numbers had actually increased to 97 nationalities, and by now must have passed the 100 mark. The Moslems, which formerly were the most fanatical in adhering to their religion, are now turning away from it in large numbers; the reasons are chiefly social and economic. To the Moslem women it means emancipation from their age-long degradation; to the men it means freeing themselves from the oppression of their former feudal lords. In joining the collective the former semi-slave farm labourer becomes independent, a new life begins for him and he readily abandons his old religion which had taught him submission to his master.

The Moslem women, particularly of Central Asia, have been roused to cast off their former bondage and degradation, symbolized in the wearing of the *parandja*, a heavy cloth covering face and body, when outdoors. On the international woman's day, March 8, the great solemn annual meeting takes place in which the women in large masses remove the *parandja* and sometimes demonstratively burn them. In 1932 ten thousand Uzbek women alone dropped the veil. This meant as much as abandoning their religion and exposing themselves to persecution from Moslem fanatics; as a result many women were beaten and 14 even were killed. Nevertheless they continue their struggle for independence. During the last (1930) elections, 126,165 Uzbek women, 16.2 per cent. of the voters, participated in the elections and elected 3,890 women delegates to the Soviets, 12 9 per cent. of the total number of seats. All this was done despite the bitter opposition of the Moslem clergy and means actually a break with the old religious taboos and traditions. Anti-religious propaganda among the minor nationalities is at the same time an agitation for a social revolution and its far-reaching consequences are widening.

THE ATHEIST INTERNATIONAL

Communists are internationalists and every aspect of their work eventually becomes international in scope. This is also true of their anti-religious propaganda, which in late years has found expression in the atheist international. Known abroad as the " International of Proletarian Free-thinkers," its aim is " to carry on a decisive struggle on an international scale against clericalization of the labour movement, against missionary activities in colonial and semi-colonial countries, against Christian pacifism and the participation of the Church in preparing a new imperialist war." [1]

In the summer of 1925 was formed, under the initiative of German and Czecho-Slovakian Atheists, the International of Proletarian Free-thinkers which at once communicated with the Soviet atheist organizations; in 1926 the Soviet Union of Militant Atheists joined the International and soon gained control of the organization, directing its efforts along revolutionary lines in opposition to the reformist tactics of the Socialists affiliating with the Second International. The controversy which arose out of these differences ended with the withdrawal of the reformist free-thinkers, who joined the so-called Brussels International consisting of bourgeois free-thinkers, and the International of Proletarian Free-thinkers came under the full control of Communist parties and of organizations sympathising with the Third International.

At first the headquarters of the International was in Germany. But later, when prohibited by the German Government, it withdrew and temporarily its address is at the headquarters of the Central Union of Militant Atheists in Moscow. The

[1] From the resolution of II Congress of the Union of Militant Atheists.

activity of the International consists in a lively exchange of experience between the different national sections and in friendly competition in carrying its propaganda amongst the masses. By 1932 two hundred and fifty local atheist organizations in the U.S.S.R. were in correspondence with foreign organizations. Of these 80 atheist youth organizations have signed competitive agreements with as many units in Czecho-Slovakia. Similar exchange is going on with Holland, Germany South Africa, Australia, South America, Japan, etc., and in all there are 31 countries which are in correspondence and which use " Esperanto " as a medium of communication.

The " International " has turned its attention to the foreign workers engaged in Soviet construction work and carries on its propaganda among them. In one of the Moscow plants, out of 150 foreign workers, 100 have joined the atheist Union, whilst in other plants and cities similar interest is found amongst foreign workers.

In the programme of activities of the " International " study is made of religious movements in capitalist countries, particularly in the U.S.A., Canada, Latin America, and most of the European countries. The results of these studies have been published in 30 different monographs and for such literature there is an increasing demand among the atheist organizations of the " International."

CHIEF CAUSES OF ATHEISM

Wherever the masses are being organized in the U.S.S.R., it entails a break with the old traditions and also with religion. Some of the surveys have brought this out clearly. The Red Army, as we have shown, carries out extensive anti-religious propaganda among its recruits. Surveys of large factories show similar results. In a factory with 12,000 workers 84.1 per cent of the non-party members in the factory are atheists and only 15.9 believers. For the party members it is taken for granted that they are all atheists. A survey in White Russia, carried out in 1930 in 20 towns and 225 villages, showed that 98.5 per cent. of the industrial workers are atheists, whilst for the rural communities the average of unbelievers is 65.4 per cent.

The performance of the rites of christening, marriage and burial by a priest, while having little to do with religious convictions, being largely a matter of social custom, is also beginning rapidly to decrease, particularly as regards Church weddings, which formerly were universal and rather an expensive performance. The present registration fees in the civil department are very small and the registration still has enough semblance of a ceremony to satisfy most people. The following figures are very characteristic of this drift from former religious customs. The data are taken for the periods of nine months, January to September 1 of each year:

For the Number of Births in Moscow

	1927	1928
1. Having no religious ceremony	33.0%	38.1%
2. Having a ,, ,,	59.7%	57.8%
3. Unknown	7.3%	4.1%

For the Number of Burials

	1927	1928
1. Having no religious ceremony	30.1%	33.3%
2. Having a ,, ,,	66.8%	65.7%
3. Unknown	3.2%	1.0%

For the Number of Marriages

	1927	1928
1. Having no religious ceremony	81.6%	86.3%
2. Having a ,, ,,	15.6%	11.8%
3. Unknown	2.8%	1.9%

If we commence an inquiry into the causes which have brought about this rupture with Religion we find them to be the results either of agitation or of disappointment in the clergy and in the power of religion to prevent the calamities of war and famine. In one of the factory surveys 96 autobiographies of atheist working men were received in which are told the stories of their severance from religion. Analyzing these testimonies we find that in 7 cases it was the experiences of the 1905 Revolution which led to the severance; in 10 cases, the World War; in 26 cases, agitation in the Red Army; in 31 cases, the experiences of the October Revolution and of Socialist construction; in 9 cases, disappointment in the clergy and revolt against the frauds of the Church; direct converts by atheist agitation, 5; and, finally, 5 cases resulting from personal experiences leading to the abandonment of God and the Church.

Here are some of these testimonies.

Writes one worker: " My doubts in the Faith date back to 1905, to the time of the shooting of workers on January 9. With Religion I broke in the shop."

Another: " My break with Religion began in 1905. I began to visit the underground groups and the May Day demonstrations, which made it clear to me that Religion is a weapon of the bourgeoisie and that we must struggle against it."

A third: " At the Front in 1915 I completely severed my relations with God. At the Front all this could be understood. Where can there be a God when people kill each other, for what reason? They don't know themselves. Now I have no doubts."

A fourth: " Before the war I was religious; during the war I saw that Religion is an opiate of the people. When the priests accompanied the army to the Front, they told us: ' You shall perish for a sacred cause, and will receive for it a heavenly reward,' but they themselves retreated to the rear."

A fifth: " The civil war made me break with Religion; because of the relation of the priest to the people during the Imperialist (World) War, and also, during 1918–19, when I saw how the priests behaved toward the Soviet Power."

A sixth: " After the Revolution I saw what was taking place. There can be no heavenly ruler. No one could stop the revolution, which was breaking down all the foundations of Religion and faith in God."

A seventh : " I read a few atheist journals and listened to lecturers, and this made me break with Religion."

An eighth : " The chief reason for my severance from Religion was the influence of my teachers and also the absurdities of the Bible, which I had read."

A ninth : " I read Darwin's book on the origin of nature, which produced a revolution in my mind."

A tenth : " Not God gave the peasants the land of the lords, but the godless Bolsheviks."

There are thousands of similar cases. We see that they are rarely of a philosophic nature, but rather the result of disappointment, or of a naïve faith and superstition, shattered by scientific facts. As illustration of the latter cause, it is recorded that in one village a group of school children, with the aid of the teacher, installed an incubator ; this apparatus was watched with curiosity and anxiety by the inhabitants, and when finally the chicks appeared, they began to doubt in God Almighty, and one of the women took all her ikons and burned them demonstratively before the whole village. These are not isolated cases ; science and the machine upset the traditional beliefs of unsophisticated peasants, particularly if scientific facts are interpreted as proof that there is no God, as in the case of the incubator.

CHAPTER XII
COLLECTIVIZATION AND ATHEIST PROPAGANDA

SOCIALISM is impossible in a country with millions of small individual peasant holdings and primitive methods of agriculture. The population of the Soviet Union is still predominantly agricultural; more than 80 per cent., or about 130 million people, are peasants living in a million small villages. Such small settlements are too poor to have any cultural activities. For centuries they lived in illiteracy, poverty and superstition, and the Church was the only institution which had access to them, though it did next to nothing for their education. On the contrary it kept them in ignorance. as the safest way to maintain authority over them.

The proletarian revolution swept away the political power of the Church together with that of the Tsars whose mainstay it was. The peasantry, generally, supported the Revolution, for they were hungry for the land hitherto held by the rural gentry and the Church. The Soviet Government nationalized and distributed the land amongst them for their permanent use, with a single tax system by which the State drew its revenue. This, for the time being, solved the problem to the peasant's satisfaction, but not to that of the city population. These small holdings, tilled by primitive methods, were too inefficient to yield a large enough surplus to provide for the needs of the city and for purposes of export. From year to year this surplus continuously decreased and the growing cities and industrial centres began to feel the shortage acutely. Two possibilities offered themselves as escape from this difficulty. One was to permit and stimulate the development of the larger holdings of the more well-to-do peasants, called the "kulaks" (i.e. "fists") because they held the poorer peasants in their control and exploited them; the other was to pool the land of the peasants and to cultivate it collectively by more efficient methods with the aid of modern machinery. The Communist Party and the Government decided in favour of the latter; to do otherwise would be to betray the aims for which the Revolution was fought. This decision was reached after profound internal party struggles and it was the most daring venture of the Bolsheviks since the early October days. Large industrialized State farms and machine-tractor stations were to demonstrate the new methods and become the leaders in the movement. In this manner the State hoped to solve the food problem for the city and also to open the way for Socialism in the village.

The industrialization of the country outlined in the Five-Year Plan was to proceed hand in hand with the collectivization of the peasant landholdings. This gigantic scheme meant equally a cultural revolution. The plough-shares, drawn by powerful tractors, were not only to till millions of acres of fertile land, some still in a virgin condition, but also to break down the old traditions with their many superstitions, religious taboos and customs. It must be remembered that the religion of the peasants is an agricultural cult in which the working seasons of the year are associated with the great Church feasts and Saints days. It was believed that the fertility of the soil and the success of the crops depended on the magic rites and the Church prayers. But now agricultural science and modern machinery, hitherto practically unknown in Russia, was let loose upon a still primitive untutored people and it went rough shod over all they cherished. It struck hard at their individual property instincts and wrought havoc in their religious and social habits and ideas. It roused enthusiasm in the younger and the poorer peasants and bitter opposition in the conservative "kulak" class.

The anti-religious movement put great faith in the tractor as a means to the eradication of Religion. Its enthusiasts jumped to the conclusion that the collective farm will end rural class differentiation and therefore Religion. Some of the new collectives were named " Godless," the peasants having voted for the closure of the Church. There are 400 such Collectives registered in the Central Union of the Militant Atheists. This is not large considering that there are over 200,000 Collectives and 5,000 State farms embracing 61 per cent. of the farming population and producing 80 per cent. of the crops of the country.

THE EFFECT OF COLLECTIVIZATION UPON RELIGION

In December, 1932, there met in Moscow a conference of rural representatives and leaders of the anti-religious movement, in all about a hundred delegates. These representatives came from practically every part of the Union and their reports were most illuminating in revealing religious conditions in the collectivized villages. The writer attended a number of their sessions, and much of what he heard was food for thought and helped considerably in the understanding of this complex problem.

With few exceptions all delegates frankly stated that their work so far had not had much effect upon the masses. The religious customs have still a strong grip upon the people. Most of the so-called " Godless " collective farms are godless only in name and do not differ actually from other Collectives; sometimes even they have no organization for anti-religious propaganda of any kind. One of the representatives of the Leningrad province reported concerning several surveys carried out in two rural districts, one of which is considered progressive and the other exceedingly backward. Here are the facts as given by the speaker. They reveal an entirely different story from that which is commonly believed concerning religious conditions in the Soviet Union, and the fact that the data were collected by an atheist organization may assure us that the report has not been coloured to favour of religion.

Of the three groups of figures given below: Group I represents the Collectives of the progressive district; Group II, the Collectives of the backward district; and Group III represents individual peasant households who have as yet not joined the Collectives. The survey sought to establish how many peasant families still have ikons in their homes, which is the first and surest indication of the Russian orthodox religious tradition, just as the family Bible was once such an indication in a Protestant farmer's household. The four following columns list the replies given to questions put to the families as to their view of Religion, whether it is helpful, harmless or harmful. The answers are given percentage of the total ikon holders:

	Ikons	Helpful	Harmless	Harmful	Undecided
Group I	77	28	30.6	18	—
Group II	98.7	26.3	39	30	6
Group III	100	82	—	7	10

In analyzing these figures we see that the collective farmers in Group II are not only beginning to discard their ikons, as in Group I, but a large percentage considers religion harmful, referring chiefly to trust in prayer to their ikons as the visible gods. While agreeing as to the harmfulness of religion they are still unable to break away from it. Group III is much more definite in its belief in the helpfulness of religion and its dependence upon the ikon. The individual farmer does not feel the strength of the Collective behind him, and therefore relies upon deity. For a peasant to discard his ikons means to become an atheist. Hence Group I is already 23 per cent. godless.

Another Leningrad Survey showed that in a district with 27 collective farms embracing 912 households, 97.4 per cent. possessed ikons, but 3.1 per cent. were atheists, showing that some professing atheism had not as yet abandoned their ikons. These Collectives kept 52 Saint Days and Church feasts, to which they devoted 117 work days, and there were only two cases where burials took place without the participation of a priest. The Church Saint and feast days are a great hindrance to scientific farming and one of the aims of anti-religious propaganda is to break down the traditions which support them.

Nevertheless, to comply with the wishes of the peasantry, the Government stipulated a seven-day week with Sunday as the general rest day for the rural districts. The cities and industrial centres have a rest day on every sixth day, reckoned according to date and ignoring the day of the week.

Another survey in 14 rural schools showed that in 94.7 per cent. of the homes there were ikons, 19 per cent. of the children declared themselves atheists, and 15 per cent. of the families. Only 25.4 per cent. kept the fasts prescribed by the Church and 57 per cent. had prayers. These figures probably compare well with any Protestant community outside of Russia. Again we must remember that most confessions of atheism, particularly from school children, are rather superficial; they are usually the result of agitation on the part of the teacher who instructs the children that science excludes God, and that the crops do not depend upon the fancies of Deity but upon the caprice of nature, much of which science can control. A visitor to one of the rural schools, which was known to be particularly atheistic, asked the children if there exists a God and all shouted in a chorus that there is none. The visitor then asked if there were witches, to which the children, after a moment's silence, shouted that of course there were, that they had two in their own village! Probably the teacher taught them only that there is no God, and forgot to tell the children that there are no witches.

Anti-religious propaganda, with all its confessed defects, is nevertheless a force which gradually undermines the foundation of the people's faith. The appearance of machinery on the farms rouses the curiosity of the peasant and there is a great search for scientific enlightenment. A group of 20 peasants of the Moscow Province walked 18 miles to the county seat to inquire from a Communist lecturer who happened to be there how men and Religion had come into the world. In another place hundreds of working men formed in line in order to look through the microscope after having heard a lecture on biology, and it was two in the morning before the last one had satisfied his curiosity. This shows that the former orthodox ideas of the universe are no longer satisfactory. The anti-religious propagandists are skilfully using scientific knowledge to discredit theology. The unsophisticated peasant is faced with the choice between God or Science, the Collective Farm and Socialism or the Church and Religion. It is not only the atheist agitator who presents the problem in this exclusive manner, it is often done by the priest and the religious fanatic. The writer once enquired of a peasant why he was so opposed to Collective farming, which promised so many advantages; his bizarre reply was that it was opposed to the will of God, for had God desired Collectives, he would have created not the individual Adam and Eve, whom he had put into the Garden of Eden, but he would have created a Collective and instructed them to work the garden as a group. Similar arguments are heard from the Evangelicals who, however, stress the fact that to enter a Collective means to associate with unbelievers.

This opposition to Collectives on religious grounds is usually either an excuse on the part of the more prosperous peasants, who withhold their co-operation because it means for themselves a personal loss, or comes from the most backward peasants, usually from those villages which were formerly in the possession of landlords under the system of serfdom, to which class of peasantry entering the Collective appears like returning to the old system of serfdom. The clergy also spreads propaganda against the Collectives because it fears its anti-religious influence; it fights the Collectives in every way and frequently turns to fraud or appeals to the superstitions of the masses. Thus in one of the Central Volga districts a " Letter from Christ " was circulated by monks and nuns which asked the faithful to keep out of the ungodly Collectives. Investigation shows that this district at the time of the outbreak of the Revolution had some 2,000 monks and nuns and hardly a single school in the whole district. The Soviet Government disbanded these monasteries and convents, with the result that their inmates spread through the neighbouring country, where they continued their agitation. Although the constitution of the Collectives prohibits religious discrimination, the fact that anti-religious propaganda has been carried on in them has been used as an argument against them. It is of course true that a Collective is a dangerous rival to the old religion even though no word against God is said there. It is a machine which ruthlessly disregards the old customs and goes roughshod over the old superstitions and taboos.

A young peasant lad of 18, visiting a rural anti-religious exhibit, writes : " I believed in God but the exhibit convinced me that the priests had deceived me. I am now declaring myself an atheist and shall enter the Komsomol and the Collective." From this statement it is clear that this youth was held back from the Collective by his traditional belief that it was incompatible with Religion. Abandoning the old faith he found the way clear to join. The Collective does affect the psychology of the peasant and the machine removes the fear of the forces of Religion against which the individual feels so impotent. This does not always mean that the peasant gives up his belief in the supernatural all at once, but he feels that the collective and the machine are strong enough to resist it. A conversation with an Uzbek farmer, in one of the Collectives in Central Asia, illustrates the point : " Tell me," asked the interviewer, " do you still believe that Shaitan (the evil spirit) exists ? "

" Oh, yes, he still exists, and he can get me, but not in the Collective ! "

" And why not in the Collective ? "

" Because there we are many, and if I should become learned and be an engineer, then he cannot get me at all ! "

Another peasant, interviewed on the existence of witches, answered in the affirmative, but added : " In the Collective they are harmless because it is a godless Collective." [1]

In another community, visited by an expedition of the Communist Academy for the study of Religion, the leader of the expedition asked a lad of 18 to go up into the belfry and

[1] From the report of A. T. Lukachevsky, quoting from materials collected by the expeditions of the Communist Academy for the Study of Religion.

ring the church bell to assemble the peasants scattered in the fields. The boy did so and afterwards said : " Two years ago I would not have climbed into the belfry for anything."

" And why not ? "

" Because there are devils up there, and they would have caught me."

" And why don't they catch you now ? "

" Because now I am doing social work and they don't dare to touch me."

Similar reactions take place in the minds of many workers recently arrived from the villages, who have never seen a machine before. One of these writes from the newly-constructed Magnitogorsk steel plant : " We build everything, there is no God." Such are the reactions of an unsophisticated people upon whom has suddenly descended a mechanical civilization. Some recoil from it in fear. Others feel its mighty challenge and creative power. They join it enthusiastically and through it they feel their own strength. " We build everything, there is no God." Such is their sweeping conclusion. As a result they drift away from the Church.

A survey in one of the rural districts in White Russia with a population of 40,000, seventy per cent. of which are in Collectives, shows that they had eight Orthodox Churches, two synagogues, and one Roman Catholic Church. Of these, one synagogue and one Orthodox Church had been closed since the collectivization movement began. The Survey shows that the Jewish population leaves its religious traditions most readily and the Roman Catholics hold to it the longest. According to actual count, after collectivization has been established in the district, not more than 10 per cent. of the population still attends church.

The drive against the old-established religions with their consequent disintegration does not always mean that the people are finished with Religion and have become permanent atheists. Very often they leave the old faith to embrace some new cult. There is, for example, a strong sectarian movement among the Moslems of Azerbaidjan. The nature of these sects has not been studied as yet, to understand in what consists their attraction during this transitional period. There is also a strong sectarian differentiation in the south of Russia and in Siberia, following the traditional lines of the apocalyptic flagellators and other trends. To the mystically inclined and discontented peasants the revolutionary changes brought about by collectivization and the whole atheistic propaganda of Communists appears to them a certain sign that Anti-Christ rules and that the world is heading towards a cataclysmic end. In some places it takes on fanatic forms, of peasants leaving their homesteads and taking to wandering, a phenomena which, as we have observed, existed during the 18th century when Peter I made his first drive to modernize Russia. This wandering mania is frequently stimulated by the monks expelled from the monasteries, who make their way through the country spreading alarm among the population. Also there are some priests who, after being driven from the parishes, take to wandering, and as they go they offer their services in performing the orthodox rites of baptism, prayers for the dead, and so on. These monks and priests mingle in the market places and seek admission and shelter in the homes of peasants and artisans who often become willing listeners to their insidious propaganda. Others of the former clergy and sectarians enter the collective farms as accountants, clerks and sometimes as full members. Possessing greater organizing skill and shrewdness, they quickly rise to leadership and influence. Other priests and sectarians openly and undisguisedly offer their service, which some Collectives and even Soviet officials accept, pressed by the shortage of experienced and literate help. The sectarians, particularly because of their sobriety and elementary honesty, rise quickly to influence and control in some of the Collectives.

NEW TACTICS OF ANTI-RELIGIOUS PROPAGANDA

All these facts compelled the atheist agitators to renew their activities and to design a programme of work which would more effectively counteract the revived religious forces. It is realized that to let things drift in the hope that Religion will atrophy by the mechanical forces of industrialization is thought to be an unsafe solution. This is called the mechanist heresy. It ignores the consciousness and the power of organization of the old religious movements, some of which have shown remarkable vitality under most trying circumstances. The anti-religious leaders argue that to leave Religion to itself will prolong its existence, and therefore something must be done to counteract it. The more impatient fall back upon repressive measures, trying to force the closing of churches and the arrest and exile of the unfriendly and fanatical leaders of religion; but by these measures they arouse ill-feeling among the followers and are apt to stimulate fanaticism. These repressive measures have contributed a great deal to stimulating the revival of apocalyptic sectarianism and have made the population believe that the Soviet Government is in sympathy with religious persecution. To avoid these harmful conclusions, repressive measures are discouraged and strictly prohibited by the Party and the Government.

The only effective thing to do is to rely on education and active counter propaganda. This is the present position of the atheist leaders and on this principle the new programme of activity is being outlined. In the resolution adopted by the All-Union Conference of Rural Anti-religious Workers, to which we previously referred, this change of policy is clearly stated. We shall quote from this document at some length, for it presents a clear picture of the situation as seen by the men engaged in the struggle against Religion. In characterizing the present situation in the rural districts, the Resolution says :

" In the given period, because of the great victories of Socialism, millions of toilers depart from Religion, casting off for ever religious customs, attending to work on religious feast days, shutting down churches and religious meeting houses, and godless collective farms are organized at the initiative of the peasants themselves. All this calls for further development of anti-religious propaganda in the villages. At the same time is observed in a number of organizations and among individual anti-religious workers, a most harmful point of view which consists in the opinion that religion is at its end and therefore no anti-religious activity is needed."

The " organizations " referred to in this paragraph, we learned from the debates on the resolution, were chiefly the public schools, which prefer to hold a neutral position in the struggle with Religion. The Resolution furthermore states : " The separation of the toilers from Religion must be deepened upon a Marxo-Leninist basis, upon the basis of scientific knowledge. The development of the dialectic-materialist philosophy of life among the working masses is a long process, it will not come by itself but calls for extensive educational work in politics and in anti-religion."

In reviewing the work of the Union of Militant Atheists in the light of these aims, the Resolution arrived at the conclusion : " The condition of the anti-religious work in the villages does not answer by any means to the demands that are placed upon it at this stage ; the Union of Militant Atheists does not cope with the organization of the masses who drift away from Religion, and in its mass activities it does not meet the growing demand of the members of the collective farms and of individual farmers."

The constructive measures suggested for improving their activities in the villages, are in seeking to raise upon a higher scientific research level all the anti-religious mass activities, making them correspond to the problems which are before the workers of the Soviet Union in the Second Five-Year Plan. The present anti-religious propaganda must start with the achievements of Socialist construction of science and technique, which, it is hoped, will further disintegrate the religious survivals. Says the resolution : " The anti-religious propaganda, in exposing the counter-revolutionary aspect of Religion and in exhibiting its anti-scientific nature, must help millions of toiling peasants to grasp, in a Marxo-Leninist way, the world of nature and of society. The materialistic conception of the world is being gradually understood by the peasants together with collectivization and the use of machine technique in agriculture. The anti-religious propaganda must strengthen and raise it to a philosophic Marxo-Leninist level. This newly developing materialistic approach to the world is gained through practice in Socialist construction."

To attain these aims the Central Council of the Union is entrusted with preparing instructions and devising methods for every form of anti-religious activity, such as textbooks, lectures and exhibits. Of interest are the themes which are to be treated in these books and lectures. Emphasis is placed upon: " Abolition of the opposing cultural standards of city and village "; " The abolition of the differences between physical and mental work "; " Collective work and the struggle with religion "; " Latest achievements in agricultural engineering and technique "; " Economic and organizational improvement of collective farms "; " Improvement of crops and the struggle with Religion "; " International education and race co-operation "; etc. In considering these subjects one begins to wonder what anti-religious interpretation the author of the subjects may give to them. It will possibly be the old charge that Religion is anti-scientific, conservative and anti-social. These accusations are generally true of organized religion in Russia and upon this anti-religious propaganda bases its stress. The problems indicated are of most vital importance, for upon their solution depends the success of the Five-Year Plan, which aims at the realization of a classless society in the Soviet Union and hence the establishment of Communism.

To meet the new demands for positive scientific knowledge, a qualified personnel must be trained, the lack of which is considered the weakest link in the chain of anti-religious activities. The leaders of the Union complain that their best converts and collaborators are taken by the Party and the Government for other work and in turn the poorly qualified and inefficient are sent to them. " On the precept," as one orator put it, " if a man is not fit for anything else he is considered good enough for anti-religious work; and yet there is no other activity which needs such high qualifications as anti-religious propaganda." Here we have the same complaint and the same difficulty which for centuries has been heard in the Church.

In listening to the frank self-criticism of the preachers of atheism and in reading their resolutions, one begins to appreciate their difficulties, which are not unlike those which any propagandist has to face whatever his message. The ignorance, indifference and frivolity of the masses seem to be their common attribute. The bold attacks of anti-religious propagandists have done, however, a great deal to awaken the peasants from their inertness. After a thousand years of Christian tradition when never a shadow of doubt darkened the minds of the masses of " Holy Russia," the peasants suddenly see their gods and sanctuaries attacked and exposed as fraud; they see great new forces released from Nature by the will and power of man; they see the machines and great power stations harnessing Nature to do their work; and naturally they begin to ask, if there is a God, why He permits all this blasphemy to His name and His sanctuaries. Why does he not smite the atheist agitator? Is God indifferent, or is he asleep, or is he an illusion? The peasant looks at his sacred ikons, to his visible gods; he recognizes in them the bearded images of his own forefathers, and at once jumps to the conclusion this is made by man and in his, man's, image. There is no God but man himself. Therefore he declares himself a *bezbozhnik*, a man without a god.

The Church expected that after the destruction of the old forces of control and the disappearance of the fear of a revengeful God, every moral restraint would disappear; yet nothing of the sort has occurred. As far as observation goes, the amount of crime and moral licentiousness has not increased but, wherever economic conditions and educational facilities have improved, men have become more civil and restrained. It is too early to generalize on the results of anti-religious propaganda in the life of the peasant. The millions of the Russian countryside see, for the first time, their gods challenged and dishonoured; the peasant is sometimes amazed, sometimes terrified by what has happened. The revolution is upon him. It attacks not only his property instincts, but all the foundations of his life. He can never return to the past and he is not certain of his future. For him the old world has actually come to an end.

CHAPTER XIII

ORGANIZATION AND METHODS OF ANTI-RELIGIOUS PROPAGANDA

THE programme and methods of the activities of the atheist societies has been rapidly developing into an intricate system which may well compare with that of any modern church organization in the West. It is supervised by the Central Council of the Union of Militant Atheists, with headquarters in Moscow. It has also a system of regional organizations spreading throughout the whole country. Associated with the " Central Council " are its " home " and " foreign " missions departments, which carry on an intensive activity among the minor nationalities in the Soviet Union and assist groups of proletarian atheists throughout the world.

Important departments of atheist propaganda are those of mass agitation, education, publications, army and navy, industrial, rural, youth and children, scientific research in religion and methods of work, training of agitators, museums and libraries, and finally the use of the fine arts in anti-religious propaganda, particularly the theatre, the cinema and the radio.

Mass agitational activities were particularly used during the first stage of the struggle of the Revolution with the Church. Lectures and debates were the favoured methods, also anti-religious demonstrations, carnivals and open-air meetings. The direct object of mass agitation was to expose the counter-revolutionary activities of the Church and the anti-scientific nature of Religion.

The coloured poster was very popular. It aimed to ridicule and expose the superstitions of the Church and the vices of the clergy. The agitation against drink was usually associated and synchronized with an agitation against great Church holidays, such as Christmas and Easter, which habitually were occasions for over-eating and drinking. Posters such as " Guard your children against Religion and Alcohol " are common ; the priest is usually pictured drunk, holding the cross in one hand and a vodka bottle in the other. It is of course true that the priests as a class were very intemperate and that the Russian Church never agitated against the liquor traffic, but on the contrary opposed the temperance movement when it was started by a number of laymen and priests. These originators of the temperance movement were finally excommunicated as dangerous sectarians.

The introduction of the Five-Year Plan and the collectivization of agriculture gave the anti-religious mass agitation a new impetus. Its posters and slogans were now directed at making the people believe that the Church was opposed to the Soviet industrialization and collectivization schemes. One of the favoured methods in this mass agitation was the printing of rhymes and verse on sweet wrappers, cigarette boxes, and the like. One of the popular brands of sweets had the following verse printed on the wrapper :

> Priests are our enemies to the grave !
> Watch them closely with both your eyes.
> In answer to the calumny of Popish nonsense
> Let us complete the Five-Year Plan in four.
> Let us drive out *Alcohol* and *Religion* with culture.

The radio was used for lectures on subjects such as " Religion and the Five-Year Plan." Two of these lectures by Z. Krainiuk were even published in English translation to be circulated among the English-speaking workers, many of whom had come to the U.S.S.R. to participate in the huge construction works provided by the Five-Year Plan. We shall briefly outline these radio lectures, since they show the methods which atheist agitators are commonly using in attacking religion :

Lecture I:

The Five-Year Plan; The Basis of Anti-religious propaganda.

1. The absence of plan in capitalist economy and the social roots of religion. The victory of Socialism leads to the abolition of exploitation and slavery. The victory of Socialism means the final destruction of all these social roots which feed religion. The fulfilment of the Five-Year Plan will not only be a victory on the economic front; it is also a cultural undertaking to free hundreds of thousands of workers from the tyranny of darkness, from religious stupefaction and ignorance.

The Marxo-Leninist view characterizes religion as the sigh of creatures under oppression, an opiate for the people, a mental intoxicant which weakens their class antagonisms and suppresses their creative initiative and their enthusiasm for work. This means that only by being freed from the yoke of capitalist exploitation and from religious, as well as every other kind of bourgeois oppression, can a higher standard of labour productivity be attained.

2. The underlying principles of the Five-Year Plan for the development of the national economy of the U.S.S.R. in the field of industry.

3. The same in the field of agriculture.

Conclusion: In developing these principles in industry and agriculture a materialist philosophy of life advocated by Lenin will be created which is irreconcilable with religion and fatal to priestcraft in all its forms.

Lecture II:

Introduction: What is the social basis of the Five-Year Plan for cultural development? In what consists the problem of cadres? The Five-Year Plan of the Union of Militant Atheists is to rid the country of the poison of religion.

1. The liquidation of illiteracy and universal compulsory elementary education. Here the problem is to compel the Commissariat of Education to change its policy from a non-religious to an anti-religious programme of education, and to

obtain teachers who would be trained and willing to carry on anti-religious propaganda among the school children. No neutrality on this question should be tolerated.

" Our task is not only to protect the rising generation from the disintegrating Church and sectarian influence, but also to wrench from the iron clutches of religion those children of workmen, peasants and toilers generally, who have been held captive by it. In the liquidation of illiteracy (i.e. adult education) we have the special task of impregnating all branches of the work with an active anti-religious content."

2. The Five-Year Plan of the Union of Militant Atheists.

In respect to members it provides an increase of membership by 1933 to 17 million members and 12 million children.

Factories, workshops, shock brigades, communal houses, ought, at the end of the Five-Year Plan, to become regular hot-beds of atheism. There should be no churches and no trace of religion in the Socialist towns for whose construction the Five-Year Plan provides. They should be centres of free and joyous atheism and genuine enthusiasm.

This very briefly is the gist of the radio lectures delivered in October, 1930. We have outlined them here showing their salient points because they are so typical of the present Communist anti-religious mass propaganda. It takes for granted that religion is a hindrance and alien to Socialism and will disappear with the realization of the latter. We may also note that the Five-Year Plan of the Union of Militant Atheists has been realized only by about 30 per cent. in the adult sector and only by about 17 per cent. in the work among children. These shortages, it is hoped, will be made good during the next Five-Year Plan which is now worked out by the leaders of the Atheist movement.

To attract the interest of workers in anti-religious problems, factory clubs are presenting courses of lectures. Thus the Moscow Automobile Works have announced for the season the following subjects :

1. Baruch Spinoza's Struggle against Religion and the Church.
2. Social Re-education of the Workers and the Struggle against Religion.
3. Science Penetrates the Atom.
4. Marxo-Leninism as Militant Atheism.
5. Modern Theories on the Origin of the Universe.
6. Origin of Life on the Earth.
7. The Modern Struggle concerning Darwinism and Biology.
8. The Rôle of Work in the Origin of Man.
9. Brain and Consciousness.
10. Origins of Religion in the Light of Marxo-Leninism.
11. The Struggle for Dialectical Materialism in the Light of the Bourgeois Crisis of Science.
12. The End of the Relative Stabilization of Capitalism and Religion.

We see here a predominance of the critique of Religion in the light of modern science. But there is still lacking a popular presentation of the positive teaching of Communism in respect to the spiritual and ethical life of man.

A similar approach still dominates the popular appeal on special occasions like the great Church feasts, which are celebrated by the atheist societies in their own fashion. We may illustrate this best by quoting extensively from an atheist Christmas Sermon :

A GODLESS CHRISTMAS MESSAGE [1]

" The struggle against Religion
Is the struggle for Socialism."

" On December 25 the Christian Church celebrates the birthday of its God, the Saviour, the birthday of Jesus Christ.

" *This holiday*, the so-called Christmas, *is a holiday of savages, of slaves, of hypocrites*. The priests assure us that this

[1] From the December (1932) number of the " Young Bezbozhniks " (Youthful Atheists), a monthly, published in Moscow.

holiday was celebrated at first only by Christians. As a matter of fact the feast of the birth of God, the Saviour, at this time of the year existed among many people long before the appearance of Christianity. All these Gods—Osiris, Thammus, Adonis, Mithras, and others are imaginary creatures, born in the heads of ancient agricultural people.

" Fortune-telling, masquerading, the Christmas tree, Christmas dinner, all these are survivals from savage times, when man populated his surrounding Nature with spirits, when the " helplessness of the savage before the forces of nature generated in him faith in gods, demons, devils, etc." (Lenin). And the savage, this helpless slave of nature, bowed before the gods he himself created, begging them aid and mercy when oppressed by the terrible phenomena of nature.

" With the development of technique the force of Nature over man weakened. Still faith in God did not diminish, but on the contrary it grew because a new yoke was laid upon helpless man. The yoke of exploitation of one man by another.

" The helplessness of exploited classes in the struggle with the exploiters inevitably produces faith into a better life beyond the grave, just as the helplessness of the savage in the struggle with Nature creates faith in gods, miracles, etc. Thus spoke V. I. Lenin.

" There never was a Jesus Christ. This even some bourgeois scholars have to acknowledge, those same learned men who, more than anything else, fear the atheism of the working masses.

" The legend about Christ the Saviour appeared in the minds of Roman slaves and paupers crushed by inhuman exploitation. These slaves and poverty-stricken people embraced the legend about God the Saviour and the tale about life after the grave ; it was the result of class oppression.

" The Christian teaching about Hell and Paradise has all the earmarks of ancient slave-holding society.

" Hell is the " utter darkness," i.e. the gaol, for the slaves, which was usually outside the town. Paradise is " eternal bliss," eternal do-nothing, the principle hope of exhausted and crushed slaves to escape the cursed labour.

"Hence the Christian religion made its start, the religion of slaves, submission and patience ; hence Christmas made its beginning, the feast of the birth of Christ who actually was never born.

"This Christmas is not only a feast day of savages and slaves, it is also a feast of utmost hypocrisy. In churches and chapels priests will shout at the top of their voices, "Glory to God in the highest." . . .

"These words sound particularly hypocritical and mean when millions of toilers and their families in capitalist countries are left without work, starving, thrown out into the Christmas cold, while thousands are committing suicide out of hopeless despair, with peasants of colonial countries selling their children, in order to maintain themselves by any means.

"The priests shout about the ' peace on earth ' which was to commence with the birth of Christ. ' Glory to God in the highest and on earth peace . . .' And yet at the same time, in spite of the economic crisis, in all capitalist countries the war industries are at work day and night, manufacturing, for the glory of God, shells and poison gas to annihilate mankind.

"A greater mockery than this preaching of peace and goodwill to man cannot be imagined. Not peace and goodwill but death and annihilation are raging in capitalist countries, camouflaged by gorgeous divine services, hypocritical sermons, lovely singing, Christmas trees, mangers, angels, Saint Nichlaus, and similar savage and slave superstitions. . . .

"The chief task of the Soviet school is to educate a strong, healthy new generation, with nerves of steel and muscles of iron, fit to establish Communism, and in this they are opposed and always will be by the class enemy in vestment and by the Cross."

We have translated this message because it is quite typical of atheist propaganda during the great Christian holidays, Christmas and Easter. The theme is always the same : that Religion is the product of man's helplessness before Nature and the strong governing classes, that it is anti-scientific and counter-revolutionary and is destined to disappear, together with the division of man into classes, with the consequent establishment of Communism.

The results of the atheist mass activities are not always easy to follow up. It has been observed however that in places where systematic anti-religious propaganda was effectively carried on, the number of absent workman on religious holidays has greatly decreased, and the forms of Socialist work such as social competition and shock brigading had improved. There appears also increased interest in the study of Dialectical Materialism and participation in the various social activities of the local atheist organizations.

The weakest link in the mass activities of the Union is considered the still small interest of women in atheist teaching with a correspondingly small membership in the Union, only 30 per cent. of the total membership.

One of the favoured and sometimes spectacular forms of anti-religious mass propaganda, are the so-called anti-religious campaigns or revival meetings. These usually are synchronized with corresponding religious revivals at the time of Lent and the great Christian holidays like Christmas. These special efforts show from season to season the success or failure of the local organizations to dissuade the masses from participating in the religious services, particularly Christmas Eve and Easter night, which to orthodox Christians are the greatest religious services of the year. To counteract the services special programmes are set up with lectures and musical entertainment, and these sometimes succeed in distracting considerable numbers of the population from the Churches. The drawback of these seasonal anti-religious campaigns is that most organizations are satisfied when they have carried through their holiday programmes and do little or nothing for the rest of the year. The Central Council is trying to overcome these defects by providing local organizations with regular weekly messages and programmes of activity. To stimulate the regular and campaign work, the Central Council of the Union has a staff of three travelling agitators and three instructors in organization, who visit the various districts in the Union with their message of atheism. These visitors usually carry with them an anti-religious exhibit and cinema films which are always an attraction to the masses.

SPECIAL EDUCATIONAL ACTIVITIES

The acute shortage of trained agitators and organizers has prompted the leaders of the anti-religious movement to create a system of anti-religious education in which lay and professional agitators could receive their training. It may be noted that among the founders of the anti-religious movement were a number who received a theological seminary training and not a few of the popular atheist agitators are former priests and monks. These men, while of temporary value, must in due time be replaced by men who have risen from the ranks of the workers and are loyal in every respect to the Party teachings and its political aims.

About a decade ago the XII Party Congress turned its attention to this problem of training a staff of anti-religious agitators. It passed a resolution which said : " It is necessary, within the whole system of Communist education, to carry on special courses in the origins, development and history of religion, of various creeds and cults and religious Church organizations, closely associating these courses with the study of human society and the class struggle of exploiters and exploited and the exposure of the manifold actual relations of Capital and religious propaganda." This decision of the Party had an enormous influence in the development of anti-religious education and clearly pointed out the lines along which it should be carried on.

The first seminar for the study of religion was organized at the Sverdlov Communist University in 1921 by E. Yaroslovsky, one of the old outstanding leaders of the anti-religious movement in Russia. By 1925 there were already 36 anti-religious courses and 6 seminars functioning in the various higher schools of learning in the Union, and in 1926 was published the first number of the *Antireligioznik*, a monthly serving the same purpose as homiletical and theological magazines do for the clergy. It carries critical articles and outlines for lectures, and book reviews on questions of religion and philosophy. This magazine has given the anti-religious propaganda unity of thought and helpful directions in the organization of the movement. In the *Antireligioznik* appeared outlines of various courses and programmes which were now beginning to be developed by special commissions appointed by the Department of Education, which also prepared three standard textbooks, one for use among industrial workers, another for the peasants, and a third for the Red Army. Simultaneously were prepared some correspondence courses on the subject " Learn to be an Atheist," which since have been greatly extended.

With the appearance of this literature the number of students of anti-religious courses rapidly increased. On January 16, 1927, there were recorded 68 anti-religious seminars, 9 propagandist circles, one special school for propagandists and one night school, besides 14 " cabinets " for the study of religion. There were also 266 study groups organized at the various workers' clubs and similar organizations. In the same year were prepared the first programmes of study for some of the national minorities in the U.S.S.R., such as the Tartar, Tchuvash, Maries, Mordva, Lettish and Esthonian languages.

In 1928 the Central Committee of the Party adopted a resolution for the organization of special chairs for the study of religion at the Communist Academy and the Institute of Red Professors, which were to train specialists in religion to be employed as curators of museums, literary workers and teachers in the training schools for anti-religious agitators. Similar chairs were organized in Leningrad, Kharkov and other of the larger Universities. Thus gradually developed a graded system of elementary, secondary and higher education in the field of religion, and not only for the study of Christianity, but also of the other great religions of the East : Christianity, Judaism, Mohammedanism and Buddhism, besides many such primitive religions as the Shaman fire-and-nature worshippers. The adherents of orthodox Christianity are the most numerous and politically they are considered the most dangerous. But agitation is carried on equally against all forms of religion and the Communist programme provides for the complete eradication of all religious ideologies and cults.

In 1929, during the great drive against religion, there were introduced a number of other forms of systematic anti-religious training. A so-called Radio University was organized which recorded about 20,000 regular listeners. In addition there were 35 so-called " Sunday Universities " which, throughout the season of 1929-30, gave popular courses of lectures in the auditoriums of the various universities of the Union. The attendance at the lectures has not been fully recorded throughout the whole country. In Moscow at the end of the session there were still 500 students attending the lectures, which shows that their number throughout the country must have been considerable.

The normal course at the " Anti-religious Universities " is two years and their purpose is to prepare district organizers for anti-religious activities, to train propagandists, lecturers, excursion leaders and general club workers for the villages and collective farms, as well as leaders for child and youth organizations.

The higher research institutes have set themselves to work along four principle lines, which A. Lukachevsky, the director of this research work, formulates in the following theses :

1. To grasp the Leninist stage of militant atheism ; to combat any distortion of Marxo-Leninism in questions of religion and the struggle therewith ; to apply merciless criticism to the work of Kautsky, Kunow and other Social Fascists ; to introduce critique of the Plekhanov position in religion and to give a complete exposure of the errors of the mechanistic materialists and Menshevik idealists, and mercilessly to expose the Trotskyist position on the questions of anti-religious propaganda.

2. To study the process of the dying out of religion. What facts contribute to the abandonment of religion, what detains

people from abandoning it ? Religion and atheism in the collective farms, religion and atheism among the old and newly-recruited industrial workers.

3. Study of the development of scientific methodology of anti-religious propaganda ? How to organize the work among the followers of different religions ? Content, methods and forms of work.

4. Study of the work of religious organizations in foreign countries. Study of everything that appears in foreign countries on the problems of religion, philosophy, history, etc.

This outline shows that the study of religion in its influence on society is being taken seriously by Communist scholars. It is checked by laboratory work and ethnographic and survey expeditions among the various national minorities, and the rural and industrial communities. In 1931 there were 19 such expeditions in which participated 56 persons, who surveyed 34 districts with 19 nationalities. This is a very hopeful sign. It will undoubtedly change that vulgar and frequently superficial attitude towards religion, which in the past has characterized the anti-religious propaganda in the Soviet Union and which chiefly was due to gross ignorance of the subtler aspects of religion in the life of the people.

ANTI-RELIGIOUS LITERATURE

Anti-religious and even critical literature in the field of religion practically did not exist in Russia previous to the October Revolution. There was a relaxation of censorship after the 1905 Revolution which permitted the publication of such works as Robertson's *History of Free Thought*, Lecky's *History of Rationalism*, Renan's *Life of Jesus*, Bradlaugh's *Science and Religion*, and a few similar books well known in the Free Thought Movement of Western countries. Communist authors, beginning to write on the subject after the Revolution, had a virgin field before them, but so far they have not produced much of value, lacking the necessary scholarship and frequently losing the necessary objectivity in the controversial atmosphere which existed in Russia after the downfall of Tsarism. M. Yakovlev, one of the contemporary students of the problem, thus characterizes the aims of Communist writers on religion :

" First, persistently and convincingly expose before the broad masses of toilers, the class and exploiting nature of religion, the counter-revolutionary rôle of the clergy and of lay theologians, the incompatibility of religious prejudices, which are a heritage of a savage antiquity, with the construction of a new socialist order ; secondly, attract the millions of toiling masses, which are being freed in the revolutionary struggle from the religious opiate, into the first ranks of that gigantic army which is struggling for the inner and outer strengthening of the Socialist fatherland of the workers of the whole world ; thirdly, in a most acceptable and intelligent form, interpret and disseminate the scientific Marxo-Leninist atheist philosophy of life." [1]

If we examine the new Russian atheist literature in the light of these aims, we must admit that, generally speaking, it relentlessly pursued these objectives, usually at the expense of scientific objectivity, but was not always very successful in giving it the necessary popular form and intelligent interpretation. In its bulk it lacks quality. Frequently it fights against theological positions which long since have been abandoned by most intelligent religious people, as, for example, the verbal inspiration of the Bible, evolutionary science, the origin of man, and the social origins of religions.

Many of the translated works are chosen from authors whose theories have long since been discarded as untenable in the light of advanced historic criticism, as, for example, the anti-religious works of the French Materialists, of Drews' and Robertson's theories denying the historicity of Jesus, the animist theory of religion by Tylor and Frazer, etc. On the other hand the strength of Communist propaganda lies in Lenin's theory, insisting on the necessity of a sociological approach to religion and finding its roots in social-economic class relations. The selection of the writings of Marx, Engels

[1] *Fifteen Years of Militant Atheism in the U.S.S.R.*, p. 386–387.

and Lenin on the subject of religion are of real value, as also are some of A. T. Lukachevsky's studies in the origins of religion and the historic works by P. A. Kranikov, B. P. Kandidov, E. Yaroslavsky, N. M. Nikolsky, M. Pokrovsky and a number of others, who have collected valuable materials on the relation of the Church to the Revolution and the place of religion in the life of the Russian people. The U.S.S.R. with its 200 racial and lingual groups, adhering to very different religions, from primitive fire-and-nature worshippers, to rationalistic sects like the Tolstoyans, are of course a huge laboratory for the study of religion and the factors contributing to changes in the thinking and customs of the people. Some of these ethnographic and religious studies, like those of Motorin, which were recently published, promise to be of real scientific value.

While there remains much to be desired in the quality of Soviet anti-religious literature, its bulk is enormous. No other country can show such circulation of publications on religious subjects as the Soviet Union. During the last decade were published 1,200 titles of anti-religious books and pamphlets not including numerous short tracts. The total number of copies distributed is given as 40,000,000, which means an average of over 235,000 for each title. This is not at all an unusual number for Soviet publications. The weekly newspaper *Bezbozhnik* has, according to latest reports, a circulation of 473,500 copies per issue, and the illustrated magazine *Bezbozhnik*, 200,000 copies. The reason for so large a circulation of books and papers lies in the Soviet system of its distribution, which is accomplished through the agency of the many local organizations of the anti-religious movement, of which, as we know, there are about 65,000 throughout the Union. While this may be an advantage to the publishing houses, it does not always mean that this literature is read. The writer has examined the anti-religious literature on the shelves of a number of Moscow libraries and found that most of the books have never been used even once. Only the manuals used in group studies are really read, and in this respect the anti-religious literature is very much like the books in the libraries of churches, which are also rarely used unless studied in young people's groups and Sunday Schools. The lack of interest in anti-religious literature is well known to the leaders of the movement and measures are taken by libraries to popularize and advertise it, for instance by organizing, in reading circles and discussion groups, disputes on the quality of certain books. This does not obscure the fact that in the consciousness of Soviet readers neither religion nor anti-religion occupies at present an important place.

ANTI-RELIGIOUS MUSEUMS

The museum as an institution of popular education has been fully recognized by atheist propagandists. During the last five years more than 100 such museums have been opened throughout the Soviet Union, in addition to many so-called travelling exhibits.

The largest of these museums are in Leningrad, housed in the great cathedral of St. Isaak and in the Kazan Cathedral. These two huge buildings were still in use for worship a few years ago, but their high maintenance cost was above the financial strength of the dwindling congregations. Therefore they were abandoned to the Department of Museums, which has converted them to anti-religious purposes.

In Moscow also there are several museums designed for anti-religious propaganda; of these the best known and best equipped is the Central Anti-religious Museum, housed in the former Strastnoi Convent Church, situated in the very centre of the city. It was opened in November, 1929, and during the first year was visited by 234,716 people, remaining ever since one of the most popular museums of the city.

Other museums of national reputation are the former famous Troitzo-Sergievo Monastery, situated about 60 miles to the north of Moscow, and the equally famous Kievo-Petchora Monastery, situated on the bank of the Dnieper in close proximity to the city of Kiev. These two ancient monastic institutions were formerly the richest and the most venerated sanctuaries in Russia, the Mecca and Medina of Russian Orthodoxy, visited annually by thousands of pilgrims.

The Petchora Monastery was the cradle of Russian Christianity; Sergievo was its northern citadel made famous by the saintly and patriotic life of Saint Sergius. Growing rich and powerful these monasteries became corrupt, and when the Revolution exposed and broke up these centres of monastic corruption and religious fraud, they were appropriated and preserved by the State from loot and destruction. Now they function as museums, exhibiting the former gorgeous wealth and power of the Church, and there they stand as sad monuments of what religion should not have been. The attractions at Sergievo are the remains of Saint Sergius, formerly fraudulently exhibited as " incorruptable "; when the sacred sarcophagus was opened by order of the Soviet Government in the presence of the clergy, the remains proved as corruptible as all flesh, and so the decayed body of the once famous saint remains to-day a symbol of a Church, itself pretending to incorruptibility, but now fully exposed of its frauds.

The attractions of the Kievo-Petchora Monastery are its catacombs, in which the " Fathers " of Russian Orthodoxy once dwelt, died and were buried. Some of them became mummified, a phenomenon which was taken to be a special sign of divine favour, thus starting the tradition in Russia that real saintliness is rewarded by incorruptibility of the flesh. Very many precious works of art were held in custody in these monastic museums, consisting of jewelled vestments, crowns, cups, old paintings and frescoes, old manuscripts, etc. They are still visited by a few pilgrims, but the majority of the visitors, who number many thousands, are excursionists who come to be shown the frauds and corruption of the Church.

If we return to the newly-equipped museums of Moscow and Leningrad we find them to be built upon a definite scheme, exhibiting departments on Science and Religion in which the evolutionary theory of the cosmos and of the origin of species is presented against the background of Biblical cosmology.

Thus in the dome of the Cathedral of St. Isaak is fastened a huge Fuco pendulum, supposedly the largest in the world, to prove the movement of the earth about its axis. The Moscow Central Museum has collections of models of the various intermediary skulls and other anthropoid relics illustrating the simian origin of man. Then there are good exhibits on the origin of religion, demonstrating the naturalistic and anthropomorphic ideas of God. The greatest emphasis, however, is placed on exhibiting the class function of religion in pre-class society, under slavery, under feudalism and in the transitional period between Capitalism and Socialism. It demonstrates the close association of the Church with the Tsarist regime and the inglorious rôle which it played in the struggle against the Revolution and the enlightenment of the people. Of course, the horrors of the Inquisition, the martyrdom of such as Giordano Bruno and Galileo, are most dramatically represented in sculptured figures and marquets, but the majority of exhibits, particularly in demonstrating the relation of the Church to Tsarism, consist of original materials and documents.

Agitation against the anti-socialist and counter-revolutionary functions of religion are not limited to the sins of the Orthodox Church. Equal emphasis is now paid to the functions of other religions, Mohammedanism, Judaism, and particularly the sectarian movement in Russia with its extreme fanatic forms of castrators, flagellators, etc.

The expositions are by no means permanent. The exhibit is continually changed to meet the current demand of anti-religious propaganda. Thus at present the Moscow Central Museum is preparing new exhibits to demonstrate the struggle of religion against industrialization and particularly the collectivization of agriculture.

The designing of these exhibits is the work of a special staff of scholars and artists, and the manufacture of the objects is carried out in special shops, where also are prepared sets of exhibits for provincial and travelling anti-religious museums. The anti-religious museums are gradually accumulating valuable paintings and sculptures illustrating one or another aspect of their propaganda.

Efforts are made by the atheist movement also to develop special anti-religious departments in the various anthropological and ethnographic museums to demonstrate the class nature of religion, and in museums of the natural sciences to show the incompatibility of religion and science. The same aim is pursued in the planetariums where the astronomic exhibits are accompanied by lectures in which the Biblical cosmogony is refuted and the conclusion drawn that religion and science are incompatible.

It must be added that all of the larger museums in the U.S.S.R. possess trained guides and lecturers, who accompany groups of visitors through the museum explaining to them the meaning of the exhibits.

There is no doubt that of all the forms of anti-religious propaganda the museums are the most effective and convincing. They visualize the anti-religious message and seek to prove it by carefully and pointedly selected facts and original evidence.

It is true that intelligent religious foreigners, many of whom have visited these museums, find nothing anti-religious about them, since they demonstrate facts most of which have for a long time been accepted by all intelligent religious people, and strike hard only at uncompromising fundamentalists and at those not wishing to accept a sociological origin and interpretation of religion. But under conditions as they exist in the Soviet Union, where there has been no modernist movement in religion, the alternative to orthodox religion, with its obscure theology and cosmology, is atheism.

The success and popularity of the anti-religious museum have prompted its development, and efforts are being made to have them organized in all larger towns and villages, transforming for that purpose and as centres of atheist education the abandoned cathedrals and churches. The greatest difficulty in realising these plans is found in the lack of a trained personnel, and of artistic exhibits. To overcome this shortage specialists are now trained for such work in the various Communist higher schools of which we already have spoken.

THE FINE ARTS AS WEAPONS OF ANTI-RELIGIOUS PROPAGANDA

It has been generally observed that the anti-religious propaganda is an appeal to reason, it ignores the emotions and is frequently dry and dull. These facts are not denied by atheist propagandists and they are making strenuous efforts to mobilize the fine arts for anti-religious purposes. The first efforts were directed to creating an anti-religious theatre and cinema; after years of trial and error they have had some success, although confessedly nothing of permanent artistic value has been created.

Play and scenario writers tried themselves in this field. During the last decade about 200 such plays and sketches have been published, but they rarely progressed beyond that anti-clerical stage which does not satisfy the anti-religious propagandist. Plays like the " Feast of St. Georgeus," " The Million of Anthony," " The March of the 14th Division to Heaven " (a musical review), " Inquisitor Torquemada," and a few others, which were staged in Moscow, had short runs and could not hold the stage. There is now no theatre which can claim to have an exclusively anti-religious repertory. But there are many plays, one might say almost every new play, dealing with Soviet life, having something anti-religious about it; the religious character in the drama is presented either as a villain or an idiot with the intention thereby to characterize religion as anti-social.

The production of anti-religious films has been more successful. Many of them are of considerable artistic quality, but they all remain within the range of anti-clerical themes and do not seriously approach the social roots of religion. Among the films which enjoyed considerable popularity were the " Feast of St. Georgeus," " The Cross and the Mauser," " The Third Wife of the Mullah," " Behind the Convent Walls," " Judas," and a number of others. The evils of the harem, and the degradation of women in Moslem communities, found its reflection in many films produced in Central Asia, Georgia and Adzerbajan. In the Far East was filmed from nature the barbaric and superstitious nature of religious customs amongst the natives and similar scenes.

But in the Soviet film, as in the stage play, it has become the rule to insinuate against religion, thus to discredit it in the eyes of the spectator. Scientific films such as the " Mechanism of the Brain," " Man and the Ape," etc., have also been produced with the insinuation that religion is opposed to and incompatible with science.

The greatest difficulty the atheist propagandist has found is in creating anti-religious music. Composers who have tried it get no further than satirizing some of the great religious tunes by working them into a pot-pouri of wild dance music. This was done by Pulver, who wrote the music to Demyan Bedny's " March of the 14th Division to Heaven." So far, however, there is no anti-religious song or symphony which has captured the atmosphere and imagination of anti-religious sentiment, and most musicians doubt whether atheism lends itself to musical expression. Atheism is chiefly an intellectual product whereas religion is chiefly emotional ; therefore religion found its most powerful expression in a music, contributed to by practically all great composers.

Our survey of anti-religious activities in the Soviet Union, though far from exhaustive, has shown us to what extent anti-religion has gripped the popular imagination and the skill with which it is carried on, using every scientific and cultural device to attain its end—the destruction of religion. Nothing like it has ever happened in the history of mankind. Surely religion under Communism is put to a test which it never before has had to face. Will it survive the ordeal ?

CHAPTER XIV
THE OUTLOOK

THE strategists of the militant atheist movement have calculated that within the next decade the power of organized religion will be broken in the Soviet Union and the roots which feed religion will wither away. Simultaneously it might seem that the militant atheist movement will also wither away because it will have fulfilled the chief task for which it was called into existence, and this actually is the opinion of some observers.

In our estimate the case is not so simple. First of all, organized religion will not disappear so rapidly as the antireligious strategists think. Even if the militant atheist movement should succeed in closing all the churches, the remaining faithful will start an underground existence which will lend to religion a new attraction, gather a new following with zeal and ardour peculiar to new converts. Then we must not forget that there are many sects which do not depend upon specially equipped buildings as does the Orthodox Church for their existence, and recent observations show that sectarianism still increases in the Soviet Union. The crux of the problem is, however, not in the liquidation of existing religious organizations. The wiser men in the Government know very well that religion will not be eradicated simply by making its organized form difficult or impossible. They know that religion will disappear only if the conditions which create and feed it disappear.

What are these conditions? In Communist opinion they are chiefly social and economic, arising from the anarchical conditions of a class stratified society, with its exploitation, uncertainties, fears, crises, and an over-emphasis of the individual as against group solidarity; then there are the great woes and calamities which from time to time overcome even modern society, such as wars, famines, pestilences, floods, earthquakes, accidents, untimely death, disappointments in love and friendship and last, not least, the eternal question of the mysterious meaning of the universe with its *whence, why* and *whither* of life. All these facts have contributed to the survival of religion. Many thoughtful, sensitive, but lonely men have again and again sought solace and an answer to the mystery of life in occult and mystic realms. Many of the causes just indicated as contributing to the development of religion, will no doubt disappear or at least will be greatly limited in a classless society, but they can never be eliminated altogether ; hence some of the roots, from which new religions will continue to sprout, will remain.

The question as to the future of religion and of atheism is in the last analysis still a theistic problem. If there is a God in the universe, men will continue to seek and worship Him ; if there is none, this greatest of human illusions will be exposed in the Communist social order which, for the first time in history, is organizing its life on the hypothesis that there is no God. We know that there were and still are many thinkers who have laid aside the problem of seeking God as a hopeless effort and have sought to re-value religion æsthetically and socially, appreciating it as a reverent, loving attitude to the universe and human society, which, God or no God, should by all means be preserved.

Such great humanists of a century ago as Ludwig Feuerbach and August Comte made desperate efforts to establish a religion without a God. After a century of the existence of the humanist movement in religion it must be confessed that it has been unable to attract any considerable following and has done practically nothing to inspire the movement for the emancipation of exploited toilers. The same is true of more recent ventures such as the Society of Ethical Culture and similar movements which have tried to preserve the ethical and æsthetical values of worship without recognizing the existence of Deity. In spite of the seeming hopelessness of discovering

God by the power of Reason, thinking men again and again resume these efforts, changing their methods but never their aim.

Man, it seems, cannot exist for long without some guiding philosophy of life, nor without some emotional stimuli which religious cult has usually been able to supply; the emotional aspect of religion has been always the more evident and appreciated. In the past religion has been predominantly an opiate, a soporific, and precisely for this very reason it is still to this day desirable to many people, despite their intellectual conviction that the metaphysics and ethics of the historic religious creeds have lost their social and rational significance. The æsthetics of religion, with its dainty mystic art, has still a tremendous attraction even to confirmed atheists. The writer knows this from many years observation of the musical life of Moscow. The great mystic musical creations like Mozart's " Requiem," Bach's " Mattheus Passion," the magnificent religious symphonies of Beethoven, and the operas of Mussorgsky, Tchaikowsky, Rimski-Korsakoff and others, remain a great attraction to Communist audiences and as yet there is nothing to take their place, for, as we have shown, modern composers have been unable to create an atheistic music.

Atheist ideology is too rationalistic. It exists in an emotional vacuum which is unsuited to human nature. The strength of the anti-religious propaganda is more in its ethical appeal than in its criticism of the obscure metaphysics and the dogmas of religion. The masses which have dropped their religious affiliations are moved at present by the pathos of the Socialist construction programme. They have embraced the " Religion of the Five-Year Plan " which has the promise of a better and happier future in the practical realization of which all can participate. Further there is the great appeal of international Communism with its great impending struggles and sacrifices. These are to many Communists an adequate substitute for religion. But everyone is not a Communist enthusiast and fighter; the majority will probably always remain indifferent and need inspiration and education, otherwise they will quickly drift into anti-social habits and become a menace to the community. Again, there are always some, disappointed and hurt in the struggle of life, the weary and the heavy-laden; to what or to whom shall they turn for solace and relief?

The Communist system has so far developed nothing which could fully replace the institution of pastoral care and of the Church. Yet some such institution is undoubtedly a human need in every form of society. All this points to the necessity of some organization which would take up these functions formerly pursued by the Church, providing emotional activities, inspiration, ethical instruction, and personal care. Who, in Soviet society, should take over these functions? So far some of them have been rendered by various non-religious organizations and institutions, although there is no single institution specially set apart with these objects in view.

The Soviet theatre and art institutions have, to a great extent, assumed the function of the ethical training and inspiration of the masses. The Soviet theatre, the cinema, the radio, the art exhibits, the concerts, even the circus and the cabaret have, apart from their æsthetic qualities, a distinctly moral and educational purpose, appealing to the best in human nature and inspiring it by challenging the intellect and the emotions. So noble a purpose in Soviet Art has many possibilities, of which Communist leadership is fully aware. The Second Five-Year Plan provides not only for a large construction programme of new buildings for Art Institutions and for the training of new artists, but it seeks also to overcome the passive nature of the theatre audience by creating social entertainments with folk dancing and singing, into which the masses are drawn in active participation. This is done particularly in the popular Parks of Culture and Rest, in the Amateur Dramatic and Musical Societies, at the Clubs, and such other places. Thus the æsthetic and emotional needs of the masses for which the Church formerly catered are now gratified by the Soviet Art institutions. In the theatres and concert halls no distinctly atheist propaganda is carried on; on the contrary free use is made of all the spiritual heritage and art of the past, presenting it in a secularized form, and while on the surface it may appear as something different, it satisfies the ethical and æsthetic needs of the masses. Some of the former pastoral functions of the Church have now been successfully assumed by the various social-service sections of the local Soviets and by the many special Soviet organizations such as the Red Cross and the children's and Mothers' Aid Societies, amongst others.

What, finally, will become of the movement of militant atheism? It is quite possible that it will gradually disappear, though more likely to change its tenets and become a popular institution for training the masses in Communist ideology, with a special emphasis on the ethical aspects; of such an institution there is a great need. The former anti-religious agitator, gradually and hardly conscious of the change, is now turning to the functions of teacher and ethical instructor. From the ranks of the more active enthusiasts students are recruited, trained in the history and psychology of religion and in the fundamentals of Communist Philosophy. These young men, by temper and qualification, under different circumstances would probably have chosen the study of theology and entered the service of the Church, but in the new social order they pursue a function similar to teachers of Communist ideology. Trained for this activity, they are forming certain mental habits which partially unfit them for any other work and for that reason they will probably stay on in this profession, which we may call Soviet Socratics, for the rest of their active life. While at present their message remains largely a critique of religion, the needs of life call more and more for the positive presentation of a theory of life and action. In this manner there develops a new institution of professional men to teach the ways of the good life in the Communist social order.

Existing as a voluntary society the Union of Militant Atheists is ambitious in building up its organization. It has already converted many of the large church buildings into premises on which to carry on its propaganda and there are plans for erecting new buildings which would suit the method of their work better than old churches. In short, step by step, the demands of life create institutions which more and more assume the functions of the discarded institutions of the Church. The weakest link in this process is the absence of a uniform æsthetic symbolic cult, appealing to the imagination of the masses, acting as an inspiration and supplying them with a much-craved-for emotional solidarity. But even here we find beginnings, in the so-called " Red Corners," with their inevitable busts of Lenin and of other popular leaders, mounted upon beautifully draped pedestals, and decorated with velvet or red silk banners, with fine gold embroideries. The Communist " red funerals," " red baptismals," " red weddings " and other dedicatory ceremonies rapidly assume the semblance of a cult and while, as yet, not properly standardized, they create the manners, language, musical accompaniments and the atmosphere generally which formerly was provided by the institution of organized religion.

Thus, step by step, in place of the abandoned cults and traditions the new life creates its own social and cultural forms. We see, therefore, no reason why the former institutions of organized religion should not disappear altogether and be replaced by something new, a higher synthesis in form and content of the obscure cults and ideologies of the past. A few centuries hence, historians and sociologists, in analyzing the superstructures of classless society, will point out that there are many survivals, rudiments and developments of what once used to be called religion.

Since the Revolution broke the bonds which tied the social life of the Russian people to its religious institutions and ideology, there is little left unchallenged which was once considered of permanent value and authority. Frankly we see no future for the former established Church of Russia ; while it may linger for much longer than its Communist gravediggers have allowed it for its death, already it has been so weakened, and its former leadership so discredited, as to render no longer dangerous as a competitor in modern Soviet life.

The Evangelical Sectarians, whilst their movement is yet vital, their appeal on the intellectual side is rather to the old ignorance and prejudice of the masses, which will doubtless hit back upon them, most painfully, as a boomerang, when a new Soviet generation, trained in modern natural and social sciences, confronts these fundamentalist Evangelicals who so far have not dared to adjust their antiquated theology.

Thus the future of religion in Russia is above all a socio-psychological problem. Organized religion is the social form in which is moulded the spiritual experience of men. The old moulds are now breaking up. This fact our study has already revealed, yet it remains to be seen whether the new generations will reveal a different psychology, not possessing those psychic traits which create spiritual religion. These latter were never at any time too common, but were as rare as other spiritual qualities, as the artistic and creative traits. If religion be only nurture then in Russia there will be no religion; but if religion in its subjective aspects is chiefly nature, that is, an innate spiritual quality of man, then, we ask how a Communist society can avoid the birth of people possessing these qualities, and what moulds the classless society will provide for its proper expression.

The science of eugenics has not discovered any method by which to select men of spiritual quality, nor do we know whether these qualities are hereditary. Religious types of genius are as much biological variants as any other type of genius. The problem is thus not one of selection but one of providing the proper nurture and a suitable environment for the unhindered development of those subtle human values which are now largely crippled or forced, as was the case in the ascetic mysticism of the Russian Church, into anti-social channels. We are confident, however, that the classless Communist order will provide an infinitely more advantageous environment for the selection, development and nurture of the subtle psychic qualities of man, than was ever possible in the class-stratified materialistic civilization of acquisitive society.

These conditions will open the era of what we may call the personal plane of society. It will show us what untapped reservoirs human nature has, and while, no doubt, many new qualities will reveal themselves, new attempts also will be made to re-value the forgotten treasures of past spiritual cultures. I cannot help thinking that future generations of Russian people will *rediscover* Jesus, whose historicity is now denied and whose gospel is now rapidly being obscured in the memory of the present generation.[1] Will the rediscovered Jesus be the crucified Son of Man, the martyred prophet of an unpopular cause, or will he be Jesus the poet, the friend of the flowers, the birds, and the little children, or will he be Jesus Christ the *logos* manifested .. who can tell? The mystery of the cross, of the innocent sufferer, may never be solved. The new social order cannot be a painless, static, fools-paradise; so long as the laws of nature continue to function, there will be inexplicable suffering to contend with. The appearance of human self-consciousness is a gloriously bright light in the shadow of the universe. Has it its constant beyond the effervescent manifestations we call Life? This will probably always remain a mystery, and hence the object of faith and contemplation.

The young Soviet people have demands and interests which to-day are not satisfied, so they reject both the existing religious teachings and the anti-religious propaganda. There is need for a message which synthetically would enrich the social message of Communism with emotional and ethical values. This message in content and form will be nothing like any of the old institutions of religion. It will be upon a much higher intellectual level, much more æsthetic in form and sentiment. It will greatly differ from the present crude presentation of atheist propaganda. We may be sure the future lies not in the *negation* of the past but in the *affirmation* of the new life for which the proletarian revolution has prepared the way, and the coming Communist classless society should be the most favourable environment for the development of a spiritual culture never before dreamed of by prophets, sages or poets.

[1] The attraction which the character of Jesus has to the poetic mind may be seen from the fact that the famous French Communist writer, Henri Barbusse, has turned to this subject in his book *Jesus*.

APPENDIX I

IMPORTANT DOCUMENTS, ISSUED BY THE U.S.S.R. COMMUNIST PARTY, RELATING TO RELIGION

A.—Programme and Rules of the U.S.S.R. Communist Party of Bolsheviks

§ 13. *In the Field of Religious Relations.*

In relation to religion the U.S.S.R. Communist Party does not limit itself to the already decreed separation of Church and State and of the School from the Church—measures which bourgeois democracy itself advances in its progress, but nowhere in the world has carried to the end because of the various actual relations of Capital and religious propaganda.

The U.S.S.R. Communist Party guides itself by the conviction that the realization of planning and consciousness, in the whole social-economic activity of man, alone will result in the complete withering away of religious prejudice. The Party strives towards a complete destruction of the relation between the exploiting class and the organization of religious propaganda, thus effecting the actual liberation of the toiling mass from religious prejudice, and towards organizing a most extensive scientific educational and anti-religious propaganda. Herein it is necessary carefully to avoid any insult to the feelings of believers, since that would only lead to the strengthening of religious fanaticism.

(*Translated from the* 16*th Edition,* 1932.)

B.—Problems and Methods of Anti-religious Propaganda

(Theses adopted at the Party Conference on Anti-religious Propaganda and at the Central Committee of the U.S.S.R. Communist Party, April 27-30, 1926.)

I. *Basic Conditions for the Proper Organization of Anti-religious Propaganda.*

1. The correct solution of the problem relating to the content and method of anti-religious propaganda depends on three basic conditions: (1) on the correct understanding of the very nature of

religion ; (2) on a correct evaluation of the objective rôle as well as the subjective aspect of religion ; (3) on the correct grasp of conditions under which the anti-religious propaganda is developed, relating it to the political and economic problems of the particular period.

II. Significance of a Correct Understanding of the Nature of Religion.

2. Success in anti-religious propaganda depends, to a considerable extent, upon a correct definition of religion, upon which our propagandists have their base and from which they proceed in their work. The struggle with religion can be successful only under conditions of a correct understanding of the very nature of the religious philosophy of life, a correct evaluation of the rôle of religion in the life of the toilers, a proper grasp of the causes which raise or lower the waves of religious sentiment among the toiling mass of the population.

Every simplification, every one-sidedness or narrowing down of definition of religion, the insufficient appreciation of any of these aspects, must inevitably lead, and actually does lead, to all kinds of " deviations " in practice.

III. Objective Rôle and the Subjective Aspect of Religion.

3. In all anti-religious activity explaining comprehensively and emphasizing the objective rôle of religion as subjugation and oppression of the toilers, it is necessary at the same time to make a distinction between this objective rôle of religion and the mode of its subjective acceptance by one or another social group (the backward strata of proletarians ; various social groupings of peasants, etc.), i.e. the subjective aspect of religion.

It is necessary, in defining the content and methods of anti-religious propaganda, to remember that the subjective aspects of religion represent :

(*a*) A philosophy of life and the universe ; that is to say, a peculiar system of fantastic conceptions of the universe, not corresponding to fact and contradictory to the data of contemporary science.

(*b*) A peculiar emotion and mystic sentiment.

(*c*) " A more or less consistent system of behaviour " outwardly expressed in " religious worship, or . . . cult " of the believers—(Plekhanov).

(*d*) A system of morals—since the concept of good and evil peculiar to one or another social group, all concepts of " duty " and all rules and opinions regulating the conduct of people, are usually presented by believers in a religious form, whilst others are transformed into a system of religious-moral concepts (i.e. into religious morals).

APPENDIX I

Naturally, between the objective and subjective aspects of religion exists a close, inseparable relation. Religion becomes an implement of class oppression through the system of religious concepts of the world, through religious emotions, and through various rules of everyday behaviour. The problem of the anti-religionist consists not only in illuminating, from the aspect of Marxism, these two aspects of religion, but also in detecting the existing inseparable and close relation between them.

Furthermore, detecting in the subjective aspect of religion its objective rôle, as an implement in the hands of the exploiters, it is necessary with sufficient clearness to extract its bourgeois kernel from the especially variable shell of mythology, and with this end in view to carry out anti-religious propaganda in every existing religion. Such an approach will at the same time prevent the possibility of the interpretation of anti-religious propaganda, by the clergy and the believing masses, as persecution of one or another creed in particular.

IV. *It is Necessary to Calculate Strictly the Peculiarities of the Situation and the Close Relation of Anti-religious Propaganda with Economic and Political Problems.*

4. A particularly important condition to the success of anti-religious propaganda, as of every agitational and cultural-educational activity, is its strict co-ordination with the conditions and peculiarities of a given moment.

At present we observe, in the toiling masses, two opposite processes in the field of religious experience. On the one hand, religion is exhausting itself, and atheism is spreading and deepening; this progress is seen in the growth of the Society of Atheists and the increasing rejection of religious ceremonies (baptisms, Church weddings and funerals, and the entertainment of the priest on feast days), as well as an increased interest in anti-religious lectures and literature. On the other hand, in some strata of the toiling population, not only among peasants but also among workers, is observed the opposite process, an increasing growth in some places of sectarianism, in others a strengthening of the orthodox parishes.

Anti-religious propaganda must be construed upon an exact computation and scientific Marxian grasp of all the peculiarities of the given moment, on which background such contradictory phenomena as the growth of atheism and the strengthening of religion are comprehensible. Anti-religious propaganda must proceed from a clear understanding " of the social roots " of religion precisely now, at the given period of socialist construction and must be closely related to the political tasks of the moment. The growth of atheism, generally speaking, is conditioned by the very process of socialist construction. The participation of the toiling masses in the administration of the State, in the trade union and co-operative movement, in political educational work, in the growth of agriculture, of technique and of co-operation in the villages, etc.—all such participation conditions the desertion of religion by the working masses. But inasmuch as socialist construction (even though in the form of agricultural producers co-operation) does not yet sufficiently embrace the broad peasant masses, and inasmuch as the poor and middle peasant still remains an individual small producer—in so far the premises of religious sentiment are for the time preserved in these strata, in the economic conditions of their existence. These sentiments are also upheld in the backward strata of the proletariat, among petty artisans and similar groups of toilers, by the comparatively high cost of living, by unemployment, by insufficient organization of this strata, and by the inadequacy of educational work among them. In this respect those new working strata, formed by peasants migrating for work to the towns without severing their relation to the village, also demand attention. However, the increased activity of priests and sectarian leaders at the present time is undoubtedly due not so much to the maintenance of religious sentiment in the various strata of the working population as to the development of the new bourgeoisie (the *Kulaks* in the villages and the *Nepmen* in the cities).[1] *Kulaks* and *Nepmen* make use of religion in new forms, under changed circumstances, for their class interests. Anti-religious propaganda must take into consideration the new forms of class utilization by the *kulaks* of the religious sentiments of the middle and poor peasants, in order thus to counteract the aims of socialist construction in the villages. Therefore anti-religious propaganda must be construed so as to be closely related to the general work of the socialist construction of the Party and Soviet power, and also with the problems and methods of this work under present conditions.

V. *Comprehensive Critique of Religion Necessary*.

5. In view of the conditions outlined above, as well as in view of the peculiar complexity of religion and its many aspects as a social phenomena, the possibility of the complete success of anti-religious propaganda is assured only by a comprehensive critique of religion; the exposition of the harmful rôle of religion in the life of society must be carried on simultaneously along *all* directions indicated above, it must embrace *all* aspects of religion.

[1] Since destroyed as a class. *Translator*.

APPENDIX I

It is necessary to struggle against religion ; firstly, by exposing the class essences of religious beliefs ; the underlying class basis of the activities of the religious organizations of both the dominant Church as well as of the sects ; by exposing religion in its rôle, in Western Europe, America and in the Orient, as the servant of capital.

Secondly, by exposing the anti-scientific nature of religion, which as such proves a trustworthy means in the hands of the bourgeoisie for obscuring the class consciousness of the toilers by idealistic notions, distorting and perverting their concept of the world, the laws of nature and the development of human society. By pointing out that objectively religion imposes upon the toilers a false concept of the world, thus preventing them from forming the concept obtained from contemporary science ; that religion shows itself as servant and weapon of the exploiters, since whilst the proletariat is mastering science and transforms it into an implement of his class struggle, religion plays the rôle of a class implement in the hands of his enemies.

Thirdly, the struggle with religion must be carried on by exposing religious morals, as a morality imposed in a special manner upon the toilers by the ruling class. (Contemporary Christianity, for example, as a system of morals, represents by itself nothing but such concept of duty as is in the interest of the exploiters. The morals, proposed to the toilers by Christianity, are bourgeois-exploiter morals, training the exploited classes for all those qualities which, from the point of view of the exploiter, his victim should have : silence, passiveness, meekness, patience.)

It is necessary to condemn categorically, as the worst type of popery, every effort or approachment of Christianity to Communism. Religion must be rejected for good, without reservation and camouflage. At the given moment this is particularly necessary since sectarianism, in its effort to hide from the toiling masses its bourgeois essence, is adopting a Communist phraseology. Every obscuration by anti-religionists in this respect will be used by sectarians against us.

Fourthly, it is necessary to point out the harmfulness to the class interests of the toilers of religious emotions and sentiment. It must be shown that the feeling of awe paralyzes human thought and results in a submissive instead of a critical attitude, produces fear and compliance and results from slavish conditions of society based upon exploitation.

Fifthly, it is necessary that anti-religious propaganda, in the conditions of the given moment, should become one of the sections of the general ideological and political struggle for the interest of socialist construction. It is necessary to expose the political rôle of religion at the given moment as the servant of Kulaks and the Nepmen bourgeoisie and their struggle against the construction of socialism. Especially is it necessary to expose the rôle of sectarian religion in the villages, which propaganda helps to strengthen the Kulaks. This should be done by exposing the class meaning of the preaching of general peace, love and co-operation under conditions of stratification in the village and the growth of the Kulaks.

VI. *The Harmfulness of Insufficient Appreciation of the Subjective Aspect and of the Objective Rôle of Religion.*

6. Insufficient appreciation of the significance of the subjective aspect of religion, in the sense of limiting our task to exposing religion as an implement for the oppression of the workers, results, in practice, in narrowing the limits of anti-religious propaganda, by which it is inevitably reduced to superficial agitation, thus objectively preparing the ground for the appearance of those mechanistically simplified, unscientific, frequently idealistic conceptions of religion, which are only a product of the fraud of the ruling classes and the priests.

This narrowing of the limits of our work deprives us of the possibility of gripping by a wide ideological influence, the toiling proletarian masses, among whom religious sentiment still persists, and thus compels the adherents of this view to concentrate themselves in their work only upon the " top layers," the vanguard of the masses. Such " proletarian aristocracy " is a great political danger under present conditions.

In relation to the strengthening of the Soviet economy and the progressive development of our industrial programme, the opening of new mills and factories results in profound changes in the composition of the working class ; new elements are added to it from the villages which have as yet not broken their relation to the peasant economy. This produces a " peasant " sentiment in the ranks of the working class. It is unpardonable, therefore, for us to forget our duty to this enormous mass of fresh poorly-qualified elements in the working class.

7. A further error is just the reverse of that above described and is due to the insufficient comprehension of the objective rôle of religion, that is, its political and class essence. According to this opinion, which may be characterized as that of " liquidation," anti-religious propaganda must be severed from the concrete problems of the class struggle advanced by life itself—disassociated from questions of social life and of politics, in other words liquidated, and

replaced by mere " enlightenment," by a dissemination of scientific and agronomic knowledge.

Such deviation is not less harmful, since it is well known that neither cultural activity nor enlightenment by themselves are the means of freeing man from the religious opiate.

VII. *Anti-religious Propaganda is Unthinkable without Relating it to the Problems of the Class Struggle and Socialist Construction.*

8. " Economic slavery is the true source of the religious humbugging of man," says Lenin, " and only socialism frees the worker from faith in a future life, by consolidating him in the present struggle for a better life on earth " (*Socialism and Religion*). " The oppression of religion over humanity is but the product and reflex of economic oppression within society, and therefore, by no books and no sermons is it possible to enlighten the proletariat, if his own struggle will not enlighten him against the dark forces of Capitalism " (Lenin). It is necessary to relate our work in the struggle with religion to the general political problems of the class struggle of the proletariat, recommending to all toilers a complete denunciation of religion, as that objectively necessary conclusion at which arrives every conscious fighter for the emancipation of the toiling part of humanity from the oppression and violence of Capital. All our atheist conclusions we must make to proceed from the class interests and demands of the toiling section of contemporary humanity.

The religious sentiments of people cannot be got rid of as a result of intellectual effort alone. Fantastic concepts of actuality persist in the people's minds because in the conditions of their lives there exists a corresponding ground for these concepts. Life does not change from reasoning about it. Only socialism, only the struggle for a thorough reconstruction of life upon socialist principles, can free man's consciousness from the mystic concepts of life. Only socialism can prove itself the force fit to remove from the path of human development the hindrances created by religion. This thought, expressed by Com. Lenin twenty years ago, finds its realization and corroboration in our days. Economic and political oppression, the struggle with nature under conditions of backward technique, isolation and the confused struggle of unorganized individuals and of petty producers, economic slavery and impotence, served as source of the religious sentiments of the toiling poor under the regime of exploiters who, with the aid of the priests, transformed these sentiments into implements of still greater enslavement and oppression. It would suffice to understand the sources of these phenomena in order that these sentiments may disappear. It was necessary to attain a real possibility to remove these causes. " Philosophers have only explained the world in one way or another, our task is to change it." (Marx.)

The possibility of " changing " the world is now gradually being realized under our dictatorship. The extensive drift from religion by the toiling masses at the present time is a fact not so much the result of atheist propaganda as it is the result of the strengthening and development of the socialist elements of our economy. Anti-religious propaganda only helps the masses to abandon religion, it accelerates the process where the conditions are ripe for it. The increase of atheism among the proletarians is conditioned by the fact that the latter participate more actively in socialist construction. This process takes place much more slowly among the peasants. But the mechanization of the whole of Soviet production, and especially the supply of tractors to the village, will mean a gigantic technical revolution in our economy. The power of nature over man, limited in his struggle with it by the capacity of his own muscles, will be replaced by a human control over nature by means of the powerful resources of electric energy. The isolated position of millions of solitary producers will be replaced by powerful co-operative unions of economic contact between the city and the village. The many millions of the village will be drawn into the construction of Socialism, which will free human consciousness from faith in God now shattered by anti-religious propaganda. Already Socialism pursues religion at every step. In this struggle each perfected machine in the factory, each tractor on the fields of the farmer, is a weapon ; electricity is his force, co-operation the way leading to victory ; the drift from religion to atheism is the ideological expression of the gigantic material changes taking place at this moment in our country.

9. " We . . . must not drift into abstract idealistic presentation of the religious problem ' by reason,' outside of the class struggle." (Lenin—*Socialism and Religion*.) We must not construct our programme merely by limiting our task to exposing the logical contradictions of priestly creeds ; we must unfold before the consciousness of the toilers those gigantic contradictions which exist between his class interest and the demands of religion.

We must construct our propaganda upon rigidly concrete material, such as the actual surroundings of the proletarian or the peasant. We must point out that religion is a handicap in the life of the toiler ; that it obscures the development of his class consciousness and thereby reinforces and strengthens the yoke of Capital over its victims ; that it hinders his abilities in the struggle for a better lot on earth ; that it hinders the development of technique, condemning the toilers to starvation and want ; that it hinders the development of the political struggle and supports the exploiters in their greedy attempts to suck out completely the vitality of contemporary proletarians.

Finally, we must emphasize the harmful reactionary rôle of religion in home and social life.

VIII. *Anti-religious Propaganda must Serve the Scientific Materialistic Philosophy of Life.*

10. Even if anti-religious propaganda presents a concentrated, combined blow at religion, its exposure does not exhaust our task. It is only one part of our work.

We reject religion in order to clear and prepare the way for injecting into the consciousness of the toilers the basic principles of Marxian science. With us exposure is no end in itself ; it is only one of the means of purging the minds of the toilers of false mystic views of life by grafting thereon the scientific materialist conception of the world, of man and human society.

" The Marxist differs from the anarchist and from the bourgeois enlightener in that he sees his task not only in destroying faith in God, but also in destroying the religious philosophy of life by scientific concept." . . . (I. I. Skvortsov-Stepanov. *Principles of Anti-religious Propaganda.*)

IX. *Anti-religious propaganda must be Construed in Consideration of the Peculiar Conditions of the lives of Toilers (Workers and Peasants).*

11. Religion is by no means the result of exceptional ignorance and darkness, just as it is not a question of simple logic, the result of false thinking. It has its roots in the social life, in the conditions of existence ; it grows upon the soil of definite social relations and is determined by the class position in society of the one or the other group.

The religious convictions of people depend on the methods of production in society, on the level of development of technique, on economic and political conditions. Therefore our task in selecting the more appropriate methods of anti-religious propaganda may, in principle, be reduced to the following : in as much as the conditions of life are not everywhere the same, there can be no uniform method of struggle with religion in all conditions of life ; the methods must naturally be selected in consideration of the situation in each particular place.

12. By inertia, backwardness, routine, primitive savage technique,

which deliver the peasant into the power of the uncontrolled forces of nature ; his ignorance of natural law ; his inability scientifically to grasp natural processes and to select the useful forces of nature serviceable to his economy ; his inability to subject them, technically to overcome them and, what is most important, his lack of means for this control ; by all such are created conditions for the appearance of faith in fortunate or unfortunate chance, in evil or good fate, or in " providence," which direct the fate of man independent of his will. All this, taken together, creates the basis of the religious sentiments of the people. In these conditions, upon this ground, appears and develops faith in God, designer and ruler of the world. Thus becomes evident the need of directing anti-religious criticism not only against faith itself, but also upon those material causes which condition the vitality and persistance of religious sentiment—namely, backward technique, backward methods of production, backward social customs, and deadening inertia and routine in the family and social habits of village life. In these conditions present-day peasant economy remains deprived of scientific efficiency. In spite of our achievements we have far from mastered in the villages the dependence upon uncontrolled nature and the slavish attitude thereto. All this, taken together, explains the difficulty of the peasant mass in understanding those processes which take place in nature and society. Therefore, in exposing religion as the implement of class oppression, as the servant of the Kulak class in its effort to subject the poor and middle peasant to its influence and control, in emphasizing the social-political rôle of religion in the present-day village, it is simultaneously necessary to lay stress upon natural science and agronomic propaganda. Anti-religious work in the village must give the peasant a materialistic interpretation of those phenomena of social life and of nature with which they come into contact. In this respect it is necessary to show the peasant that the religious interpretation of the phenomena of nature and society is false, depriving him of the possibility of a correct concept of life, and how it might be changed to his advantage. It is necessary so to formulate anti-religious propaganda in the villages that the peasant rejection of religion would be a logical conclusion from the point of view of his interests, resulting from his own reasoning and calculation of what would be profitable to his economy. It is necessary to correlate anti-religious propaganda with the problem of the peasant economy from the point of view of its development towards Socialism.

13. Anti-religious propaganda in the village must have the nature of a quiet, cautious talk, a deepening propaganda influencing the mind of the hearers.

APPENDIX I

With no less caution it is necessary to carry on anti-religious propaganda among the workers, particularly at present when is observed a considerable influx of peasantry into the working class. It is our duty not to repulse but to attract these fresh elements in the working class, to attach oneself closer to them and subject them to our influence. The old rule of Lenin, " better to move slower but with the whole mass," is of exceptional significance at the present moment. Our programme must be thoroughly saturated in the spirit of uniting ourselves to the proletariat and the principle body of the peasants, in the spirit of consolidating these two groups of toilers in our Union.

Problems in discrediting and exposing methods, passion for offensive tactics and its over-estimation in anti-religious propaganda results in ugly phenomena as :

(*a*) Struggle against religion by external pressure (administrational method ; closing of churches ; removing of church bells ; etc.).

(*b*) By shocking (carnivals and demonstrations), and even, in isolated cases, by terror.

Particular caution must be maintained toward debates, which frequently yield results contrary to those for which they were organized.

X. *In Anti-religious Propaganda National Peculiarities must be taken in Consideration.*

14. The fact of the existing influence of the clergy upon national minorities, among which are adherents of Islam, Lamaism, Judaism, Catholicism ; the fanaticism of the believing masses, which is frequently exploited by the clergy for organizing resistance to Soviet construction ; the increased propaganda, directed to associate the concept of nationality with religion ; these create special difficulties in work among these nationalities. These difficulties may be overcome only by a careful, thoughtful approach in this work.

The methods of propaganda among the nationalities of the U.S.S.R. are conditioned by :

(*a*) The form of the economic life of the nationalities among which are distributed the religions mentioned above ;
(*b*) The remnants of semi-feudal class relations existing locally ;
(*c*) The historic past ;
(*d*) The degree of participation in Soviet construction ;
(*e*) The degree of influence of religious organizations and religion.

XI. Practical Conclusions.

1. A widely-spread development of anti-religious propaganda is necessary both in the city, among the backward strata of the working-class and particularly among its new strata immigrant from the villages, and in the villages, where religion, particularly sectarianism, and the religious sentiments among the village poor and middle peasants are used by the Kulak class for increasing their influence upon the peasant mass, for struggling with Soviet society and for counteracting Socialist construction.

2. Anti-religious propaganda in city and village cannot and should not be carried on by the forces of the Party alone; in the interests of this propaganda a wide, non-party, active atheist group of workers and peasants should be created, organized in the local unions of atheists.

3. In these unions all Party organizations should establish firmer direction than heretofore, for which purpose it should

(a) form Communist sections therein;

(b) obtain regular reports from these sections of the work accomplished;

(c) establish an ideological control over the anti-religious literature published by the unions of atheists;

(d) strengthen the unions by qualified Party workers;

(e) consider active work in the unions of atheists, as well as the anti-religious work of party men generally, as party work which is to be credit as such.

4. Provincial and regional committees must participate directly and through the medium of the atheist unions in the training of anti-religious propagandists, by organizing special seminars and by developing more than heretofore a system of propaganda study-circles among workers and peasants, transforming them into schools of political literacy and into cells for the propagation of Marxian ideas in problems relating to religion.

5. The Central Council of the Union of Atheists, together with the Chief Department of Political Education of the R.S.F.S.R., must prepare, and harmonize with the propaganda department of the Central Committee, typical programmes for seminars of anti-religious propagandists in towns and villages. These to be ready for the winter season of 1926-27. In addition, to prepare, and similarly harmonize with the propaganda department of the Central Committee, a plan for publishing special teaching manuals for these seminars and circles, having these manuals prepared and edited by qualified persons and their publication completed by the beginning of 1927.

6. Moreover, the Executive bureaux of the Central Council of the Union of Atheists, together with the Cultural Department of the All-Union Council of Trade Unions and the Chief Department of Political Education of the R.S.F.S.R., must prepare and distribute locally by the autumn of this year instructions for the organization of anti-religious propaganda in workers' clubs on the basis of the present theses. In these instructions it is necessary to consider the organic relations of anti-religious propaganda with all forms of club work, particularly of mass activities, the work of club libraries, red corners, and wall newspapers in the enterprises; in particular it is necessary to give attention to the closest relation of anti-religious propaganda with problems of the worker's social and home life; especially to set apart the problem of the " atheist corners " in the clubs, indicating the necessity of reviving their work by transforming them into corners of consultation relating to anti-religious questions, under direction of an anti-religious propagandist, demonstration of pictures, placards, etc.

7. Instructions of the same kind, in the same order, must be prepared by the autumn of this year for anti-religious propaganda in the cottage reading rooms, houses of peasants and the " atheist corners " attached to them.

8. The Executive Bureau of the Central Council of the Union of Atheists should also plan and take the necessary steps to organize an anti-religious museum and establish it in Moscow.

9. The Commissariat of Education of the Republics of the Union should provide anti-religious repertories for all kinds of theatrical productions (particularly for the workers' clubs, houses of the peasants and cottage reading-rooms), also prepare lantern slides and cinema films with an anti-religious content.

10. On the part of these Commissariats it is necessary, for the school season of 1926–27, to improve the programmes of Soviet Party schools, institutes of political education, pedogogical technicums and pedogogical faculties, by inserting elements of an anti-religious character, problems of content and method of anti-religious propaganda, in order to train party propagandists, political educators and teachers for spreading anti-religious propaganda among workers and peasants, as well as work out the problem of organizing at the Higher Schools research work in the anti-religious field.

(*Translated from " Antireligioznik," N.* 8. 1926.)

APPENDIX II

DECREES AND STIPULATIONS OF THE SOVIET GOVERNMENT RELATING TO RELIGION AND THE CHURCH

A.—DECREE OF JANUARY 23, 1918, " ON FREEDOM OF CONSCIENCE AND RELIGIOUS SOCIETIES."

1. The Church is separated from the State.
2. Within the limits of the Republic it is prohibited to publish any kind of local laws or orders which would hinder or limit the freedom of conscience, or would establish any kind of preference or privilege on the basis of the denominational adherence of the citizens.
3. Every citizen may adhere to any religion or adhere to none. Any limitations before the law relating to adherence to any kind of faith or non-adherence to any faith are abolished.

Note.—From all official documents are excluded every reference to religious adherence or non-adherence of citizens.

4. All State and other public and social functions before the law are not to be accompanied by any religious customs or ceremonies.
5. Free practice of religious customs is safeguarded in so far as it does not disturb the public peace and does not infringe upon the rights of citizens of the Soviet Republic. Local authorities have the right to take all necessary measures to safeguard public peace and security in all such cases.
6. No one may evade his civil duties on religious grounds. Exemptions from these, on condition of substituting one form of civil service by another, in each separate case must be granted by a decision of a people's court.
7. The religious oath is abolished. In necessary cases only solemn promises are given.
8. Records of civic states are kept exclusively by the civil authorities, by departments of marriages and birth.
9. The School is separated from the Church; the teaching of religious confessions is not allowed in State, public and private schools where secular subjects are taught. The citizen may teach or be taught religion in a private capacity.

10. All Church and religious societies are subject to the general status existing for voluntary societies and unions and do not enjoy any privileges or subsidies from the State, nor from local autonomous and self-governing bodies.

11. Compulsory collections or assessments for the benefit of Church or religious societies, as well as measures of compulsion or punishment on the part of these societies over their members, are not permitted.

12. No Church and religious societies have the right to own property. They have no rights of juridic persons.

13. All property of existing Church and religious societies is declared the people's property. Buildings and objects specially designated for divine service are given for free use to corresponding religious societies on the basis of special ordinance of the local or central State authorities.

B.—Decree of the All-Russian Central Executive Committee and Council of Peoples Commissars of the R.S.F.S.R. about Religious Organizations.

Author's Note.—This decree contains 68 paragraphs of which we translate fully those of special interest, for the rest we only indicate the content.

The All-Russian Central Executive Committee and Council of People's Commissars of the R.S.F.S.R. decrees:

1. Under the jurisdiction of the decree of People's Commissars of the R.S.F.S.R. from January 23, 1918, on the separation of the Church from the State, and the school from the Church, come churches, religious groups, sects, religious trends and other organizations of cult of all denominations.

2. Religious organizations of believers of all cults are registered into religious societies or groups of believers. Each citizen can be a member of only one religious organization (society or group).

A religious society is a local organization of believing citizens, not under eighteen years of age, of one and the same cult, creed, opinion or sect, in numbers not less than twenty persons, who unite for the common satisfaction of their religious needs.

Believing citizens who, due to their small number cannot form a religious society, have the right to form a group of believers.

A religious society or group of believers has no right of juridic person.

4. A religious society or group of believers can commence their activities only after registration of the society or group in a given

administrative department of a local Executive Committee or city council of a city, which is not the administrative centre of a region or of a county.

5. For the registration of a religious society its initiators, if not less than twenty persons in number, apply to the organs indicated in the previous (4) paragraph, according to a registration form fixed by the People's Commissariat of the Interior of the R.S.F.S.R.

6 refers to place of presenting applications.

7. The organs indicated in (4) are obliged, within a month from the day of the filing of the application, to register the society or group of believers or inform them of refusal of registration.

8. The composition of the religious society or group of believers, as well as their executive and controlling organs and servants of the cult, is presented to the organ with which it is registered according to the time and form prescribed by the People's Commissariat of the Interior of R.S.F.S.R.

9. In the lists of members of religious societies or groups can be entered only those believers who have given their consent to it.

10. To satisfy the religious needs of believers who have composed a religious society a special building for service and equipment, exclusively designed for purposes of the cult, may be received for free use from the township, or regional executive Committee or City Council.

In addition, believers who have formed a religious society, or a group of believers, may also use other premises for the purpose of worship, obtained from private individuals at local Soviet and Executive Committees. For these premises are applicable the same rules as for special buildings of cult; leases for the use of such premises are signed by separate believers under their personal responsibility. In addition, these premises must be satisfactory in the technical and sanitary sense.

Each religious society or group of believers cannot use more than one set of premises for worship.

11–16 refer to the signing of contracts and the election of control organs of the societies.

17. Religious organizations are prohibited: (a) from forming mutual aid associations, co-operatives, productive associations, and generally making use of the property in their care for any purpose except the satisfaction of their religious needs; (b) from rendering material aid to their members; (c) from organizing special children's, youth, women, prayer and other meetings as well as general bible studies; also literary, handiwork, industrial, teaching of religion and other meetings, groups, circles, departments, as well as organiz-

ing excursions and children's playgrounds, opening libraries and reading-rooms, organizing sanatoria and medical aid.

In buildings and premises for worship may be kept only books needed for the celebration of the cult.

18. It is prohibited to teach any religious creed in State, social and private schools and educational institutions. Such teaching may be permitted exclusively in special theological courses, opened by citizens of the U.S.S.R., with the special permission of the People's Commissar of the Interior of R.S.F.S.R., and on territories of autonomous republics with the permission of the Central Committees of the corresponding autonomous republics.

19. The region of activity of servants of the cult, of preachers and teachers, is limited to the residential area of the society served by him and the location of the place of worship.

The activity of servants of the cults, of preachers and teachers of religion, who permanently serve two or more religious units, is limited to the territory on which the believers are living who enter into these units.

20. Religious societies and groups of believers may organize local, All-Russian and All-Union, religious conferences and conventions on the basis of special permission in each case, obtained : (*a*) from the People's Commissariat of the Interior of R.S.F.S.R., when the conference is called for Russia or for the whole Union upon the territory of the R.S.F.S.R. ; or if the conference embraces a territory or two or more provinces, regions and governments ; and (*b*) from the corresponding regional or territorial, governmental or district administrative departments, if the conference is local, etc.

21–24 deal with organization and functioning of conferences.

25–44 deal with the care of property given for use to religious cults and the provisions of contract related to them and the liquidation of contracts.

45. The building of new places of worship may be permitted at the request of religious societies on the common basis and technical provisions, as well as in accordance with special regulations fixed by the People's Commissariat of the Interior.

46–53 refer to repair and maintenance of property used for worship.

54. Members of groups of believers and religious societies have the right to make and collect voluntary contributions in their place of worship as well as outside it, but only among members of a given religious unit and only for the purpose of maintaining the buildings of worship, objects of the cult, engagement of servants of the cult, and the maintenance of their executive organisations.

Every compulsory collection in favour of religious units is prosecuted by the criminal code of the R.S.F.S.R.

55–56 refer to the accounting of collected funds.

57 refers to sanitary conditions of property used for the cult.

58. Prohibits religious functions in State, social, co-operative and private enterprises.

This prohibition does not refer to requests of the dying and the sick in hospitals and prisons; religious cult in these cases is permitted in isolated rooms as well as on cemeteries and in crematoriums.

59–61 refer to regulations of religious processions.

62–63 refer to stipulations in the accounting of religious societies and groups.

64.–The control of religious units, their property, etc., is laid upon the departments which registered them.

65–66 demand re-registration within one year of the issue of this law; societies failing to do so are considered liquidated.

67–68 refer to annulling of previous stipulations contradicting this decree.

Signed by the Chairman, V.C.I.K.,
M. KALININ.
Vice-Chairman of the S.N.K., R.S.F.S.R.,
A. SMIRNOV.
Vice-Secretary, V.C.I.K.,
A. DOSOV.

April 8, 1929,
Moscow, Kreml.

Author's Note.—On the basis of this law have developed commentaries and instructions, issued by the Central Administrative organs directing the affairs of religious organizations, which serve as precedents in the application of the law.

DECREE

C.—OF THE ALL-RUSSIAN CENTRAL EXECUTIVE COMMITTEE AND THE COMMITTEE AND COUNCIL OF PEOPLE'S COMMISSARS OF R.S.F.S.R.

Relating to the Formation of a Central Commission on Religious Affairs.

On the basis of the decree of the Central Executive Committee and Council of People's Commissars of the U.S.S.R. from December 15, 1930, " concerning the liquidation of the People's Commissars of the Interior of the Union and Autonomous Republics (Isvestia C.I.K. of the Union and V.C.I.K. of December 16, 1930, No. 345), and in correspondence with the decision of the Presidium of V.S.I.K. of December 20, 1930, the All-Russian Central Executive Committee and Council of People's Commissars of the R.S.F.S.R. *decrees* :

The handling of affairs related to cults to rest upon the Commission for dealing with religious problems at the Presidium V.S.I.K. in the Centre, and locally upon the Presidiums C.I.K. of the Autonomous S.S.R., the Executive Committees and Councils through the corresponding part of the apparatus.

Chairman of the All-Russian Executive Committee,
M. KALININ.
Chairman of Council of People's Commissars R.S.F.S.R.,
D. SULIMOV.
Secretary of the All-Russian Central Executive Committee,
A. KISELEV.

December 31, 1930,
Moscow, Kreml.

DUTIES

of the Permanent Central and Local Commissions for dealing with Religious Problems.

1. The Permanent Central Commission on problems relating to organizations of cult is attached to the Presidium V.C.I.K. as the organ upon which are laid the duties of the general direction and surveillance for the correct realization of the policy of the Party and the Government in the *application* of the laws relating to cults upon the whole territory of the R.S.F.S.R.

2. The Permanent Central Commission consists of a chairman (member of the Presidium V.S.I.K.), a responsible secretary and members, personally appointed by the Presidium V.S.I.K.

3. The Permanent Central Commission is charged :

(*a*) With preparing and previously examining projected legislative acts and ordinances on questions relating to cults, and their presentation for decision to the Presidium V.C.I.K. ;

(*b*) With the general direction in the correct application of projects of legislative acts by the People's Commissariat of C.I.K., of autonomous S.S.R.s, by territorial and regional Executive Committees in legislation relating to questions of the cult, and in giving directions and assistance in these problems ;

(c) With the systematization of legislative acts and ordinances of V.C.I.K. and R.S.F.S.R. on questions relating to cults ;

(d) With the presentation of conclusions on questions of cults to the Presidium V.C.I.K. ;

(e) With dealing with complaints concerning incorrect actions of C.I.K.s of the Autonomous S.S.R.s, of territorial and regional Executive Committees, on questions related to the functioning of cults, on the closing of buildings for worship and the cancelling of contracts with religious societies and groups of believers.

Note.—The decisions of the Permanent Commission at the Presidium V.C.I.K., cancelling the decisions of Executive Committees, are subject to ratification by the Presidium V.C.I.K.

(f) With the recording of religious unions and preparation of statistical data presented by local organs.

4. In order to accomplish the task placed upon the Permanent Central Commission it has the right :

(a) to place responsibilities upon all central organs of the R.S.F.S.R. within the limits of their competence on problems related to cults ;

(b) to demand from central and local organs necessary information and materials on problems relating to cults ;

(c) to demand from Republican territorial and regional Commissions reports on their work in the field of cults ;

(d) to print and publish materials on questions of legislation related to cults ;

(e) to form Sub-Commissions, with the right of including in them representatives of departments, who are not members of the Commissions, to treat special problems related to cults.

5. All Government Departments of the R.S.F.S.R. have previously to harmonize their measures directly relating to cults with the Permanent Central Commission at the Presidium V.C.I.K. on dealing with religious problems.

6. All directive ordinances, as well as demands, of the Permanent Central Commission, relating to problems of cult are obligatory to all local organs.

7. The Permanent Central Commission on dealing with religious problems has its stamp and seal.

8. The Permanent Central Commission has its staff consisting of a responsible secretary, consultants and the necessary office assistants.

Author's Note.—Analogous regulations are given to the Local Commissions with the Central Commission as the last court of appeal.

(*Translated from Bulletin No. 2, 1932, of the Permanent Central Commission.*)

INDEX

ABRAMOV, 85
  Aethos, Monastery of Mt., 24
Albinsky, John, 212
Alexander I, 59, 69, 70, 98, 105
Alexander III, 52
Alexander-Svirsky Monastery, 206
Alexandra, Tsarina, 53
Alexis I, 24, 43, 47
American Revolution, 96
Andrew of Ufa, Bishop, 202
Anti-Christ, 48, 51, 56-57, 60, 61, 63, 64
Anti-Religious Agitators, Training of, 254-257
—— Campaigns, 253
—— Movement, The, 215-231
  Beginnings, 10, 92, 101; numerical strength, 218-220; youth organisation, 220-223; in the Red Army, 223-224; amongst Minor Nationalities, 224-227
Anti-Religious Propaganda:
  New tactics, 240-245; organisation and methods of, 246-265; problems and methods of, 275-287
Anti-Religioznik, The, 254
Arius and Athanasius, 27
Antonine, Bishop, 209, 211
Arsenius of Novgorod, Archbishop, 198
Artsybashev, *Sanine*, 136
Atheism in the Soviet Union:
  chief causes, 228-231; future of, 266-273
—— and Education, 220-222
Atheist International, The, 11, 227-228
Avvakum, Arch-Priest, 47-48

BACON, FRANCIS, 87
Bakunin, M. A.:
  Aristocratic origin, 120; early religious passion, 121; dialectic negation of religion, 121;
  as militant anarchist, 122; opposition to religion, 122-124; other references, 108, 127, 128
Baptists, 70-72, 74
Barbusse, Henri, 273
Basil of Moscow, Prince, 22
Bayle, Pierre, 87
Belinsky, V. G.:
  Early influences, 109-110; as idealist, 110-111; as materialist, 111; as revolutionist, 112; negation of religion, 113; controversy with Gogol, 113-114; denies religiosity of Russian people, 113-114; other references, 108, 125, 127
Belkoff, Priest, 209
Benjamin, Metropolitan, 209, 211
Berdyaev, N.:
  Religious position, 147-149; relation to Communism, 129, 149-150, 188; aristocratic individualism, 150-151; on Slavophilism, 131; other references, 138, 140, 143, 152
Bestuzhev, A. F., 99
Bezbozhnik, The, 215, 259
Bible in Russia, The, 26, 45-46, 69, 70, 106-107
Bielo-Krinitza Monastery, 58
Black Hundred, The, 193
Block, Alexander, 138
Blount, Charles, 78
Borisov, Peter, 105-106
Bradlaugh, *Science and Religion*, 257
Brahminism, 77
British and Foreign Bible Society, 69
Bruce, General Jacob, 85-86
Bruno, Giordano, 262
Buddhism, 11, 77
Buechner, 118
Bulgakov, Sergius, 129, 143-144

297

INDEX

CAIRD, *The Evolution of Religion*, 3
Castrators, 61, 66–68
Catechism of a Free Man, The, 106–107
Cathedrals :
    Assumption, of the, Moscow, 19, 20, 21, 23, 31–32, 40–41 ; Christ the Saviour, Moscow, 117 ; Kazan, Leningrad, 260 ; St. Isaak, Leningrad, 260, 262
Catherine II :
    Liberal enthusiasms, 62, 81, 84, 88–92, 96 ; attempts to reform the Church, 91–92 ; reactionary phase, 92–93, 97–99 ; bans masonic order, 92, 94–95, 105 ; other references, 18
Ceremonies, Decline in Religious, 229, 277
Chalcedon, Fourth General Council at, 28
Chancev, John, 212
Christianity, introduction of, into Russia, 13
—— and Paganism, Syncretism of, 14–18
Christmas Message, A Godless, 250–252
Civil War, 1919–1920, 207, 223
Collectives, Godless, 234, 241
Collectivisation :
    Hostility of sectarians to, 73 ; effect on religious beliefs, 234 ; and atheist propaganda, 226, 232–245, 247
Communism amongst Sectarians, 63, 66, 68, 70–73
—— Berdyaev on, 149–150, 188
Communist Party Conference, 1926, 216 ; theses adopted at, 275–287
—— Philosophy of Life, 179–182
—— Theory of Religion, 1–2, 5–9, 174–188
—— Writers on Religion, 258
—— Academy for the Study of Religion, 238, 255
Comte, Auguste, 1, 113, 118, 267
Condorcet, 95
Conscientious Objectors in Russia, 74
Copernicus, 86
Council of 1666–67, 47–48

D'ALEMBERT, 89, 95
Dancers, The, 66
Darwin, 118
Dead, Prayer for the, 32–33
—— Slavic Cult of the, 16–17
Decembrists :
    Their purpose, 102 ; their leaders, 103–104 ; views on religion, 104 ; aristocratic composition, 104–106 ; reasons for collapse, 107–108 ; Herzen on, 114–115 ; other references, 93, 99, 125, 189
Declaration of the Rights of Man, 98
Deism, 76–78, 88
—— Voltarian, 93, 96
de Maistre, Joseph, 79
Denyers, The, 64
Descartes, 87
d'Holbach, Baron P. A., 83–84, 94, 105
Dialectical Materialism, 174–176, 176, 179–182, 253
Dialectics, Laws of, 6, 182–185
Dictionary of Foreign Words, Petrashevsky's, 126
Diderot, Denis, 81–84, 89, 94, 95
Dietzgen, Joseph, 187
Dmitrievitch, Prince Vasily, 23
Dolgoruky, Prince Ury, 22
Dostoievsky, F., 139–143
    religious complex, 113, 126, 129, 138 ; religious outlook as expressed in his novels, 139–143 ; sentenced to death, 125, 139
Drama, Anti-Religious, 264
Dukhobury, The, 68, 70
Durkheim, 2

ECCLESIASTICAL Culture, 18–20
Ecumenical Councils, The Seven, 27, 28, 30, 32
Edinovertsy, The, 59
Elagin, 94
Ellwood, Charles A., 2–3
Encyclopædia, French, 81
Encyclopædists, French, 90, 94, 103, 174
Engels, F., attitude towards religion, 174–175 ; Anti-Duerig, 177 ; other references, 181, 258

298

INDEX

Enlightenment, French, in Russia, 77–84, 89–93, 93–95, 96, 100, 103, 105, 111
Ethics of the Russian People, 33–36
Euphemius, 62
Evangelical Christians, Union of, 72
Evangelical Sects, 10, 56, 69–75
    Increase since the Revolution, 71–73, 266, 271–272 ; increase since checked by Soviet, 71, 73–74
Extremist Sects, 62–69

FAMINE, 1921, The, 207–210
Feudalism, 38–39, 103
Feuerbach, L., 121–122, 126, 174
    Wesen des Christentums, 112, 118, 176–177
Fichte, 108, 110, 120, 121, 160
Films, Anti-Religious, 264–265
Fine Arts, Anti-Religious Use of, 264–265, 270
Five Year Plan, 217, 218, 222, 224, 225, 233, 242, 243, 247, 249, 268, 269
Flagellators, 64–65
Fontenelle, 88
Fourier, 108, 126
Fox, George, 119
Frederick II of Prussia, 78, 80, 81, 89
French Encyclopædia, 81
—— Encyclopædists, 90, 94, 103, 174
—— Enlightenment in Russia, 77–84, 89–93, 93–96, 100, 103, 105, 111
—— Revolution, 77, 81, 92, 93–95, 97, 98, 120, 182
Friends of the Newspaper Bezbozhnik 215–216
Franklin, 95

GALILEO, 86, 262
Galitzen, The Brothers, 98
Gandhi, Mahatma, 155
Gapers, The, 63
Gapon, Father Gregory, 190
George of Vladimir, Prince, 22
Georgian Church, 50
German Idealist Philosophy in Russia, 108
Giddings, Franklin H., 2
Gironde, 112
God-Builders, Socialist, 185–188

Godless at the Bench, The, 215
God-Wrestlers and God-Seekers, Intellectualist, 10, 128–154
Gogol, 113, 138
Going Amongst the People, The, 128, 135
Gorky, Maxim, 129, 186–187
Goudonov, Boris, 43
Grimm, 89

HEGEL, 2, 108, 110, 120, 121, 124, 174, 181, 182, 184
Hegelians, Young, 121
Helvetius, 84, 90, 95, 96, 105
Herbert of Cherbury, Lord, 78
Herzen, A. I. :
    Early influences, 114 ; Decembrist uprising, 114–115 ; influence of St. Simon, 115–117 ; exile, 117 ; religious dramas, 117–118 ; *Northern Star* and *The Bell*, 118 ; critic of the Church, 118–120 ; other references, 108, 127, 128
High Procurator, Functions of, 50–51, 196
Hiliodor of Tsaritsin, 53, 54
Hinduism, 77
Hlesty, The, 64–68
Hobbes, Thomas, 78, 87
Holy Alliance, 102
Holy Synod :
    Foundation and functions, 49–55 ; other references, 69, 71, 91–92, 192–193.
Huxley, Julian, 1

IBERIAN Virgin, Ikon of, 20, 24–25
Ikon Worship, 20–26, 30–32, 91, 235
Illuminates, The, 95
Industry, Heavy, Commences in Russia, 107–108
Institute of Red Professors, 255
Intellectuals and Religion, 128–154
International, Second, 227 ; third, 227
—— of Proletarian Free Thinkers, 227

JEREMIAH, Patriarch, 43
Jews, 11, 19, 52, 239
Job, Patriarch, 43
Jonah, Metropolitan, 40

INDEX

John III, 40–41
John IV, 41–42
Joseph I of Austria, 89
Jumpers, The, 65–66
Justinian, Emperor, 27

KANDIDOV, B. P., 259
Kant, 2, 6, 160, 182
Kantemir, Antioch, 88
Kautsky, 256
Kerensky régime, 195, 199
Khomyakov, A. S., 29, 108, 130, 134
Khrapovitsky, Antonius, 193–194, 196–198
Kidd, Benjamin, 2
Kiev-Petchora Monastery, 206, 260, 261
Kniggen, Adolf von, 95
Kornilov, General, 196
Kranikov, P. A., 259
Kraniuk, Z., 247
Krasnitzky, Vladimir, 209, 211
Kremlin, 19, 20
Kroner, 184
Kunow, 256

LAMETTRIE, 80–81, 89
Lecky, *History of Rationalism*, 257
Lectures, Anti-Religious, 248–250
Leibnitz, 96
Leipzig, University of, 96
Lenin :
  on Religion, 11, 177–179, 251, 281–282 ; Dialectical Materialism, 181–182 ; on Tolstoy, 156–157 ; controversy with Gogol and Lunacharsky, 187–188 ; other references, 83, 259, 271, 285
Leningrad Anti-Religious Museums, 260–262
Leonid, Archbishop, 211
Literature, Anti-Religious, 257–260
Living Church Movement, 210–212
Locke, 79, 87
Lopuchin, I. V., 94, 95
Lublinsky, Julian, 105
Lukachevsky, A. T., 238, 256, 259
Lunarcharsky, A., 129, 186–189
Luther, Martin, 160

MABLI, 96
Makarius, Bishop, 54
Marat, 111

Marx, Karl, 99, 112, 128, 129, 160, 174–177, 258
Das Kapital, 177
Marx and Engels, 113
German Ideology, 175
Masonic Order in Russia, The, 92–95, 105
  Reactionary tendency, 93–95 ; banned by Catherine II, 92, 94–95, 105
Masonic Order, The British, 94
Merezhkovsky, D. S., 138, 140, 143, 144–147, 152
Methodosius, St., 30
Michael I, 37, 43, 133
Military Training, Sectarians and, 74
Miliukov, P., 29, 32
Minor Nationalities, Atheism amongst, 224–227, 239–240, 285
  Cultural advances since Revolution, 224–225
Minsky, N. M., 153
Moleschet, 118
Molokans, The, 69–71
Montesquieu, 88, 90, 92, 96
Morris, William, 160
Moscow, Religious Splendour of, 18–20
Moscow Art Theatre, 59
—— Central Anti-Religious Museum, 260, 262
—— University, 115
Moslems, Atheism amongst, 226
  Sectarian movement, 239–240
Motorin, 259
Muraviev, Colonel N. M., 104, 106–107
Muraviev, S., 107
Murry, Middleton, 11
Museums, Anti-Religious, 260–264
Music in the Soviet Union, 265, 268, 269
Mutes, The, 63

NAPOLEON, 102, 130
Narodnik Movement :
  Origin, 107–108 ; two trends, 108 ; the Westernists, 108–127 ; Slavophilism, 108 ; movement breaks up, 127–129
Neo-Christians, The, 140, 143–154
New Israel, The, 72
Newtonian Physics, 78, 79, 181

INDEX

Nicæa, First and Seventh General Councils at, 27, 28, 30, 32
Nicene Creed, 27, 28
Nicholas I, 50, 51, 59, 63, 102, 108, 121, 125
Nicholas II, 52–55
Nicholas, The Grand-Duke, 54
Niebuhr, Reinhold, 2, 7–8
Nikhon, Patriarch, 24, 43–44, 46–48, 51, 57, 59
Nikolsky, Professor N. M., 17, 259
Nine Sisters, The Lodge of the, 95
Nonconformism, Belinsky on, 114
Nonconformity in Russia :
  Beginnings, 56–57; the Old Believers, 57–62; various extremist sects, 62–69; the Evangelical Sects, 69–75; Communist trends, 63, 66, 68, 70, 71, 72–73; pacifism, 68, 70, 74
Non-Prayers, The, 63–64
Novgorod, the Baptism of, 18
Novikov, Nikolai, 95

OGAREV, NICHOLAS, 115
Old Believers, The :
  Beginnings, 46–48; differentiation, 56–62; split over episcopate, 57–58; priestly faction, 58; Edinovertsy faction, 59; priestless faction, 59–61; radical factions, 63; prosperity of Old Believers, 58–59; service to culture, 59; as colonisers, 61–62; their Moscow settlements, 62; decline, 68–69
Olga of Kiev, Princess, 13
Oman, Professor John, 3, 5
Orthodox Church, The Greek, 13–14 26–28, 30, 32, 60
—— —— The Russian :
  Foundation, 13; close organic relation to the State, 10, 13–14, 37–55, 84, 136–137; doctrinal peculiarities, 26–33; apostolic origin theoretically established, 42; separation from Byzantium, 40–43; position under Feudalism, 38–39; relationship to Serfdom, 44–48; its wealth, 17, 18–20, 38, 44, 194, 200, 203, 209; the illiteracy of the clergy,
  and its intellectual backwardness, 15–16, 28–29, 33, 39, 46, 84, 86, 88; Slavophil idealisation of the Church, 131–134; the future, 55, 271
Orthodox Church and the Revolution, The conflict of :
  Conflict prior to 1917, 189–195; 1917–1918 Council of the Church and the re-establishment of the Patriarchate, 195–198; the Sobor, 195–198; 1917 Constitution of the Church 197; counter-revolutionary offensive of the Church, 199–202; counter-offensive of the revolutionists, 202–207; separation from the State, 202–205, 208, 290; nationalisation of Church property, 203–205, 290; relic frauds exposed, 206, 260; attitude during the Famine of 1921, 207–210; capitulation, 210–214; Living Church Movement, 209–214

PACIFISM, 68, 70, 74, 155, 170–171, 224
Pagan Survivals, 14–18
Pakhomius, 24–25
Patriarchs, Institution of, 28, 43
Patriarchal Messages, 1918, 200–201 February, 1922, 208–209
Patriarchate, Re-establishment of, 195–198
Paul the Apostle, 45
Paul of Kolomna, 57
Paul I, 99
Penn, William, 118–119
People's Liberty Party, The, 129
Pestel, Colonel P. I., 104
Petchersky Monastery, 29
Peter I, 49, 51, 55, 84–87, 88, 89, 240
Peter III, 67, 91
Peter of Moscow, Metropolitan, 202
Petrashevsky, N. V., 108, 125–127
Petrov, Gregory, 53, 137
Philaret, Patriarch, 37, 43
Philip, Metropolitan, 47
Philippovitch, Daniel, 64–65
Philotheus, 41
Plekhanov, 256
Pnin, I. T., 99–100
Pobyedonostzev, K. P., 16, 52
Pokrovsky, M., 259

INDEX

Processions of the Cross, 19–20
Prokhanov, I. S., 72
Prokopivitch, T., 85, 87, 88
Protassov, Count, 50
Protestants, 19, 45–46
Proverbs, Slavic, 33–36
Provisional Government, 1917, 195, 199
Pugatchev, 92
Putilov Strikes, 190–192

QUAKERS, 66, 68, 69

RADIO used for Propaganda, 247–249, 256
Radischev, A. N., 95–99
Ralcevitch, V., 185
Rasputin, Gregory, 53–55
Raven, Canon C. E., 1
Red Army:
  Sectarians and, 74; atheism in, 223–224, 228, 255
Relic Worship, 20–21, 30
—— frauds exposed, 206, 260
Religion:
  Nature and origins of, 1–9; Communist theory of, 1–2, 5–9, 174–188; Feuerbach on, 176–177; Gorky and Lunacharsky on, 186–188; Hegelian view of, 184; Lenin on, 11, 177–179, 251, 281–282; Marxian view of, 174–177; future of, in Russia, 9, 266–273; Communist Party Documents relating to, 275–287; Soviet Government Decrees relating to, 289–295; its special study in Communist Universities, 11, 254–257
Religion and the Revolutionary Movement, 102–127
Religious and Philosophical Society, The, 145
Renan, Life of Jesus, 257
Revolution, 1905, 71, 129, 143, 156, 200, 257
  Spiritual depression following, 135–136
—— 1917, 45, 52, 54–55, 71, 102, 135, 257
Revolution and the Church, The, 215

Revolutionary Year, 1848, 122, 125, 126
Robertson, History of Free Thought, 257, 258
Robespierre, 112
Roman Catholic Church, 19, 80, 85–86, 179, 239
Romanov, Lord Yamblikon, 25
Romanovs, The, 37
Rosanov, V. V., 138, 140, 143, 151–152
Rosenkreuzer, The, 94–95
Rostov, Baptism of, 18
Rousseau, 90, 96, 160
Rural Anti-Religious Workers Conference, 241
Russo-Japanese War, 136.
Rychin, F. I., 23

ST. ANDREW in Russia, Legend of, 42–43
St. Petersburg Academy of Science, 88
St. Petersburg Journal, The, 99
St. Petersburg Strikes, 1905, 189
—— University, 126
St. Sergius, 206, 260
Saint-Juste, 112
Saint-Simon, 108, 115–117, 126
Samarin, High Procurator, 54
Sanineism, 136
Sankya, 77
Schelling, 108, 110, 120
Scherbatov, Prince, 90
Schleiermacher, 2
Sectarianism, 56–75
  Increase since 1917, 71–73, 268, 271–272, 277; since checked, 71, 73–74
Self-Burning, 48, 67
Semenov, S. M., 70, 103
Sergievo Monastery, 206, 260, 261
Serfdom, 44–48, 88, 103, 156
Seventh-Day Adventists, 72
Shaw, G. Bernard, 1
Sholopats, The, 66
Skvortsov-Stepanov, I. I., 283
Slavophilism, 108, 130–134
Sobor, The, 59, 195–207, 212–214
Socialist God-Builders, 185–188
Solovetsk Monastery, Revolt of, 47–48
Soloviev, 29, 138
Soroky, Nil, 43

302

INDEX

Soviet Decrees:
  1918, 202-205, 289-290; 1929, 73-74, 214, 217, 290-293; 1930, 293-294
Spengler, Oswald, 3-4
Spinosa, 79, 171
Stankevitch, S., 109-110, 120, 125
State and Church, Close Organic Relation of, 10, 13-14, 37-55, 84, 136-137
Steklov, J., 121
Storchevsky, I, 122
Straniki, The, 62-63
Strastnoi Convent Church, 260
Stretensky Monastery, 23
Strigolnik Movement, 45
Stroganov, T. A., 98
Suicides Following 1905 Revolution, 135
Suslov, Ivan, 65
Sutayev, Ivan, 161
Svirsky, St. Alexr., 206
Swedenburg, Emanuel, 117

TAMERLAINE, 22-23
  Tatischev, Vasily, 87-88
Theatre, The, 264, 269
Theodosius, Emperor, 21
Theodosius, 61
Tikhon, Patriarch, 198, 202, 207-210, 213-214
Tikhovinsky, Father, 53
Tolstoy, Count Leo:
  His religious anarchism, 155-173; religious development, 157-161; anti-revolutionary position, 160-161; contact with the people, 161-163; principles of religious philosophy, 163-173; pacifism, 155, 170-171; present position, 173; *Childhood, Boyhood, Youth*, 158; the novels, 159; autobiographical nature of characters, 159; *Confession*, 159, 160; Lenin on Tolstoy, 156-157; other references, 68, 113, 129, 138

Tolstoyans:
  Soviet Government and, 155; foreign influence, 155, 163
Tverentinov, Dr., 70

UKLEYN, SIMON, 70
  Union of Benevolence, The, 105
  —— —— Militant Atheists, The, 215, 218-220, 221-222, 227, 234, 242, 246, 249, 253, 270-271 (See also *Anti-Religious Movement*)
  —— —— the Godless, The, 216-217
United Slavs, The, 105-106
Universities, Anti-Religious, 254-257
Utopian Socialism, French, in Russia, 108, 126

VEDENSKY, Priest, 209-211
  Vladimir of Kiev, Prince, 13, 14
Vladimir Virgin, The Ikon of, 20, 21-24, 41
Voltaire, 78-80, 81, 83, 84, 88-93, 95, 103, 104, 105, 122
Voltairians, The Russian, 89-93

WANDERERS, The, 62-63
  Weisshaupt, Adam, 95
Wesley, John, 160
Whitberg, A. L., 117
World War, The, 135

YAKOVLEV, M., 258
  Yaroslovsky, E., 254, 259
Youth Movements, Communist and Atheist, 73, 220-223

ZADONSKY, TIKHON, 206
  Zakrzhevsky, *Religion*, 134
Zemstvos, Suppression of, 52
Zubatov, 189